A HISTORY OF BIG RECESSIONS
IN THE LONG TWENTIETH CENTURY

This book examines the array of financial crises, slumps, depressions, and recessions that happened around the globe during the twentieth and early twenty-first centuries. It covers events including World War I; the hyperinflation and market crashes of the 1920s; the Great Depression of the 1930s; the stagflation of the 1970s; the Latin American debt crises of the 1980s; the post-socialist transitions in Central Eastern Europe and Russia of the 1990s; and the great financial crisis of 2008–2009. In addition to providing wide geographic and historical coverage of episodes of crisis in North America, Europe, Latin America, and Asia, the book clarifies basic concepts in the areas of recession economics; high inflation and hyperinflation; debt crises; political cycles; and international political economy. An understanding of these concepts is needed to comprehend the big recessions and slumps that often lead to both political change and the reassessment of prevailing economic paradigms.

Andrés Solimano is the founder and chairman of the International Center for Globalization and Development (CIGLOB). His most recent books include *Global Capitalism in Disarray: Inequality, Debt, and Austerity* (Oxford University Press, 2017); *Pensiones a la Chilena* (Editorial Catalonia, 2017); *Economic Elites, Crises, and Democracy* (Oxford University Press, 2014); *and International Migration in the Age of Crisis and Globalization* (Cambridge University Press, 2010).

A History of Big Recessions in the Long Twentieth Century

ANDRÉS SOLIMANO

International Center for Globalization and Development

CAMBRIDGE
UNIVERSITY PRESS

CAMBRIDGE
UNIVERSITY PRESS

University Printing House, Cambridge CB2 8BS, United Kingdom

One Liberty Plaza, 20th Floor, New York, NY 10006, USA

477 Williamstown Road, Port Melbourne, VIC 3207, Australia

314–321, 3rd Floor, Plot 3, Splendor Forum, Jasola District Centre, New Delhi – 110025, India

79 Anson Road, #06-04/06, Singapore 079906

Cambridge University Press is part of the University of Cambridge.

It furthers the University's mission by disseminating knowledge in the pursuit of education, learning, and research at the highest international levels of excellence.

www.cambridge.org
Information on this title: www.cambridge.org/9781108485043
DOI: 10.1017/9781108755276

First published 2020

Printed in the United Kingdom by TJ International Ltd. Padstow Cornwall.

A catalogue record for this publication is available from the British Library.

Library of Congress Cataloging-in-Publication Data
Names: Solimano, Andrés, author.
Title: A history of big recessions in the long twentieth century / Andrés Solimano, International Center for Globalization and Development.
Description: New York : Cambridge University Press, 2020. | Includes bibliographical references and index.
Identifiers: LCCN 2019029219 | ISBN 9781108485043 (hardback) | ISBN 9781108485043 (ebook)
Subjects: LCSH: Economic history--20th century. | Recessions--History--20th century.
Classification: LCC HC54 .S59 2020 | DDC 338.5/42--dc23
LC record available at https://lccn.loc.gov/2019029219

ISBN 978-1-108-48504-3 Hardback
ISBN 978-1-108-71913-1 Paperback

*This book is dedicated to my wife Bernardita and daughters
and son: Gracia, Pedro, and Paula*

Contents

Figures

Tables

Boxes

Acknowledgments

I would like to acknowledge the support of Cambridge University Press, in particular of Karen Maloney, executive publisher for business, management, finance, and economics, and of Rachel Blaifeder, editorial assistant, for their good advice on the preparation of the book. Grace Morris and Priyaa Menon also provided useful assistance in the editing and production of the book. A special mention is due for Javier Galaz, who provided untiring support and excellent assistance in the long preparation of the book. His contribution to data research and analysis, gathering historical material, and locating some difficult to find bibliographical references was outstanding. Damian Gildemeister also provided effective assistance in the final stage of preparation of the book.

1

Introduction

The long twentieth century, from World War I to the second decade of the twenty-first century, has been a period of significant wealth creation and technological breakthrough, but also of booms followed by sharp contractions of output, investment, and employment. The century witnessed two world wars; the rise and fall of Soviet-type socialism; episodes of hyperinflation, depression, and stagflation; collapses of exchange-rate regimes; and a host of financial crises. Extreme monetary episodes were pervasive in different decades. There was hyperinflation in Germany, Austria, Hungary, Poland, and Soviet Russia in the early 1920s; in Greece and Hungary in the 1940s; in Argentina, Bolivia, Peru, and Nicaragua in the 1980s; in Yugoslavia and Bulgaria in the 1990s; in Zimbabwe in 2008; and in Venezuela since 2017. The toll in terms of economic activity, investment, and human welfare of these episodes was large.

The US stock market crash of 1929 was followed by the Great Depression of the 1930s, and then by World War II, which entailed unprecedented destruction of human lives and physical assets, and changed the geopolitical landscape of the world. Postwar reconstruction and recovery in the Western world under US hegemony was followed by a sustained period of steady growth from around 1950 to 1973, the so-called "golden age of capitalism." This was a period of high employment, more balanced labor-capital relations, and virtually no internationally transmitted financial crises. After World War II, a Socialist camp was formed around the Soviet Union although the Sino-Soviet schism in the 1960s and 1970s distanced Communist China from the USSR.

From the 1970s onward, there have been frequent episodes of financial crises and cycles of expansion and output contraction, in the periphery and the center world economy (also affecting Socialist countries in Central and Eastern Europe) culminating in the Great Recession of 2008–2009 and its aftermath.

Big recessions can have complex political repercussions and spearhead changes in dominant paradigms in economics and social sciences. At the political level, hyperinflation and unemployment in the Weimer republic and the economic slump of the early 1930s paved the way for the accession of Hitler to power in Germany. In the United States, triggered by the hardship of the Great Depression, a federal system of social security, deposit insurance, and various legal acts was established to guarantee economic prosperity, security, and price stability. In France, a protracted compression of economic activity between 1930 and 1936 preceded the victory of the left-wing Popular Front.

The Great Depression also prompted revolutions in economic thinking. The previous faith in the self-correcting abilities of the free market system to restore prosperity and employment after an adverse shock was replaced by state intervention to stabilize the economy. Keynesian economics recommended active stabilization policies to guarantee jobs and opportunities for everyone. In contrast, the stagflation of the 1970s was accompanied by a "crisis in Keynesian economics" to borrow the phrase of Sir John Hicks (see Hicks, 1974). The recommendations of Keynesianism were replaced by several brands of free market macroeconomics such as rational expectations, monetarism, supply-side economics, real business cycle theory, and the efficient market hypothesis. These views, often presented in elegant mathematical formulas but without much resemblance to real world situations, became very influential within academia and governments eager to find quick solutions to the maladies of stagnation, inflation, and monetary instability. The policy recipes were market deregulation, privatization, macro stabilization and trade, and financial integration. Left behind were policies of full employment, the strengthening of the welfare state, controlled private capital mobility, and cooperative labor–capital relations. In contrast with the 1930s and 1970s, the Great Recession of 2008–2009 has so far not led to a change in dominant macroeconomic paradigms.[1]

1.1 Intensity and Determinants of Contractive Episodes

A main focus of this book is the frequency and intensity of episodes of recession and slumps. To put these episodes in perspective, it is worth noting that close to 80 percent of the 744 recessive episodes in the

---

[1] In the 1990s and early 2000s, macroeconomists in center economies proclaimed that we were living in an era of "great moderation." Prevailing macroeconomic approaches were not paying much attention to the ample supply of bank credit, going to speculative real estate activities, soaring asset prices, and high wealth concentration at the top. This complacency ended abruptly with the eruption of the sub-prime crisis of 2007–08 in the United States.

Table 1.1. *Frequency of episodes of recession and depression in the long twentieth century (declines in GDP per capita)*

Type of decline		1900–2017		1900–1950		1951–2017	
		Obs.	Percent	Obs.	Percent	Obs.	Percent
Recessions	Mild recession (less than 3%)	335	45.0%	115	32.7%	220	56.1%
	Moderate to large recession (between 3% and 10%)	261	35.1%	141	40.1%	120	30.6%
	Severe recession (between 10% and 15%)	61	8.2%	42	11.9%	19	4.8%
Depressions	Depression (between 15% and 30%)	59	7.9%	34	9.7%	25	6.4%
	Mega depression (more than 30%)	28	3.8%	20	5.7%	8	2.0%
Total		744	100.0%	352	100.0%	392	100.0%

Source: Author elaboration based on data from Maddison (2013); World Development Indicators, The World Bank 2017; OECD (2017a, b); National Accounts Main Aggregates Database (United Nations); and World Economic Outlook, FMI October, 2018.

period 1900 to 2017 for 56 countries[2] examined in this book correspond to declines in per capita GDP below 10 percent with episodes of decline in per capita GDP below three percent representing 45 percent of the sample, the event of highest frequency (Table 1.1). On the other hand, depressions defined as declines in GDP per capita above 15 percent account for near 12 percent of the sample. Furthermore, very large economic contractions, say "mega-depressions," defined here as cuts in per capita GDP over 30 percent, represent only 4 percent of the sample.

The frequency of mild recessions increased in the second half of the twentieth century and the early twenty-first century. On the other hand, all other categories of recession/depression declined in importance in that period.

---

[2] Some of these countries are no longer political entities (Yugoslavia, the USSR, and Czechoslovakia)

This suggests that governments, when it was financially feasible, learned the lessons of the Great Depression and implemented countercyclical demand policies to stabilize the macroeconomy. During the golden age of capitalism, financial markets, a source of economic crisis and financial destabilization when they do not work properly, were better regulated and restricted in their reach particularly at global level. Conversely, the impressive growth and deregulation of international financial markets since the 1970s have been accompanied by many financial crises and episodes of large output contraction.

Not only do the intensity of recessions and depressions matter but also their *frequency*. In the Latin American region, we find the highest frequency of ups and downs in the level of aggregate economic activity. Venezuela, for example, experienced episodes of negative growth in approximately 57 percent of the years between 1970 and 2018. In Argentina, the share of years with negative growth in the same period was 36 percent. Paradoxically, these two economies were among the most prosperous in Latin America in the early to mid 20th century.

1.2 Events and Shocks Leading to Slumps

We can identify several factors of economic and noneconomic nature that prompt cycles of contraction (and expansion) of economic activity. The main noneconomic events that have consequences upon economic activity are *armed conflicts or wars*. The American and British economies were stimulated in the run- up to World War I and World War II by the increase in defense spending. Germany, in the second half of the 1930s, also experienced rapid expansion stimulated by rearmament, although it suffered immense economic and human loss in the final phases of both World War I and World War II. World War I led to economic disintegration and massive output contraction in Russia and the former Austro-Hungarian empire.

Turning to economic causes of slumps in developing countries they are often associated with the final phase of a *cycle of intense external borrowing*.

A debt cycle is a situation of initial borrowing (that helps in sustaining growth) followed by a decline/stop of borrowing that can cause a recession and/or a financial crisis. The borrower may be the state, the enterprise sector and households or a combination of the three. The typical debt cycle runs as follows. In the initial phase, there is an abundance of foreign (and domestic) credit that stimulates demand, production, investment, and employment. Foreign capital arrives to a country following new investment possibilities, ambitious policy reforms, the discovery of valuable natural resources, with a wave of optimism developing on the economic future of the country. The counterpart of the intense foreign borrowing is internal overconsumption and overinvestment. At some point, the boom runs out of steam and the accumulation of foreign debt generates uncertainties among lenders regarding the capacity of a country to repay debt. This is the syndrome of the "*sudden-stop*," a term used to describe the effects of a sudden cutoff of foreign lending to countries experiencing *unsustainable external current account deficits* (excess of investment over domestic savings) and/or large *short-term foreign debt* relative to the level of international reserves (indicating a liquidity problem). Examples of sudden stops in recent decades include crises in East Asia (1997–1998); Mexico (1994–1995); Argentina (1995 and 2001–2002); Ecuador (1999); and Greece and Latvia (2008–2009). Swings in foreign capital flows were also destabilizing in Latin America, Australia, and Europe in the late 1920s and early 1930s.

When a current account deficit cannot be financed with new external credits and/or by selling international reserves held by central banks, the bulk of adjustment is placed upon the trade balance and internal economic activity. A real depreciation of the national currency often accompanies adjustment to generate a trade surplus (an excess of exports over imports) and improve the current account of the balance of payments.

Another way to look at the adjustment process in the external accounts is the balance between investment and domestic savings. When the former exceeds the latter, the difference is met by foreign savings. If foreign savings are not forthcoming, the domestic economy will have to adjust, and the typical adjustment to a balance payments disequilibrium is through a cut in investment leading to a decline in output and employment, say a recession or a depression. The so-called *smoothing* of adjustment, say a gradual correction of an imbalance supported by external credit is very often a luxury that many developing/emerging economies and the European periphery cannot afford because of constrained access to international financial markets at the time of uncertainty and crisis.

Debt cycles were a crucial determinant of the macroeconomic adjustment process in the 1980s in Latin America, Turkey, the Philippines, Poland, Hungary, Yugoslavia, and other economies in Central and Eastern Europe. In the context of advanced economies, the saving and loan financial crisis in the United States in the late 1980s, and the financial crisis of Sweden of the early 1990s, were also cases of debt cycles.

An important economic factor that causes recession and depression is the occurrence of episodes of *extreme monetary instability*. The lack of control of the printing of paper currency to cover large fiscal deficits can lead to uncontrollable processes of currency depreciation and price increases known as *hyperinflation*. Rampant inflation destroys the contract structure of an economy creating very strong incentives *against* wealth creation, along with un-desired income and wealth redistributions. Extreme inflation, however, is a highly complex process with several intervening causes and a focus only on "purely" monetary factors may be insufficient to fully understand it. History shows that high inflation is often accompanied by unstable external sector conditions and internal disarray. For example, war reparations, economic embargoes, cutoffs in foreign lending, and drops in export revenues can all provoke a sharp decline in the value of local currency that contributes to inflationary impulse. For hyperinflation to take place, of course, requires very rapid money growth, but this may be an accommodating process for other shocks rather than the only and exogenous source of a process of hyperinflation.

The state of public finances is an important factor underlying situations of exacerbated monetary and price instability. Behind the hyperinflation of the 1920s in Poland, Austria, Hungary, Germany, and Russia, there was a *fiscal crisis of the state*. The dismembering of the Austro-Hungarian empire after World War I and the ensuing territorial and asset losses of newly formed countries clearly affected the tax base and increased public spending commitments of Austria, Hungary, and Poland. In Germany, the loss of former colonies and the shrinking of its commercial navy, along with the imposition of war reparations (in kind and money) had a crippling effect on the German economy. This was exacerbated by the distributive conflicts about who would pay for the reparations, say workers or capitalists and renters, and manifested in a wage-price spiral leading to explosive inflation. In Soviet Russia after the Bolshevik revolution, civil war, external intervention, a weak taxation base, and increased public spending contributed to create hyperinflation in the early to mid 1920s.

The stabilization of rampant inflation in Austria, Hungary, and Germany involved legal reforms in fiscal and monetary areas (prohibition of rediscounting of treasury bills by the central banks and policies of fiscal balance). In addition, exchange-rate stabilization was critical for the stabilization of the price level supported by external credits and surveillance missions by the League of Nations. Poland adopted similar reforms but initially without the supervision of the League of Nations. Russia stabilized rampant inflation by introducing a hard currency, the chevornet, and its value was strictly tied to holdings of foreign exchange and gold. To support the stability of the chevornet, the Bolshevik government moved also to reduce fiscal and monetary imbalances.

Another source of economic slumps and crises is the *collapse of fixed-exchange rate regimes and currency boards*. Managed exchange-rate regimes may help to reduce inflation but also can generate overvaluation of the real exchange rate (currency appreciation), creating trade and balance of payments imbalances. In addition, the external imbalance encourages borrowing in foreign currency, making the banking system and the corporate sector that contracted these loans very vulnerable to adjustment in the value of the local currency. When the currency regimes crash, output and investment suffer badly.

Cycles of expansion and contraction in aggregate economic activity can have an origin in *over-expansionary fiscal, monetary, and wage policies* that are adopted in periods of democratization and economic redistribution to low income groups. In the early 1970s, in the southern cone of Latin America (Argentina, Chile, and Uruguay), popular/socialist experiments took place with the objective of rapid redistribution of income and wealth to the urban working class and the rural poor. In Chile, the redistribution of assets was carried out through nationalization policies in industry, banking, and mining, along with agrarian reform. In addition, redistribution of income was attempted through wage policies and aggregate demand measures that created initial gains for wage earners, but after a year or two, redistributive policies were followed by large macroeconomic imbalances that invited sharp policy reversals.

During Salvador Allende's presidency in Chile, in the early 1970s, the balance of payment deficits could not be funded by official lending from multilateral organizations, a policy urged by the US government, unhappy with having a leftist government in south-America. External "strangulation" and internal resistance to redistribution and democratization by company owners, economic elites and the upper middle class often led to disruption of production chains, food shortages and economic sabotage, prompting currency depreciation, and inflation. Eventually, the ensuing economic crises and internal polarization led to a right-wing military coup in September of 1973 and the collapse of democracy in Chile. Once in power, the military and their economic technocracies adopted neoliberal policies of monetary and fiscal restraint that produced slow disinflationary results, but were costly in terms of output losses, investment declines, and unemployment. Political economy factors and geopolitics should not be disregarded when analyzing the adoption of apparently irrational economic policies that contribute to collapses in economic activity.

Summarizing, we can identify a set of causal factors that are associated with economic slumps:

- War and armed conflict.
- Episodes of extreme monetary instability and hyperinflation.
- Adverse external shocks, debt cycles, and cutoffs in foreign credit ("sudden stops").
- Collapse of fixed exchange-rate regimes and currency boards.
- Premature financial liberalization, credit booms, and asset price overvaluation.
- Overexpansionary demand and wage policies that become unsustainable.
- Political destabilization and economic uncertainty.

1.3 Organization of the Book

The book is comprised of nine chapters including this introduction. Chapter 2 provides an overview of theories and empirics of recessions and depressions; examines the conceptual impact of external shocks, inflation, and other factors on economic activity; and looks at the shapes of business cycles (v, u, L and w recessions). Chapter 3 studies the impact of World War I, the hyperinflation of the 1920s, and World War II on aggregate economic activity of countries engaged in these armed conflicts. The chapter shows a variety of effects on output (expansions and contractions) resulting from both World War I and World War II across different countries. Chapter 4 focuses on the causes and consequences of the Great Depression of the 1930s; the role of the gold standard in leading to the depression; the period between abandoning the gold standard and the start of recoveries; the severity of the contraction worldwide; and the depression's impact upon industrial production, exports, and the phenomenon of price deflation. The chapter discusses various conceptualizations of the effects of price deflation and the role of fiscal and monetary policy, including war preparation, to take some economies out of the slump. Chapter 5 focuses on the transition from the golden age to the stagflation of the 1970s and then the neoliberal era in the core economies of the USA and western Europe along with economies of the European periphery. The chapter also identifies main recessive episodes in terms of impacts on per capita GDP and investment ratios from 1970 to 2015. Chapter 6 examines two depressions of the early twenty-first century, in Latvia and Greece. It documents the various policy choices faced by these economies at the time of the crisis and effects on output, investment, fiscal budgets, external current account, balance of payments, and private and public debt. The chapter also critically examines the role played by the International Monetary Fund (IMF) and European institutions in the design and implementation of austerity in these two economies and draws lessons from these policies. Chapter 7 focuses on the rise and fall of growth in centrally-planned socialist regimes in Central and Eastern Europe and the former Soviet Union. It studies the period of rapid growth and socialist industrialization in the 1950s and 1960s, the stagnation of the 1970s, and the decade of stagnation in the 1980s. Then it turns to the "transformational recession" of the early 1990s and the causes of these slumps. It also studies how these economies were impacted by the crisis of 2008–2009. Chapter 8 centers upon the episodes of growth crises, recession, and depression in Latin American and East Asian economies, along with other emerging economies from 1970 to 2015. The chapter discusses the cases of Argentina, Venezuela, Chile, Mexico, Indonesia, Korea, and other nations. The book closes with Chapter 9, summarizing and interpreting the main findings of the book.

Recession and Depression

An Overview of Theories and Empirics

2.1 Introduction

Before continuing with the analysis of actual experiences of economic slumps (recessions and depressions), this chapter reviews main conceptual approaches to understand slumps and the interactions between policies, shocks, and recessionary cycles.

2.2 Business Cycles, Recessions, Depressions, and Recoveries

The amplitude and duration of a *whole* business cycle can be measured from *peak to peak* or from *trough to trough*. In addition, a distinction is made between the phase of *expansion* of a cycle – running from trough to peak – and the phase of *contraction* (recession) that is measured from peak to trough (see Figure 2.1). A trend line often represents the medium-run evolution of output, around which we observe short-term fluctuations.

Another way to see a business cycle is as a temporary deviation in the level of output (total Gross Domestic Product (GDP), per capita GDP, industrial production) from the trend (Figure 2.2a) or a more permanent reduction in the level of output (Figure 2.2b).

Empirically, using quarterly data, a common definition of a *recession* is a sequence of negative growth lasting for at least *two consecutive quarters*.[1] Some add to this definition an unemployment rate approaching 10 percent. If we use annual data, we may define a recession as at least *a year of negative growth*. Economists tend to distinguish between mild to moderate recessions and *depressions*, with the latter describing deep

---

[1] See the methodology of the National Bureau of Economic Research of the United States.

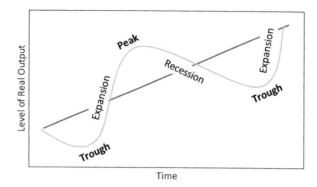

Figure 2.1. The phases of a business cycle.

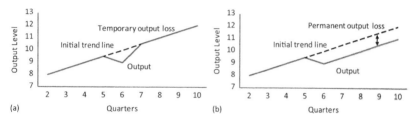

Figure 2.2. Transitory and permanent deviations from trend.

and protracted contractions in economic activity. Some may apply the term "depression" to permanent decelerations in output growth relative to some historical averages. The term "depression" is often attributed to US president Herbert Hoover who used it to describe the *slump* affecting the US economy in the period between 1929 and 1933, characterized by massive bank failures, output contraction, high unemployment, plummeting investment, and pessimistic expectations (see Chapter 4).

In the nineteenth century, when the system of national accounts as we know it today was in its infancy (or simply it did not exist), the term "depression" was used to describe episodes of financial instability, bank failures, and market panic. For example, the panics of 1819, 1873, and 1907 were defined as "depressions."

Nowadays, a Great Depression encompasses an economy in serious distress, a situation that combines severe features of market destabilization, panic, and stress along with company bankruptcies, output contraction, investment collapses, rising unemployment and poverty.

Box 2.1. Recession and Depression Shapes

Four shapes of recession and depression can be distinguished with corresponding letters of the alphabet.

(a) *V-shapes* are intended to reflect a sharp contraction in GDP (or another indicator of economic activity) followed by a strong recovery. These recessions could be sharp but of relatively short duration, as recovery is fast.

(b) *U-shapes* are often part of long-duration cycles with a contraction that may last several years, followed by a gradual recovery.

(c) *W-shapes* are also known as "double-dip recessions" or recurrent recessions.

(d) *L-shapes* are a fall in output that is followed by no (or little) recovery for a period of several years. This could also be interpreted as a cut in GDP followed by a period of stagnation.[2]

Economists have developed alternative empirical definitions for classifying an event of economic contraction as a *depression*. To quote at least three of them:

Definition I: a drop of total GDP above 10 percent combined with an unemployment rate over 20 percent of the labor force. In chapter 1 we define depression as a decline in GDP per capita above 15 percent.

Definition II: a decline in GDP that lasts at least three years.

Definition III: a situation in which pre-crisis trend growth is not restored before a period of a decade or more.

Economic contractions can come in varying forms and shapes, as we shall see in this book when reviewing several historical events (see Box 2.1 and Figure 2.3a–d).

The assumption of a linear trend line may be unrealistic to describe the evolution of trend/potential output when a big recession followed by a sluggish recovery hits the economy (Figure 2.4). There are several mechanisms through which a prolonged recession or depression may negatively affect the level of potential output: (i) a decline in the rate of capital formation; (ii) de-skilling of a labor force that remains unemployed for a period of time; (iii) a lower rate of innovation and technical improvements; and (iv) flight of human capital and qualified human resources out of a country to escape

---

[2] See Roberts (2016).

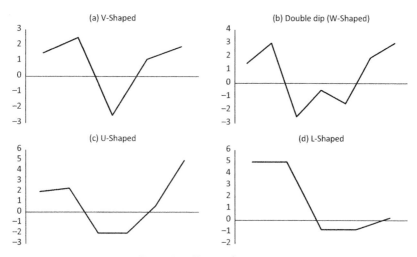

Figure 2.3. Types of recession.

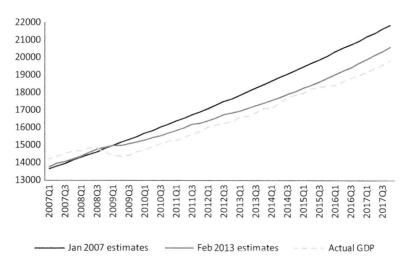

——— Jan 2007 estimates ——— Feb 2013 estimates – – – Actual GDP

Figure 2.4. Potential output affected by a severe and protracted slump: Downward revision in US potential GDP (Billions of dollars, 2007–2017). *Source:* US Congressional Budget Office and U.S. Bureau of Economic Analysis.

a big slump. These factors are often known as "hysteresis effects," as there is a feedback effect between the trajectory of the economy and long-run values of potential output and trend growth.[3]

---

[3] See Cerra and Saxena (2016).

In the case of temporary output losses, output recovers to the trend line reflecting the pre-shock, long-run growth rate of GDP.[4] In the case of permanent output losses, after a recession, output *fails to return to the trend line*, although it may keep growing at the same pre-recession rate, but along a permanently lower *level* of GDP (Figure 2.2b). So, recessions may have long-run effects on living standards, as the economy may fail to recover the output losses incurred during a crisis's episode.[5]

When there are hysteresis effects, the traditional concept of the *output gap* becomes less precise as the level of potential output also declines as a consequence of a severe recession. A permanent output loss calculated with a trend line unaffected by the recession will not reflect the actual degree of unused capacity that can accurately guide fiscal and monetary policy. This may induce a government to undertake a fiscal over-expansion as the output gap is overestimated (potential GDP is not adjusted downward).

A good calibration of the output gap becomes challenging. Recalculations of the output gap in the United States and Europe undertaken by Cerra and Saxena (2016) for the period 2000–2009 show that there was no "over-heating" prior to 2008 when calibrated with *adjusted* potential output.

Regarding the *intensity* of output contractions, different empirical studies show that the size and persistence of the declines in output and investment are larger, and the speed of recovery slower, when a recessionary cycle is accompanied by financial crises, currency crises, and twin crises (Calvo, 1998, 2007, 2016; Bordo, 2006; Cerra and Saxena, 2008, 2016; Solimano, 2017). In fact, financial crisis often involves excessive debt accumulation by households, enterprises, and the government, which acts as a drag on the recovery of consumption and investment after negative shocks have occurred. In addition, the process of restoring solvency and reducing debt –"improving the balance sheets" – is often slow when there has been a financial sector crisis. Typically, firms and corporations are reluctant to invest if they have high levels of debt; at the same time, households postpone consumption (mainly of durable goods) at times of low employment and high debt. In addition, if a slump is accompanied by deflation in prices, the real value of debt increases, worsening the prospect for recovery.

---

[4] In the recovery phase GDP may overshoot its long-run growth rate.
[5] Middle income "growth traps" are examined in Eichengreen et al. (2013) and episodes of "growth accelerations" and "growth collapses" are studied in Hausmann et al. (2005, 2006).

2.3 Causes and Context of Recessions and Depressions

There are several strands of thought regarding the causes of the Great Depression of the 1930s, a paradigmatic case of a severe output slump. Monetarists such as Milton Friedman and Anna Schwartz argued that the US Federal Reserve (the Fed – the American central bank) played an important role in turning a confidence crisis into a period of massive output contraction and bankruptcies. The chief mechanism was a *cut in the money supply*, depressing nominal spending. The monetarist view of the Great Depression stresses the role of *mistakes* in monetary policy and it is largely drawing on the US case, although the Great Depression was, indeed, a global phenomenon.[6]

Another conceptual framework for understanding the Great Depression is Irving Fisher's theory of *debt deflation*. Fisher was a close observer of business cycles and also a participant in the stock market (albeit not always with successful financial results).[7] He placed an important emphasis on the evolution of debt during booms and busts. For example, the boom in the housing sector in Florida and New York in the first half of the 1920s, followed by an economy-wide stock market boom later in the decade.[8] Fisher noted that credit creation by banks and other financial intermediaries in the booming phase of the cycle leads to debt accumulation (by households, firms, and the government), a process that is coupled with rising asset prices (stocks, real estate, and land that appreciates in value) and booming economic activity. However, booms do not last forever and when there is a bust: investors start selling their assets in haste, deflating their prices and increasing the real value of debt held by individuals and corporations, impairing household consumption and corporate investment. Fisher outlined a dynamic for a downturn involving debt liquidation and distress selling, a contraction in credit supply as bank loans are paid-off, decline in asset prices, pessimism, loss of confidence, and a decline in the value of wealth.

Different from monetarist and debt-deflation theories are the views of the British economist, policy advisor, art collector, and cosmopolitan figure, John Maynard Keynes.[9] In the 1930s, Keynes focused on the role of *aggregate demand* in output determination and stressed investment as the most volatile component of effective demand. He formulated also the

---

[6] Romer (1990 and 1992) discusses the US case in great detail.
[7] Cassidy (2009).
[8] See Solimano (2017, chapter 7).
[9] See Taylor (2010).

"consumption function" with income as its main determinant, setting a marginal propensity to consume below one. There is a "multiplier" that amplifies the effect of demand disturbances on output, whose value is proportional to the propensity to consume. Keynes emphasized that the "general" (normal) state of a capitalist economy is *below* its potential; in this context we observe both excess capacity (unused capital stock) and unemployment. The *General Theory*, inspired, in part, by the real-life experience of the slump of the 1930s in the United Kingdom, United States, and other countries, underscored the *lack* of self-correcting mechanisms for imbalances between intended savings and desired investment plans in a capitalist economy. In contrast, classic economists such as Arthur Cecil Pigou see flexibility in real interest rates, wages, and prices as the mechanism to ensure the ex-ante equality between desired savings and planned investment *at full employment*. For Keynes, variations in output and employment levels were the key adjustment variable to produce an equilibrium between savings decisions and investment plans. The lack of effectiveness of monetary policy that he observed in the early 1930s in the United States and the United Kingdom led him to propose a *fiscal stimulus* to get the economy out of the slump. Keynes envisaged investment as determined by the expectation of future profits and sales: in a situation of stagnation and liquidity traps, low interest rates will do little to stimulate a resumption of capital accumulation and economic growth if they do not reignite the "animal spirits" of entrepreneurs and investors.

More recently, Ben Bernanke developed his "non-monetary theory of depression."[10] It combines elements of the monetarist and debt deflation explanations of the Great Depression and adds the dimension of the *credit crunch* by the banking system – and not only a decline in the money supply engineered by central banks – as an important factor that triggered the Great Depression. Banks, when faced with a lower probability of recovery of their loans from distressed borrowers, react by curtailing the supply of credit to corporations and households, squeezing aggregate demand and leading to an economic slump. Bernanke developed the notion of a "financial multiplier" that can amplify adverse confidence shocks with negative consequences for employment, output, and investment, chiefly acting through the *credit mechanism*. This can also be relevant at a global level. For example, speculation against the US dollar taking place in international markets when the British government depreciated the pound

---

[10] Bernanke (2000, 2004).

sterling and left the gold standard in 1931 aggravated the slump in the United States by generating panic in the banking system.

In the realm of *financial theories of recession,* we have to add the work of Hyman Minsky, who emphasized the way the structure of financing of firms (hedge, Ponzi, and speculative) is critical for generating financial fragility. Key actors were central banks (the "big bank") and "big government" that invited speculation and financial fragility as their policies were internalized by the private sector; this included accommodative money supply policies – including rescues of banks in trouble – and fiscal activism to maintain full employment. He coined the phrase "stability is destabilizing" to convey the notion that practices of debt speculation and Ponzi financing were the consequence of authorities guaranteeing stability in almost all circumstances.

Several episodes of big contractions of economic activity were preceded by booming asset prices and debt accumulation (Reinhart and Rogoff, 2009). For example, the Great Depression of the early 1930s in the United States (and other capitalist economies) was preceded by a crash in the stock market in October, 1929, that shattered confidence and led to cuts in consumption and investment. Nonetheless, in conventional macroeconomic textbooks, depressions are assumed rarely to be connected with a financial crash. They are largely explained by exogenous declines in aggregate demand.

Minsky's insights, along with the study of many actual crises throughout history, led MIT economic historian Charles Kindleberger to stress the role of financial markets in generating *manias and panics.* For Kindleberger, economic crises are often surrounded by *psychological factors* and thus are not entirely "rational" in the sense economists often use this term.

A theme of historical significance is the effect of *war* on economic activity. We can identify both demand and supply effects. An increase in defense spending tends to be stimulative if the economy is operating below full capacity (there is idle labor and capital). However, if the economy is on the production possibilities frontier, the defense sector will compete with the civilian industry, developing a trade-off between "guns and butter" in the example of Samuelson's early editions of his famous *Economics* textbook written in the 1940s. Further, if the economy is engaged in an armed conflict, and is a net importer of armament and inputs, the *availability of foreign exchange* will be a crucial determinant of the resources available to buy military equipment. The effects of war on economic activity will depend upon which *phase* of the war in a country: war preparation, actual war, and post-war demobilization and reconstruction. The pre-war preparation phase may be expansionary if the demand for military equipment produced at home increases and the economy is in an under-employment equilibrium (for example, the United States and Germany in the mid- to late 1930s). In turn, the waging of war will often destroy human lives and productive capacities affecting the supply side of the economy. The post-war situation can be, initially, contractive as defense spending is reduced, orders to the armament industry are cut, and soldiers are demobilized, creating pockets of unemployment and lack of purchasing power. Also, the shift of capital and labor between the defense sector to the civilian sector may not be automatic, creating friction in the inter-sector reallocation of factors of production. In addition, when liquid assets that are often accumulated during the war period due to food shortages and price controls (e.g. money overhang) are spent in the goods market, this creates inflation.

Depressions and recessions may be accompanied by periods of *price deflation* or *price inflation*. The long depressions of the nineteenth century and the Great Depression of the early 1930s were, in general, accompanied by price deflation (e.g. a decline in the price level; see Chapter 4). However, a depression or recession can come with *price inflation*, as was the case of the stagflation of the 1970s in advanced economies, the Latin American debt crises of the 1970s and 1980s, and the transformational recessions of the post-socialist transitions in the 1990s. In the 1950s and 1960s, the dominant view was of a trade-off between inflation and unemployment. This is the so-called "Phillips curve," an empirical regularity that established a *negative* relation between inflation and unemployment. In this context, policymakers could choose different combinations of unemployment and inflation. Within this framework, a cut in inflation would lead to an increased output gap – say a recession – and higher unemployment; contrarily, a country could attain a higher level of economic activity but pay the cost of living with higher inflation. This regularity and its implications were questioned, independently, by Nobel prize winners Milton Friedman and Edmond Phelps. They showed that the Phillips curve would be vertical in the long run. The alleged trade-off between inflation and unemployment/output gaps would vanish once expectations, wages, and prices have enough time to adjust. The Phelps-Friedman view predicted that stabilizing inflation could, in principle, be costless in terms of lost output and unemployment, if the economy is on the vertical Phillips curve.

The experience with inflation since the 1970s showed that the *level* of inflation matters for the output costs of inflation and stabilization, and there was a need to distinguish between low, intermediate, high, and extreme inflation. Currently, annual inflation rates below 2 to 3 percent per year are considered acceptable for policymakers and rates of inflation

above 5 percent are deemed as excessive, not only for advanced economies, but also for more stable emerging economies. However, in the 1980s
and 1990s, the perception of what constituted tolerable inflation, at least
in developing countries, was different (Solimano, 1989). Writing at that
time, MIT macroeconomists Rudiger Dornbusch and Stanley Fischer
considered four categories of annual inflation: (i) moderate, between 15
and 30 percent per year, (ii) high, between 30 and 100 percent per annum,
(iii) extreme, between 100 and 1,000 percent and (iv) hyperinflation, above
1,000 percent per year (Dornbusch and Fischer, 1986).[11] In contrast, low
inflation rates are in the one-digit range and governments should aim at
having these rates of inflation when setting their objectives for anti-
inflationary policies.

In this approach, the cost of bringing inflation down is dependent upon
the level of inflation, its inertial mechanisms, the credibility of monetary
authorities, wage and exchange-rate rules, and institutions. In general,
stabilizing moderate to high inflation, particularly when inflation is well-
entrenched, would be more costly than stopping extreme inflation and
hyperinflation that had already destroyed the contract structure. In fact,
Thomas Sargent, in his classic study "The Ends of Four Big Inflations"
(Sargent, 1982) of how "big inflation" ended in Germany, Austria,
Hungary, and Poland in the 1920s, argued that the stabilization of inflation was almost costless once the public had high credibility in a new
monetary and fiscal regime (see Chapter 3). Sargent's emphasis was on
credibility and institutions rather than on wage contracts and indexation
rules. In this book, we examine cases of extreme inflation and hyperinflation, showing that *during* hyperinflation output collapses, as it occurred
in Austria, Hungary, Poland, Germany, and Russia in the early 1920s; in
Argentina, Peru in the late 1980s; in Zimbabwe in 2008; and in Venezuela
in 2017–2018.

A related theme is the *collapse of exchange-rate regimes* such as fixed
rates, exchange-rate bands, and currency boards. The output effect of
collapses in exchange-rate regimes can be serious, as governments bet
their credibility to the permanence and stability of these exchange-rate
regimes.

---

[11] The classic definition of hyperinflation by Cagan (1956) is rates of over 50 per cent *per
month* lasting around 9 to 10 months. More recently, in a study on world hyperinflation (Hanke and Krus, 2013) offer other criteria for classifying a situation as hyperinflation, including daily rates of inflation and the number of days required for prices
to double.

If the national currency is devalued, firms and households see the local currency value of their debts increased with adverse effects on consumption and investment. In addition, foreign lenders will reduce their loans in the expectation of currency collapses, bringing a "sudden stop" with sharp declines in output, investment, and employment.

2.4 International Dimensions

The international spread of economic slowdowns and contractions across nations was an important feature of the Great Depression of the 1930s, the stagflation of the 1970s, and the great recession of 2008–2009. Real sector linkages across economies include falls in quantity of exports and imports and drops in terms of trade and changes in investment levels. In turn, financial mechanisms transmitting losses of confidence from one country to another include changes in asset prices, international interest rates, and shifts in the size and direction of capital flows. Analysts of the Great Depression have stressed the importance of the gold standard (a regime in which the domestic currency price of a unit of gold is fixed and central banks and government commit to defend that parity by selling and buying the required amounts of gold) – or more generally the *international monetary regime* – in precipitating a global slump (see Chapter 4).[12] Under the gold standard (and other fixed-exchange-rate regimes) a deficit country will experience a decline in the supply of money, while surplus countries will see their money supply expanding. In an ideal world of full wage and price flexibility (both downward and upward) – that clearly ceased to be the case after WWI – changes in the money supply associated with balance of payments imbalances would have only transitory effects on real output and employment affecting mostly wages and prices.

The literature on the relation between the gold standard and severity of recessions and depressions has stressed the *timing* of devaluing national currencies or exiting the gold standard. Historical studies by Eichengreen (1992) and Eichengreen and Sachs (1985) found that, in the 1930s, the longer countries remained in the gold standard, the more severe were the effects of the Great Depression (and the more delayed the recovery of economic activity). In contrast, countries that left the gold standard earlier, such as Great Britain and Scandinavian countries in 1931, recovered sooner

---

[12] See Kindleberger (1973) and Eichengreen (1992).

than France and Belgium, which stayed on the gold standard until 1935 or 1936.[13] The United States decided only in 1933 to float the dollar relative to other currencies and gold.

Another theory of the causes of the Great Depression is of an international political economy nature and refers to the *lack of a hegemon* (a political entity with authority and influence on other nations). Kindleberger (1973) argues the relative decay of Great Britain in the early twentieth century (accentuated after the end of World War I) and the reluctance of the United States to play an effective leadership role at the international level in correcting international disequilibria contributed to the onset of the Great Depression. The contrast between the reconstructed gold standard of the mid-1920s and the Bretton Woods system established in the mid-1940s is evident, as the latter was supported by an unchallenged leadership of the United States in the capitalist world, spurred the conditions for a quarter of a century of steady growth, lack of international financial crises, and lower inequality. At the same time, the socialist block remained, largely, outside the international monetary system put in place by the West, although Romania and Yugoslavia entered the International Monetary Fund (IMF) and the World Bank in the 1970s during their socialist periods (see Chapter 7). This was not the case, however, with the Soviet Union and other socialist countries in central Europe. After the fall of the Berlin Wall this changed and former socialist nations became full members of the Bretton Woods institutions.

2.5 Policy Responses to a Slump

A controversial topic in economic policymaking is how governments and central banks should respond to an economic slump. In the 1930s, Austrian economists Friedrich von Hayek, Ludwig von Misses, and Joseph Schumpeter, along with British economist Lionel Robbins, in general, favored a *liquidation approach*. In the United States, Secretary of the Treasury (finance minister) Andrew Mellon also adopted this view. The various individuals tended to coincide that the depression was the consequence of loose monetary policies pursued by central banks prior to the slump. This led to excessive credit creation, generating an unsustainable boom of economic activity and rising asset prices above the levels dictated

---

[13] China was in the silver standard (not in the gold standard) and avoided almost completely the Great Depression. Spain refrained to enter into the gold standard.

by real profitability and productivity. In this view, recessions and depressions are direct consequences of a "maladjustment of investment" induced by wrong policies of central banks, with the economy accumulating organizational and productive inefficiencies along the way. In the liquidation approach, recessions are not necessarily bad outcomes. On the contrary, they can play a *useful role* (as a "cleansing device") by allowing the release of capital and labor from socially unproductive activities to more efficient sectors, spurring an economic recovery.

In the words of Andrew Mellon:

Liquidate labor, liquidate stocks, liquidate farmers, liquidate real estate . . . It will purge the rottenness out of the system . . . People will work harder, live a more moral life. [Economic] values will be adjusted and enterprising people will pick up the wrecks from less competent people.[14]

In 1931, John Maynard Keynes was sarcastic about the prescriptions of the liquidation approach:

austere and puritanical souls [who] regard [the Great Depression] as an inevitable and desirable nemesis on so much "over-expansion" as they call it . . . It would, they feel, be a victory for the mammon of unrighteousness if so much prosperity was not subsequently balanced by universal bankruptcy. We need, they say, what they politely call a "prolonged liquidation" to put us right. The liquidation, they tell us, is not yet complete. But in time it will be. And when sufficient time has elapsed for the completion of the liquidation, all will be well with us again.[15]

Although, nowadays, few would recommend doing nothing in a slump, an orthodoxy recommends avoiding use of countercyclical fiscal policy, preferring monetary expansion (e.g. "quantitative easing"). In recent times austerity (liquidation?) policies are endorsed by the IMF and some European governments for highly indebted countries. That was the case with Greece in the aftermath of the 2008–2009 crisis (see Chapter 6).

Regarding monetary policy, there is much consensus now that, to stem a financial panic, monetary authorities must *increase* liquidity (rather than reducing it, as was done in the United States in the beginning of the Great Depression) to counteract the tendency of banks to reduce the supply of credit in conditions of economic uncertainty. In 2008–2009, central banks of advanced economies provided additional liquidity to commercial banks, and later applied the mechanism of quantitative easing to keep interest rates low with the hope of stimulating private investment

---

[14]   Taken from De Long (1990).
[15]   Keynes, 1931: vol. XII, Pt1, p. 349.

and growth. Contrary to some fears, monetary expansion did not conduct to inflation in the price of goods and services but led to a revaluation of stocks and financial assets. Mass bankruptcies of commercial banks, such as those that occurred in the 1930s, were avoided, although the rescue packages to banks benefitted more bank owners and top executives than the indebted middle and working classes that in several countries lost their homes and jobs.

2.6 Constraints for Countercyclical Demand Policies

In the Great Recession of 2008–2009, the IMF recommended to economies with "fiscal space," undertaking a fiscal expansion, to restore growth and reduce unemployment. However, in the European countries at the periphery (southern Europe, the Baltic region), the scope and space for fiscal expansions were far more limited (see Chapter 6). Governments faced the dilemma of generating a surplus in the primary fiscal budget (e.g. before interest payments) to pay interests on external public debt, or to run a fiscal deficit to stimulate aggregate demand and help the economy to pull out of stagnation. The option of the fiscal surplus requires increasing taxes and reducing public spending (or a combination of both) that are politically difficult and socially costly. On the other hand, the fiscal expansion enters into conflict with debt servicing, as resources start to be used to increase public investment and/or to spend more on education, health, and pensions. Greece and Latvia faced this stark dilemma during the crisis of 2008–2009 and its aftermath (more dramatically in Greece, see Chapter 6). A similar dilemma was present in the early 1980s at the time of the debt crisis in Poland, Hungary, Mexico, Argentina, Chile, Brazil, Peru, and other nations. The historical record shows that developing countries are typically pressured by external creditors and the IMF to choose the austerity route, and try to run primary fiscal surpluses, putting the servicing of their external debts ahead of restoring economic growth, protecting domestic investment, and employment creation.

Monetary policy also faces constraints. If a country has a fixed-exchange-rate regime, a currency board, or has joined a common currency (e.g. the Euro), the money supply is endogenous. Consequently, it is no longer a policy instrument at the discretion of central banks that can be used to stimulate aggregate demand and restore growth and full employment. The money supply will increase only if there is an increase in international reserves due to an improvement in the trade balance and/or capital inflow that is not sterilized. In addition, low inflation has reduced the effectiveness of "quantitative easing," as nominal interest rates are close to zero, leaving little space for cutting *real interest rates* and stimulating investment and consumption of durable goods, boosting spending in a depressed economy.

2.7 Secular Stagnation and the Complex Recovery after a Slump

In the late 1930s, Alvin Hansen coined the term "secular stagnation" to describe the prospect of slow economic growth and stagnation in the aftermath of the Great Depression. He identified three main factors producing this result: (i) a slowdown in population growth; (ii) a dimming of investment opportunities; and (iii) a limited ability to absorb technological breakthroughs. In the 2000s, Lawrence Summers, formerly Secretary of the Treasury under President Bill Clinton and a Harvard economics professor, reformulated Hansen's secular stagnation theory in light of the economic realities of the period surrounding the Great Recession. Summers (2014) stressed the difficulties to attain a macroeconomic equilibrium that satisfies three simultaneous conditions: (i) an equality between savings and investment at full employment; (ii) equilibrium at a positive real interest rate; and (iii) financial stability (no bubbles, say an increase in the price of an asset beyond its "fundamental" value). In fact, the macroeconomic configurations observed in advanced capitalist nations in the first and second decades of the twenty-first century have been characterized by various periods of an excess of savings over investment and chronic underemployment of resources as, for example, in the aftermath of the Great Recession of 2008–2009. In addition, Summers argues that economic growth in the United States in the period preceding the Great Recession was stimulated by *price bubbles*, first in the stock market (the IT bubble of the late 1990s) and then the real estate market bubble of 2003–2007. Nonetheless, growth resulting from bubbles is not sustainable and fails to satisfy Summers's third condition for a sound macro-equilibrium. The debate still continues about the plausibility of the secular stagnation hypothesis.

3

World War I, Hyperinflation in the 1920s, and World War II

3.1 Introduction

The first half of the twentieth century was a very complex period for the world economy and society. The first wave of globalization under the aegis of the gold standard was followed by World War I, the use of modern weapons that entailed the death of more than 12 million people (other estimates may give higher numbers), and the destruction of physical infrastructure and valuable economic assets USD 250 billion in dollars of 1914.[1] The economic variables that matter for the capacity of a country of winning a war include availability of economic resources (population, territory, and level of total GDP), its level of economic development (per capita income, level of technological advance). These variables, in turn, interact with military strategies, fighting morale of the population, and sheer luck. World War I changed the geopolitical landscape of the world. From the collapsed Austro-Hungarian,[2] Russian, Ottoman, and Prussian empires, new national borders emerged, spurring population movements and new economic relations among nations. The Bolshevik revolution perhaps would not have been possible without the collapse of the Tsars's empire, brought about by the economic crisis and social exhaustion stemming from World War I. Germany emerged from the conflict burdened by external debts and reparations payments imposed by the Treaty of Versailles and the peace treaties of Saint German and Trianon. The rise of Adolf Hitler is sometimes depicted as the result of explosive inflation in 1922 and 1923, along with other destabilizing factors present in the Weimar Republic. Extreme monetary instability and

---

[1] Broadberry and Harrison (2005) and Eloranta (2007).
[2] The end of the Austro-Hungarian empire after World War I gave rise to six successor states: Austria and Hungary (both ending up much diminished in both territory and population) and Czechoslovakia, Poland, Romania, and Yugoslavia.

hyperinflation also affected various countries of Central Europe and Soviet Russia in the early 1920s. The reconstruction of the international monetary system along the lines of a "gold exchange standard," resembling the pre-1914 gold standard, was very problematic, as we will discuss in Chapter 4. The world had changed substantially due to World War I and previous exchange-rate parities were obsolete. In 1929, a serious stock market crash affected the United States and various European countries. Misaligned exchange rates, financial fragility, a slump in aggregate demand, and a lack of international coordination in trade and financial policies opened the door to the Great Depression of the early 1930s. Then, a host of other economic and political factors configured to produce a new world conflict between 1939 and 1945. The death toll from World War II was between 55 and 60 million people and 70 percent of the industrial infrastructure in Europe was destroyed.[3] The international economic order that emerged after World War II restricted private capital flow among countries. When the conflict was coming to an end, a new monetary system of fixed-exchange rates among main currencies emerged: the Bretton Woods system that created the World Bank and the International Monetary Fund were established operating in Washington, DC. The United Nations succeeded the League of Nations and its headquarters was placed in New York City, reflecting the dominant global economic and political influence of the United States. This chapter focuses on the economic effects of World War I and World War II and of hyperinflation in Central Europe and Soviet Russia in the early 1920s in Central Europe. High inflation was related to the aftermath of World War I and its effects upon public finances and monetary institutions. The causes and consequences of the Great Depression and the subsequent period are examined in Chapter 4.

The effects of war on real economic activity in the various intervening countries were highly differentiated. World War I entailed initially expansionary effects on the economies of the United States (that joined the conflict in 1917) and Great Britain, although the dumping of U.S. stocks and bonds by Europeans in 1914 had created bouts of instability in the United States. World War I had devastating effects on the economies of the Austro-Hungarian and Russian empires, which could not withstand the stress of reorienting their economies toward the defense sector, the burden of fighting, food scarcities, and the administrative weaknesses of declining empires. The French economy also suffered, quite significantly in 1914–1919. The economic cycle in Germany was more complex, with alternative estimates yielding different output paths, for the period covering from 1913 to 1924.

---

[3] Pilisuk and Rountree (2008).

The onset of World War II also generated initial economic expansions in the United States, Britain, and Germany. In contrast, in the Soviet Union, agriculture, civilian industry, construction, and GDP contracted sharply between 1940 and 1942 to start recovering afterwards.

The overriding economic priority in various countries as World War II approached was the defense industry. France was negatively affected by the occupation by Germany that extracted food and raw materials from the French to send to Germany. The end of World War II, in turn, led to downturns in the United States and Britain (both economies had expanded during wartime) but enabled strong recoveries in France and Italy (that had contracted) in the second half of the 1940s. Nonetheless, recoveries were less strong in Germany and Japan after the termination of World War II. A variety of economic outcomes related to the war preparation, war, and postwar phases were observed in the different belligerent countries.

3.2 Empire, Globalization, and the Run-Up to World War I

The period from around 1870 to 1913 was accompanied by a liberal economic order with rising prosperity, although not evenly distributed within and across countries. Price stability and monetary predictability were pursued through the operation of the gold standard. Trade tariffs were low and there were few restrictions upon the mobility of capital and people across national boundaries (except upon the Chinese and other Asian people attempting to settle in countries such as Australia and the United States). Economic historians label this period as "the first wave of globalization" in which the levels of trade openness and capital flow (relative to GDP or savings) exceeded those of the second wave of globalization that started in the 1980s (Solimano, 2010).

Nonetheless, the first wave of globalization was not free of its own internal contradictions. On one side, trade and capital market integration brought an enhanced diversity of goods and services and spurred productive dynamism. However, there was also a process of property and market concentration in productive and financial spheres and the formation of monopolies and oligopolies. In turn, the benefits of globalization were accrued unevenly between labor and capital, generating significant levels of inequality.[4]

The global economy was embedded into a larger system formed by empires and influential nations. The dominance of Britain in the first wave

---

[4] Analysis of inequality in that period include Hatton and Williamson (2005) and Picketty (2012).

of globalization was underpinned by its large influence on the global trade system, supply of loanable funds, and foreign direct investment. British influence was reinforced by two important factors: naval superiority and the role played in steering the gold standard. However, this started to be challenged by rising powers. New contenders were the recently unified nations of Germany and Italy, along with France. The Russian, Ottoman, Habsburg, and Japanese empires also had a role in the division of the world into colonies, protectorates, and areas of influence. Another potential challenger was the United States, endowed with vast territory, an enterprising population, new technologies, and natural resources.

The first wave of globalization, embedding strengths and weaknesses, was followed by the outbreak of World War I. This unexpected turn of events invites important questions on the relationship between globalization, empire, and war. How was it possible that the first wave of globalization and its intended overall economic benefits ultimately ended up in a global conflict that created large scale human and economic destruction? How did the dynamics of various empires overlapping with globalization influence the run-up to "total war"?

There are competing views on these issues. One view is the hegemonic approach developed by historian Paul Kennedy (Kennedy, 1989)[5] and economic historian Charles Kindleberger (Kindleberger, 1986) in which main nations pursue internationally dominant positions through various means such as military power and defense spending ("hard power") and through international economic influence ("soft power") manifested in international trade, capital mobility, foreign direct investment, and their various influences on the working of the international monetary and reserve currency systems.

Another view, earlier developed in Angell (1911)[6] and largely endorsed by trade economists, stressed that economic interdependence in trade and finance is a powerful deterrent of war, as it increases its opportunity cost in terms of lost gains of trade and foregone unexploited investment opportunities. In this approach, economic integration will rarely be followed by armed conflict.

Another approach was the theories of imperialism in different guises. An important theorist in this vein was the British liberal and social reformer John A. Hobson (1902 [1988]), who in his classic book *Imperialism: A Study* argued that economic expansion by Britain and other big powers through the export of goods and capital was the consequence of the excess of production over internal demand along the lines of the underconsumption

---

[5] Kennedy (1989).
[6] Angell (1911).

hypothesis (see Solimano, 2017). In addition, Hobson noted the growing importance of financial capital over productive capital that needed external outlets in its pursuit of profit. In modern terminology, to avoid a "savings overhang" (e.g., an excess of national savings over investment at macro level) countries seek new external markets and territories to overcome limited internal investment opportunities.

The Hobson study was the basis for Vladimir Lenin's book *Imperialism, the highest phase of capitalism* (Lenin, 1939 [1972]). In his book, Lenin stressed that in the early twentieth century, the "highest stage of capitalism" was characterized by a growing concentration of production in monopolies and oligopolies. Financial resources were centralized by commercial banks owned by a small economic oligarchy. The author underscored the growing importance of the export of capital, over the export of goods, along with the growing rivalry among imperialist powers competing for new areas of influence and access to raw materials, land, and foreign markets.[7]

In the first and third approaches – hegemonic theories and approaches of imperialism – the sequence of globalization then war can be observed in practice. In contrast, in the economic integration approach, globalization and war would be highly unlikely events as economic globalization needs peace to flourish, with wars creating enormous cost for an economically interdependent world. In this approach, the sequence of globalization followed by war should be explained, largely, by the occurrence of noneconomic factors.

3.3 World War I

These approaches can shed light on the causes of World War I. Economic factors include the level of economic resources such as population, size of the territory, total GDP, and the effectiveness and productivity at which these resources can be mobilized (summary variables could be the GDP per capita and also the stage of development of technology). Noneconomic factors include the rise of nationalism, competition among powers and empires, diplomatic failures, military strategies, and political intrigue. There is a vast literature on World War I including interesting general

---

[7] Another important theorist and activist was Rosa Luxembourg, of Polish origin, killed by the German police in 1919, in her book *The Accumulation of Capital* developed a dynamic theory of the expansion of capitalism based on the under-consumptionist hypothesis. This created surplus of production that could be exported abroad along with an excess of national savings over investment that would lead to the export of capital to other nations along the lines of Hobson and Lenin.

narratives provided by Ferguson (1998) and Macmillan (2014).[8] References
to the economic approach to the conflict include those by Harrison (1998a);
Feinstein, Temin and Toniolo (2008); and Eloranta (2007).[9]

As of 1913, the world became divided into three camps whose country
composition and other features evolved as the war developed: (i) the
Allied Powers comprising, in the first phase (1914/1915) the countries of
the triple entente – France, the United Kingdom, and Russia – to which
were joined in a second phase (1915/16) by Italy, Portugal, and Romania.
In a third phase (1917/1918), Russia dropped out but the United States
joined, along with Brazil, Greece, Siam (now Thailand), and China; (ii)
the *Central Powers,* at the start of the war in 1914, included Germany,
the Austro-Hungarian Empire, and the Ottoman Empire. They were
joined also by Bulgaria in 1915 (iii) neutral nations such as Sweden and
Switzerland. To this list we have to add also the colonies and protectorates of the ruling empires that provided raw materials and food to help
the war effort.

The Allied camp, including the colonies, had a greater population than
the Central Powers (around 1.2 billion people in 1914); the Central Powers,
in turn, had a total population of 151 million. The Allied camp also held
more territory and a larger total GDP. Therefore, as measured by population, territory and level of GDP, the Allied camp had greater economic
resources than the Central Powers. However, the average GDP per capita
of the Allied camp in 1914 was around USD 1,400 in dollars of 1990, while
the average GDP of the Central Powers was USD 2,500 (see Table 3.1). The
entry of the United States into the Allied camp in 1917, along with the
departure of Russia, increased the average GDP per person for the Allied
camp, as Russia had a GDP per capita that was around one-third of
Britain's, while the GDP per capita of the United States was slightly above
that of Britain. Germany, in turn, was the most advanced economy of the
Central Powers but its per capita GDP was below that of Britain at the start
of the conflict (see Table 3.1).

Nevertheless, wars are not decided only by economic factors. The final
outcome of an armed conflict is critically affected by elements of military
strategy, the morale and fighting mystique of the population, and other
intervening factors.

In summary, we can identify the following economic aspects and consequences of war. First, war effort often requires substantial resource

[8] Macmillan (2014).
[9] Broadberry and Harrison (2005).

Table 3.1. *Initial economic conditions during World War I (select countries, 1914–1918)*

	Population (millions)	GDP (in 1990 int. billion dollars)	GDP per capita (in 1990 int. dollars)
Russian Empire (1914)	176.4	264.3	1,498
France (1914)	39.8	138.7	3,485
United Kingdom (1914)	46.0	226.4	4,921
Allies, Total (1914)	793.3	1,096.5	1,382
Italy (1915/16)	35.6	91.3	2,564
United States (1917/18)	96.5	511.6	5,301
Allies, Total (1918)	1,271.7	1760.5	1,384
Germany (1914)	67.0	244.3	3,648
Austria-Hungary (1914)	50.6	100.5	1,986
Ottoman Empire (1914)	23.0	25.3	1,100
Central Powers, Total (1914)	151.3	376.6	2,489
World (1913)	1,810.3	2,733.9	1,510

Source: Author's elaboration based on Broadberry and Harrison (2005).

mobilization (workforce, production, fiscal revenues) and the reallocation of resources away from the peacetime economy (agriculture, civilian industry, construction) toward the production of weapons and munitions by industry. In less developed economies, defense equipment, along with energy and food, often need to be imported and external suppliers have to be willing to do this during war conditions. The domestic economy needs liquid foreign exchange. In World War I, the United States and the United Kingdom were important foreign creditors for belligerent nations on the Allied side.

Second, war often leads to an increase in public spending, particularly associated with the rise of military outlays. For example, Germany increased the share of overall public spending from near 10 percent in 1913 to 50 percent in 1918; in turn, France also increased its government spending from around 10 percent in 1913 to 53.5 percent in 1918, with Britain increasing that ratio from 8 to 35 percent of GDP, with the United States rising public spending from near 2 percent to 16.6 percent in 1918.[10] To accommodate such large shifts of resources, private consumption and private investment often must contract, at least relative to GDP. A greater reliance on the state in resource allocation implies diminishing the influence of market during wartime. Price controls and administrative priorities for industrial production of military equipment and weapons are employed during situations of armed conflict.[11]

[10] Ibid.
[11] Eloranta (2007) and Feinstein et al. (2008) are other sources of estimates for the shares of military spending and total public spending in GDP for these countries.

Third, the issue of how to finance the war effort is important. The accompanying increases in public spending we have mentioned – often of large magnitude and carried out in a relatively short time span – can be financed through a combination of increased taxation (direct and indirect), issuing internal debt securities (war-bonds), external borrowing, and money-printing (this is the way the central bank pays for treasury bills (government bonds)).

When war ceases, economic conditions can be dire, as belligerent countries often have accumulated internal and external debts; need productive capacities restructured; need to provide income and housing support to demobilized war combatants; and need to jump-start the civilian sector. In addition, some countries like Germany and former Austro-Hungarian empire lost territories and were forced to pay war reparations to victor nations.

As mentioned, and explored in this book, hyperinflation was observed in countries that were more economically affected in the early 1920s by World War I. Czechoslovakia was the exception as this country avoided the monetization of fiscal deficits and violent inflation in that period (Solimano, 1991).

Fourth, World War I interrupted economic globalization and led to abandoning the gold standard, two cornerstones of the global economic order prevailing until 1913. As we discuss in Chapter 4, the restoration of a modified gold standard was fraught with difficulties and contributed to the onset of the Great Depression in the early 1930s.

Fifth, wars entail serious human and economic costs such as the loss of human lives, misery, the destruction of physical capital and infrastructure, damage to housing and housing shortages, and the damage of fertile agricultural lands and the natural environment.

3.4 The Consequences of World War I on Economic Activity

The effects on economic activity, say GDP per capita, of the events surrounding World War I varied substantially across different countries of the Allied camp and the Central Powers. As shown in Table 3.2a, in France, Germany, Italy, Austro-Hungary, and Russia, per capita GDP was lower in 1918 than in 1913. The magnitudes of the contractions in GDP per head go from 5 percent in Italy to 53 percent in Russia, with France's per capita GDP in 1918 being 31 percent lower than in 1913. In contrast, in 1918 the per capita GDP of Britain was 11 percent higher and near 7 percent higher in the United States than in 1913, according to Maddison's data.

Table 3.2b and Figure 3.1 identify several episodes of output expansion (trough to peak) and output contraction (peak to trough) related to the

Table 3.2a. *Real per capita GDP by country, 1913–1920 (1913 = 100)*

	Italy	United Kingdom	United States	Germany	Austro-Hungary	France	Russia
1913	100.0	100.0	100.0	100.0	100.0	100.0	100.0
1914	94.5	100.1	90.5	83.9	83.0	92.9	95.5
1915	89.8	107.5	91.8	79.5	76.6	93.2	98.3
1916	97.2	109.4	103.0	80.4	75.8	99.4	87.4
1917	97.5	110.2	99.0	80.9	74.6	85.5	76.7
1918	95.0	110.9	106.8	81.8	73.7	68.7	47.0
1919	91.2	99.0	107.2	70.9	65.2	80.7	40.5
1920	93.4	92.4	104.7	76.6	69.6	92.6	40.7

Source: Author's elaboration based on Maddison (2013).

Table 3.2b. *World War I-related expansions and contractions (percentage change in GDP per capita)*

	Expansion (trough/peak)		Contraction (peak/trough)	
	Years	Variation	Years	Variation
Italy	1915–1917	8.6	1913–1915	−10.2
	1919–1920	2.4	1917–1919	−6.4
United Kingdom	1913–1918	10.9	1918–1921	−18.7
United States	1914–1916	13.7	1913–1914	−9.5
	1917–1919	8.2	1916–1917	−3.9
	—	–	1919–1921	−6.3
Germany	1915–1918	2.9	1913–1915	−20.5
	1919–1922	28.8	1918–1919	−13.3
Austria-Hungary	1919–1922	27.4	1912–1919	−35.6
France	1914–1916	7.0	1912–1914	−7.9
	1918–1920	34.7	1916–1918	−30.8
Russia	1914–1915	2.9	1913–1914	−4.5
	1919–1920	0.4	1915–1919	−58.8

Source: Author's elaboration based on Table 3.2a and Maddison (2013).

hostilities of World War I in seven countries. In general, we observe a complex pattern of ups and downs in economic activity with output expansions during wartime in the United States and Great Britain.

The breakout of World War I in 1914 found the US economy in a recession affected by financial instability. In fact, the stock market sharply declined at the beginning of World War I as Europeans started a sell-off of

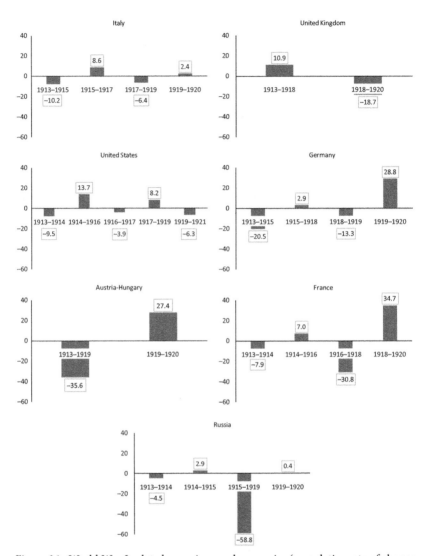

Figure 3.1. World War I-related recessions and recoveries (cumulative rate of change in GDP per capita). *Source:* Own elaboration based on Table 3.2b.

US stocks. Also, a run on commercial banks occurred. Nevertheless, things turned around thereafter, led by increased European demand for food and munition (the counterpart was an increase in US exports) that were needed to support the population and military. From the viewpoint of the United States, this created an economic stimulus (i.e., agricultural goods and industrial output rose to meet the external demand for military equipment).

As the United States entered World War I in 1917, the associated increase in government spending was financed through a combination of: (i) increased taxes on excess profits of firms and surtaxes on incomes of the rich; (ii) a rise in excise taxes on tobacco, alcohol, and luxuries (including jewelry and chewing gum); (iii) issuing of liberty bonds in 1917–1918, followed by victory bonds in 1919; and (iv) some extra money creation. According to Rockoff (2005), the size of the World War I economic expansion in the United States is roughly comparable with two previous booms: the gold rush of 1848–1853 and the American Civil War expansion of 1861–1865.[12] In Great Britain, World War I came along also with an expansionary cycle in 1913–1918 that entailed a sharp rise in military spending, the reallocation of labor and capital to the sector producing defense material, and enlarged public spending.

The behavior of output went into a stop and start pattern in Russia and France, which both experienced economic expansions in 1914/15 and 1914/16, respectively. However, the continuation of World War I led to massive output contractions in the two countries, with estimates of per capita GDP falling by 58.8 percent in Russia in 1915–1919 and by 26.2 percent in 1915–1918 in France. The Tsar Nicholas II empire in Russia was clearly disintegrating due to economic and social conditions as the war led to food and material input shortages, a declining morale of the population, and a difficult reconversion process from civilian to military production. In February of 1917, the Russian Provisional Government formed by the Duma (parliament) and led by Alexander Kerensky came into power after the collapse of the Romanov dynasty. The provisional government lasted until October 1917 (old calendar), when the Bolsheviks ascended, pulling Russia away from the international conflict. However, this was not the same as ensuring peace and the October revolution was followed by civil war and foreign intervention. Output stopped falling and then stagnated in 1919–1920 at a depressed level. Before, between 1915 and 1918 the GDP per person of Russia declined sharply (see Table 3.2b and Figure 3.1).

There are various estimates of German national income in the period 1914–1924. Box 3.1 presents seven alternative estimates. Graham's (Column II in Table B3.1.1) shows the most severe contraction during World War I (and also in 1919). According to Graham's data, Germany would have experienced six consecutive years of national income decline since the start of World War I. In fact, in 1919, Germany's national income was 45 percent below its level in

---

[12] Rockoff (2005).

Box 3.1. Alternative Income and Output Estimates for Germany, Austria-Hungary, and Russia in World War I

In this box, we present different estimates of real national income, GDP, and per capita GDP for Germany, Austria-Hungary, and Russia. Table B3.1.1 provides various estimates for Germany[13] that show national income falling between 1913 and 1918. Estimates go from a lower-bound decline of 12 percent (Column I) to a drop of 34 percent (Column 3). Maddison's estimate (Column V) shows a more conservative fall of 18 percent in national income between 1913 and 1918.

For Austria-Hungary's economy, the estimate of Schulze (2005) is of a fall of 38.5 percent in GDP between 1913 and 1918 and 37.4 percent for per capita GDP (Table B3.1.2).[14] In contrast, Maddison's estimate (presented in Tables 3.2a and 3.2b) are more conservative, yielding a decline of 26.3 percent (1913–1918) for per capita GDP.

Russia also suffered serious losses in national income in the order of 32 percent between 1913 and 1917 (Table B3.1.3 from Gatrell, 2005).

Table B3.1.1. *Germany: alternative estimates of real national income during and after World War I, 1913–1924*

	Henning	Graham	Roesler	Witt	Maddison	Ritschl and Spoerer	
	I	II	III	IV	V	VI	VII
1913	100	100	100	100	100	100	100
1914	96	82	83	90.2	85.2	90	92.3
1915	96	74	67	81.4	80.9	81.1	84.8
1916	92	69	64	80.2	81.7	75.8	80.9
1917	88	67	62	78.5	81.8	73.5	78.9
1918	88	66	57	74.7	82.0	71	76.8
1919	72	55	—	67.1	72.3	60.8	68.3
1920	74	66	—	74	78.6	70.7	76.5
1921	80	73	—	79.3	87.5	76.3	81.1
1922	83	80	—	82.6	95.2	81.4	85.9
1923	72	61	—	74.4	79.1	68.7	74.7
1924	82	74	—	87.3	92.6	80	83.2

Source: Ritschl (2005), chapter 2, table 2.1.

[13] This is based on Ritschl (2005).
[14] Schulze (2005).

Table B3.1.2. *Habsburg empire: GDP (1913 prices, 1913 = 100)*

	GDP	GDP per capita
1913	100.0	100.0
1914	89.8	89.5
1915	89.2	89.6
1916	80.2	80.5
1917	69.6	70.2
1918	61.5	62.6

Source: Schulze (2005), chapter 3, table 3.7.

Table B3.1.3. *Russia: estimate of national income, 1913–1917*

1913	100.0
1914	94.5
1915	95.5
1916	79.8
1917	67.7

Source: Gatrell (2005).

1913 (see Table B3.1.1, Column II). Other estimates, except for Maddison's, also present a continuous process of income decline between 1914 and 1919. It is only in 1920, according to all the estimates, that the German economy starts its recovery. However, this proves to be short-lived, as the economy will contract again in 1923 at the time of hyperinflation, (Table B3.1.1).

The Austro-Hungary economy, in turn, suffered a major collapse with per capita GDP falling by 35.6 percent between 1912 and 1918 (Table 3.2b). The economic and political collapse of the Habsburg empire throughout World War I is attributed to the operation of several factors: a shrinking resource base associated with the war effort; a severe foreign exchange constraint that limited its capacity to import foodstuff and war material; internal administrative complexities of the empire; and general exhaustion of the population (Schulze, 2005). Several of the same factors were also present in the disintegration of the Russian empire.

3.5 The Role of Military Spending

The evolution of military expenditure in World War I is important, as this variable is bound to have an important influence on economic cycles. In the period 1900–1913, *before* World War I, the "normal" ratios of military

Table 3.3. *Real defense burden before World War I, 1900–1913 (military spending as a ratio of net national product, percentage)*

	Britain	France	Russia	'Austria'	Germany	Italy
1900	6.9	4.4	4.0	2.7	—	3.1
1901	7.1	4.6	3.9	2.7	4.1	3.2
1902	5.8	4.5	3.7	2.7	3.9	3.3
1903	4.2	4.1	4.1	2.8	3.6	2.9
1904	3.9	4.0	9.2	2.8	3.6	3.0
1905	3.5	3.9	13.8	2.5	3.6	2.9
1906	3.1	3.9	8.7	2.3	3.8	2.7
1907	2.9	4.2	5.4	2.2	4.2	2.7
1908	3.1	4.1	4.7	2.4	3.8	2.8
1909	3.3	3.8	4.3	3.0	4.0	2.9
1910	3.4	4.1	4.0	2.6	4.2	3.0
1911	3.4	4.1	4.3	2.4	3.9	3.3
1912	3.3	4.0	4.5	2.6	3.8	4.0
1913	3.4	4.3	5.1	3.5	4.9	5.1

Source: Stevenson (1996).

spending in Britain, France, Russia, "Austria," Germany, and Italy were in the range of 3–4 percent of net national product, although in some specific years and countries the ratio was much higher, for example in Britain with the Boer-War in 1900–1901 and in Russia in 1904–1906, associated with the Russo-Japanese War (see Table 3.3). The Boer-War was between 1899 and 1902 but the higher increase in military spending for the U.K. (see Table 3.3) is in 1900–1901.

The onset of World War I led to sharp increases in military spending across most belligerent countries, although the magnitude of the increase varied considerably across nations for which we have data (see Table 3.4). In the United Kingdom, military spending increased from about 4 percent of GDP in 1913 to 38 percent in 1916–1917. After World War I, military spending declined to 4 percent of GDP in 1920, after having reached 32 percent in 1918. Military expenditure in the United States went up from 1 percent in 1914–1916, to 6 percent in 1917, and to 13 percent in 1918.[15] It is very likely that the rise in military spending stimulated *aggregate* economic activity in Britain and the United States. One additional reason for the economic booms in the United Kingdom and the United States, lies in the fact neither country suffered foreign occupation during World War I, thus avoiding destruction of their physical infrastructure.

[15] These figures are taken from Table 2.1 in Feinstein et al. (2008). Also Rockoff (2005).

Table 3.4. *Real defense burden during World War I and its aftermath, 1913–1920 (military expenditure as a ratio of net national product at factor cost, percentage)*

	United Kingdom	United States	Russia	Germany	Austro-Hungary[a]
	World War I				
1913	4.0 (3.4[b])	1	5.1[b]	4.9[b]	4.3
1914	9	1	—	14	30.2
1915	34	1	—	41	26.8
1916	38	1	—	35	26.2
1917	38	6	—	53	17.2
1918	32	13	—	32	—
1919	13	9	—	—	—
1920	4	3	—	—	—

[a] Schulze, M. (2005).
[b] Stevenson (1996).
Source: Author's elaboration based on Feinstein, Temin and Toniolo (2008).

Germany engaged in the most ambitious increase in defense spending during World War I with a rise from 4.9 percent in GDP in 1913 to 53 percent in 1917. This implies the redeployment of both labor and capital towards armament factories, chemical industries, shipyards, and other activities linked to the military preparation for World War I. Interestingly, the sustained increase in military spending in Germany coincided with a *drop* in output/income with magnitude varying according to the different estimates.

In Austro-Hungary, there was a very sharp increase in defense spending, with the ratio of military outlays to GDP increasing from about 4 percent in 1913 to 30 percent in 1914 and stabilizing at 26 percent in 1916–1917. This swift resource reallocation toward the defense sector was also followed by a *steady decline* in national income from 1914 to 1918 of a significant magnitude, resembling closely the German situation. Of course, World War I was fought in Germany and Austro-Hungary and this did contribute to the decline in aggregate output in these countries.

3.6 The Aftermath of World War I

The year 1919 – the first after the armistice signed in November of 1918 that ended World War I – was one of recession (a decline in per capita GDP relative to 1918) in Italy, Germany, the United Kingdom, Austria, and Russia. In the United Kingdom, there was a severe contraction in GDP per capita of 16.7 percent in 1918–1920. In the United States, per capita GDP declined by 6.3 percent in 1919–1921 (peak/through, table 3.2b and figure 3.1). In contrast, the end of World War I brought about a strong recovery in France and a mild rebound in Italy (see Figure 3.1).

The decline in military spending after World War I probably created recessionary impulses.[16] There are various reasons why this happened. On the one hand, the return to a peace economy is not an automatic process and can produce frictional unemployment and supply disruptions. On the other hand, the decline in military spending is bound to reduce the demand stimulus to the economy. In addition, inflation following the phase out of price controls reduced the value of liquid savings accumulated during World War I, creating a negative wealth effect. Also, private investment took time to recover, likely due to various uncertainties such as the size and timing of war reparations (in Germany), the new trade relations of newly emerging countries after the breakup of the four empires (Austro-Hungarian, Prussian, Ottoman, and Russian), more active labor unions, and doubts on the ability of governments to maintain monetary stability, among other factors.[17] In addition, the lack of complementary physical infrastructure (roads, ports, telecommunications) damaged by World War I, also must have hampered the recovery of private investment.

Box 3.2. The Recession of 1920–1921 in the United States

A "deflationary depression" developed in 1920–1921 (two years of negative growth) in the United States, in which output and sales contraction were accompanied by a generalized decline in the price of goods, services, and assets. The exact magnitude of the contraction of 1920–1921 is subject to controversy. According to the statistics of the US Department of Commerce, total output declined by 6.9 percent in 1920–1921. However, revised estimates by economic historian Christine Roemer yield a decline in GDP of only 2.4 percent during those years. Given this moderate size of GDP contraction, Roemer downplays the importance of the "depression of 1920–1921" compared with the "Great Depression of 1930–1933."[18] In turn, the output data from Maddison show a decline in US per capita GDP of 2.3 percent in 1920 and 4.1 percent in 1921, figures closer to the original Department of Commerce estimate.

---

[16] We have data for cuts in military spending after 1918 but only for the United States and Britain. Britain sharply reduced its defense spending to GDP ratio from 32 percent in 1918 to 13 percent in 1919 and further to 4 percent in 1920. The United States cut military expenditure from 13 percent of GDP in 1918 to 3 percent in 1920.

[17] Pindyck and Solimano (1993) show the value of *waiting* for irreversible investment under uncertainty.

[18] Roemer (1988).

A monetary interpretation of the causes of the contraction in 1920–1921 was advanced by Milton Friedman and Anna Schwartz in their *A Monetary History of the United States: 1867–1960*. They point to a still inexperienced Federal Reserve (the United States central bank established in 1913) as provoking the slump due to an unnecessary contraction in the money supply originated to abate potential inflationary pressures. A similar monetarist explanation of the slump during the Great Depression of the 1930s was given by Friedman and Schwartz (see Chapter 4).

Other observers have stressed the fact that the depression of 1920–1921 apparently "cured itself" – a case of a self-correcting slump – through the operation of downward price and wage flexibility, without having to resort to a fiscal expansion.[19]

3.7 Hyperinflation in Central Europe

The restoration of macroeconomic equilibrium and social balance after World War I was not easy. As noted before, extreme monetary instability and hyperinflation affected Germany and Russia and the countries that emerged from the dismemberment of the Austro-Hungarian empire such as Austria, Poland, and Hungary. Hungary experienced a virulent hyperinflation in 1946 and similarly Greece in the first half of the 1940s. The most studied case is Germany.[20] Classic references are Graham (1930) and Bresciani-Turroni (1937). More recent analysis includes Sargent (1982) and Dornbusch and Fischer (1986), and Végh (1992). A critical year in Germany was 1923. The country suffered an economic contraction as France occupied the Ruhr and was hit by hyperinflation (Figures 3.2a and 3.2b). In fact, the price level of goods and services increased sharply between June of 1922 and December of 1923. Escalating inflation was accompanied by exorbitant increases in the money supply and even more rapid depreciation of the Reichsmark vis-à-vis the US dollar and other main currencies. Hyperinflation sharply diminished the incentives to produce and invest, reduced the real value of the money supply and nominal spending, and curtailed real economic activity. According to Maddison, per capita German GDP fell by 17 percent in 1923. Other estimates provide a range of

[19] Grant, J. (2014). The US economy had experienced a series of contractions in 1907 and 1908 – associated with the "financial panic of 1907" (see Bruner and Carr 2009) and in 1914; in these episodes GDP per capita fell by near 10 percent.

[20] Accurate data on prices, money and the exchange rate in Russia for the early 1920s are not easily accessible.

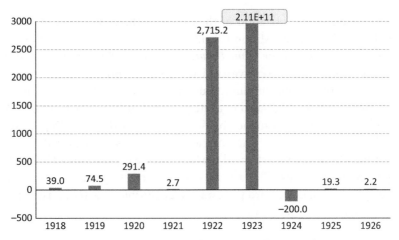

Figure 3.2a. Inflation in Germany (annual percentage change in the consumer price index, 1918–1926). *Source:* Reinhart and Rogoff (2010).

Figure 3.2b. Variation in GDP per capita in Germany (annual percentage change, 1918–1926). *Source:* Maddison (2013).

output decline in *real national income* that year between 10 percent (Witt, Column III) and close to 24 percent (Graham, Column II) (see Table 3.5).

The German economy in the 1920s was affected by debilitating conditions including large war debt and war reparations, along with an environment of social conflict. The British economist John Maynard Keynes

Table 3.5. Germany: alternative estimates of real national income, 1920–1924

	Henning I		Graham II		Witt III		Maddison IV		Ritschl and Spoerer V	
	Level	(% rate of change)	Level	(% rate of change)	Level	(% rate of change)	Level	(% rate of change)	Level	(% rate of change)
1920	100		100		100		100		100	
1921	108	8.11	111	10.61	107	7.61	111	11.32	106	6.01
1922	112	3.75	121	9.59	112	4.16	121	8.80	112	5.92
1923	97	−13.25	92	−23.75	101	−9.93	101	−16.91	98	−13.04
1924	111	13.89	112	21.31	118	17.34	118	17.07	109	11.38

Source: Own elaboration based on data from Ritschl (2005).

(1920) in *The Economic Consequences of Peace* (1919) accurately described the crippling effect of the reparations imposed by the Treaty of Versailles.[21]

The Weimar Republic showed that achieving a consensus between capital and labor and/or among industrialists, financiers, and landowners on how to share the cost of the servicing of public debt acquired during the period 1913–1918 and the war reparations was very difficult – if not impossible – to attain. The result of the impasse eventually brought very high inflation, internal economic disorganization, and political uncertainty.

There are at least two schools of thought proposed by economists studying the German case regarding the origin of the hyperinflation in the 1920s:[22] one view, represented by Graham (1930), is the *balance of payments theory* or passive money theory that stresses the fact that war reparations and uncertain external financing led to a very steep depreciation of the German mark, which fed into higher wages and prices, validated by an accommodative monetary policy followed by the Reichsbank (the German central bank). In this context, the increases in the money supply followed increases in prices and the exchange rate. The other school of thought, presented by Bresciani-Turroni (1937), is in line with the *quantity theory of money* (money times velocity equals prices times output) and the links between money creation and the financing of the fiscal deficit. In this case, the central bank prints money in exchange for bonds issued by the treasury. This is a fiat money system that relies on the legal tender status of paper money that is unbacked by real assets such as gold. In the quantity theory of money, money printing feeds not only price increases but also an increase in money velocity (due to expectations of future inflation), which contributes to inflation. The rise in velocity has, as a counterpart, a decrease in the demand for money as people economize the use of cash balances heavily taxed by high inflation. In this situation, the price level grows at a rate above the money supply, a fact observed in Germany in 1923. In turn, the lag in tax collection in conditions of very high inflation reduces the real value of tax receipts by the treasury deteriorating the fiscal

---

[21] Victorious armies also invaded the Ruhr region to make sure coal deliveries and other reparations were paid. In addition, the international community entertained serious doubts related to the capacity and willingness of Germany to comply with war reparation payments. The London Schedule of Payments, the Dawes Plan, and the Young Plan were all oriented to avoid an eventual repudiation of the Versailles Treaty conditions.

[22] Analysis of German hyperinflation of 1922–23 can be found in Graham (1930) favoring the passive money school and Bresciani-Turroni (1937) supporting the quantity theory approach. Solimano (1991) offers an international perspective on this and other Central European hyperinflationary episodes.

budget. On the expenditure side, the burden posed by war reparations, debt payments, and support spending for social needs also put extra pressure on the budget. An influential interpretation of the end of hyperinflation was Sargent (1982) in which he argued that, once there was a *regime change* in Germany in 1923 (and in other Central European nations) that undertook serious institutional reforms – such as a fiscal policy of balanced budgets and an independent central bank that would no longer rediscount government bonds unless backed by gold and commercial paper – the public understood that the main source of money creation had come to an end. In addition, credibility was strengthened by a foreign loan conditional on monetary and fiscal reforms supervised by the League of Nations. Sargent's narrative is that the stabilization of exchange rate and internal prices took place without an apparent cost in terms of loss of output and rise in unemployment once new credible monetary and fiscal rules were in place. The facts show that, while per capita GDP rose in 1922, a year of escalating inflation, in 1923 output fell substantially (stabilization took place in October, so perhaps the annual data reflects some contraction at the end of the year) but 1924 and 1925 were years of positive growth (see Figure 3.2b). However, other studies such as Wickers (1986) showed evidence that tend to contradict Sargent's claims of costless stabilization.

3.8 Hyperinflation in Austria, Poland, and Hungary

Austria also suffered high inflation in the first nine months of 1922 (the exchange rate stabilized in September and inflation stabilized in October). Austria was economically debilitated by the fact the country lost significant parts of its original territory and resources after the demise of the Austro-Hungarian empire. In addition, Austria faced war reparation payments as a loser in World War I and had to absorb part of the government bureaucracy of the old empire and support a large pool of unemployed people. Between January of 1919 and December of 1922, about 57 percent of public spending was financed by money creation issued by the Austrian section of the Austro-Hungarian central bank.[23] Inflation was stabilized more or less along the same lines of the German case: by the passage of new legislation prohibiting the rediscounting of government debt with the (reformed) central bank, by balancing the fiscal deficit, the approval of a foreign loan, and a stabilization plan monitored by the Council of the League of Nations.

---

[23] Table A.1 in Sargent (1982).

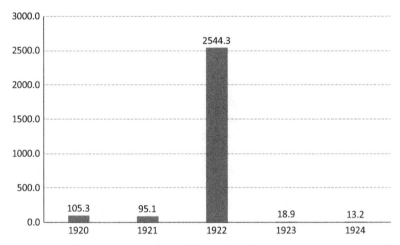

Figure 3.3a. Inflation in Austria (annual percentage change in consumer price index, 1920–1924). *Source:* World Development Indicators, The World Bank 2018.

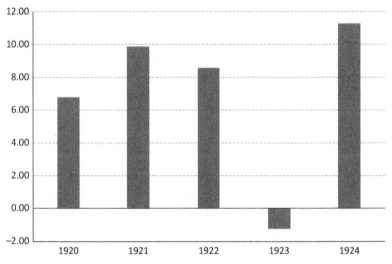

Figure 3.3b. Variation in GDP per capita in Austria (annual percentage change, 1920–1924). *Source:* World Development Indicators, The World Bank 2018.

Sargent (1982) presents the Austrian case as an example of almost instantaneous stabilization due to regime change. While hyperinflation concentrated in 1922 (2,544 percent), there was no decline in GDP per capita, with a modest fall in GDP taking place in 1923, when inflation reached 19 percent on an annual basis. Growth resumed in 1924 (see Figures 3.3a and 3.3b).

Hungary, like Austria, also suffered important losses of population and territory after World War I and experienced political turmoil in 1919, as the short-lived Bolshevik republic of Bela Kuhn was followed by the repressive right-wing regime of Admiral Horthy. From 1914 to 1924, Hungary ran substantial fiscal deficits that were largely monetized by the Hungarian section of the Austro-Hungarian bank, which dissolved in late 1919. In 1924 the Hungarian National Bank (Central Bank) was created. The period of more rapid exchange-rate depreciation and inflation in domestic prices was from January, 1922 to March, 1924, when the goods price index increased by a factor of 263.[24] The stabilization came in March, 1924, and involved similar elements of the stabilization programs in Austria and Germany: broad fiscal and monetary reform, stabilization of the exchange rate, the support of a foreign loan, and the general supervision of the Council of League of Nations.

Poland came into existence after World War I, and was formed by territories formerly belonging to Austro-Hungary, Germany, and Russia. Initially, German marks, Russian rubles, and crowns from the Austro-Hungarian bank went into circulation, in addition to Polish marks. This contributed to monetary confusion in the newly formed nation. In addition, Poland continued war with Soviet Russia until 1920 and suffered the stripping of its machinery and material by the Germans during World War I.

The country-run fiscal deficits up to 1924 were largely financed by money printing by the Polish State Loan Bank in a pattern of unbacked money creation similar to that by Germany, Austria, and Hungary. The most intense period of exchange-rate depreciation, money creation, and price level increases took place between January, 1922 and December, 1923 (see Figure 3.5) with price increases and exchange-rate depreciation strongly declining in January of 1924. The reforms that enabled stabilization of prices and the exchange rate also involved closing the fiscal gap and creating an autonomous central bank, in which the Bank of Poland replaced the Polish State Loan Bank. The new bank could not discount government debt (unless supported by gold). In this case, no foreign loan was initially arranged and external direct supervision by the Council of League of Nations was absent in the Polish stabilization process.

Although there are no reliable estimates of per capita GDP for Hungary and Poland in 1920–1924, using data on unemployment (based on registered

---

[24] Sargent (1982), p. 61.

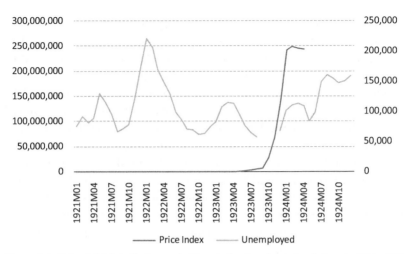

Figure 3.4. Poland: high inflation cycle (the wholesale price index, left-axis, 1914 = 100, and number of unemployed, 1921–1924). *Source:* Sargent (1982).

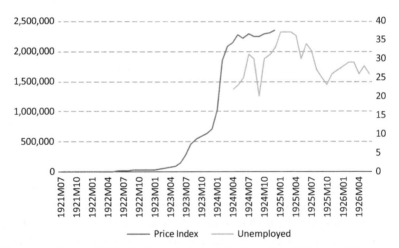

Figure 3.5. Hungary: high inflation cycle (price index, from July 1921 through November 1923, retail prices, 1914 = 100; from December 1923 through March 1925, wholesale prices, 1913 = 100 and number of unemployed, 1921–1924). *Source:* Sargent (1982).

unionized workers shown on the right-hand axis of Figures 3.4 and 3.5) we can see that the stabilization of the price level (left-hand axis) was followed by initial increases in unemployment in Poland during 1924 (Figure 3.4). An increase in unemployment also takes place in Hungary but it tends to decline from mid-1925 onwards (Figure 3.5).

**Box 3.3. Multiple Currencies, Inflation, and
Stabilization in Soviet Russia, 1914–1924**

The Russian ruble was a stable currency during most of the nineteenth century. The monetary reforms of the imperial government's finance minister Sergei Witte undertaken in the early 1890s strengthened a ruble–gold parity that lasted until the outbreak of World War I. Thereafter, convertibility was suspended and the imperial government started to run large fiscal deficits to finance Russia's involvement in World War I. The deficit was covered by money creation leading to depreciation of the currency in terms of domestic goods and foreign currencies including gold (Table B3.3.1). The imperial government lost power in February, 1917, replaced by the Kerensky provisional government, which introduced a new currency (the *kerenki*) that failed to stop inflation. In October, 1917, the Bolshevik took power, replacing the provisional government and in January–February of 1918 suspended the servicing of foreign debt acquired by the imperial and provisional governments. There were several currencies in circulation from 1918 to 1924. During foreign intervention and civil war, various belligerent parties, including foreign powers, issued their own money that coexisted with the official Soviet ruble or *sovznaks*. As of April 1920, around 68 percent of the currency in circulation was constituted by the *sovznavk*. During war-communism and after, there were heated debates on the most adequate monetary regime for Soviet Russia. In 1919–1920, an attempt was made to reduce the use of money and have a barter socialist economy. When the New Economic Policy that reintroduced elements of a market economy was launched in March–August, 1921, it was accompanied by a dual monetary system in which a "hard currency" (the *chevornetz*) backed by gold coexisted with the paper currency (the *sovznak*) that was used in the state sector (ministries, public enterprises) and in rural areas. In 1922, a currency reform was undertaken due to the rapid depreciation of the *sovznak*. The central bank (*Gosbank*), the treasury (*Narcomfin*), and the planning committee (*Gosplan*) each had a say on monetary matters and conflicts over the monetary regime continued. In February 1924, the *chevornetz* became the only legal tender and the printing of *sovznaks* was stopped. In addition, the Soviet government moved to close the fiscal deficit in fiscal year 1923/24 and to run a surplus in 1924/25. This contributed to the stabilization of the *chevornetz* in terms of foreign currency and of domestic prices. Given the hostility of foreign powers toward the Soviet regime, besides the suspension of foreign debt in early 1918, no foreign loan supported the stabilization process undertaken by the Soviet government.

Table B3.3.1. *Fiscal deficit, currency, and prices in Russia, 1914–1921*

Year	Fiscal deficit (% of public spending)	Currency issue (Millions of rubles)	Real money supply (1918 = 100)
1914	39.1	1,283	
1915	74.0	2,670	
1916	76.0	3,480	
1917	81.7	16,403	
1918	66.6	33,500	100.0
1919	77.3	164,200	28.0
1920	86.9	943,600	7.0
1921	84.1	16,375,300	5.0

Source: Author's elaboration based on Katzenellennbaum (1925), Nenovsky (2015).

3.9 World War II

World War II was the second large-scale armed conflict at a global level in the first half of the twentieth century. It brought immense destruction and had far-reaching consequences for the international economy. It consolidated the geopolitical and economic hegemony of the United States, fostered the ultimate demise of the Japanese empire, and diminished the relative position of Great Britain as a hegemonic power. At the same time, it divided the world into two competing economic camps, capitalism and socialism, exemplified by the United States and the USSR, respectively. The warring factions were the Allied countries, initially formed of the United Kingdom, France, Czechoslovakia, and British and French territories, and the Axis countries, formed of Austria, Germany, Italy, Japan, and their areas of influence. Later, the Allied camp was joined by the United States, China, and the Soviet Union, with their vast economic power (the United States) and enormous territory, resources, and fighting resolve (the USSR). In 1938, the Allied countries had a population of nearly 690 million while the population in the Axis countries was 259 million (Table 3.6). The population of the Allied increases to nearly 1.2 billion people, if we add China. In turn, between 1938 and 1942, the absolute level of GDP and the average GDP per capita of the Allied countries was higher than that of the Axis countries. The wealthiest countries were the United Kingdom and United States.

The superiority in population, territories, and combined GDP of the Allies were all important factors in their eventual victory against the Axis countries. However, winning World War II was not easy, due to the considerable capabilities in military planning and armament of Germany and

Table 3.6. *Initial economic conditions in World War II (select countries,*
1938–1942)

	Population (millions)	GDP ($ billion)	GDP per capita ($ per head)
United Kingdom (1938)	47.5	284.2	5,983
France (1938)	42	185.6	4,424
USSR (1938)	167.0	359.0	2,150
United States (1938)	130.5	800.3	6,134
China (excluding Manchuria, 1938)	411.7	320.5	778
Czechoslovakia (1938)	10.5	30.3	2,882
Poland (1938)	35.1	76.6	2,182
Allies, Total (1938)	689.7	1,024.30	1,485
Allies, Total (1942)	1195.2	2069.3	1,731
Germany (1938)	68.6	351.4	5,126
Austria (1938)	6.8	24.2	3,583
Italy (1938)	43.4	140.8	3,244
Japan (1938)	71.9	169.4	2,356
Axis, Total (1938)	258.9	751.3	2,902
Axis, Total (1942)	634.6	1552.0	2,446

Source: Author's elaboration based on data from Harrison (1998a).

Japan. Also, their early and swift initial attack in the Western and Eastern Fronts gave them a critical advantage in the initial years of the war (from 1939 to 1941/42). German expansionism was contained by the fighting ability and mystic of the Soviet Union and Britain among other nations.

Preparation for war started in Germany and Japan in the second half of the 1930s, with the share of military spending in national income, reaching 17 percent in Germany in 1938 and 13 percent in Japan in 1937 (the year of the escalation of the Second Sino-Japanese War). In contrast, the ratio of military spending to GDP was 2 percent (1939) in the United States and 7 percent in Britain in 1938.

The peak levels of military spending, as shares of national income, in World War II surpassed those of World War I. In Germany, spending reached a peak of 53 percent in 1917, while the peak in 1943 was 76 percent. These higher ratios of defense spending were also observed in Britain, the United States, and the Soviet Union. The USSR had a GDP per capita roughly one-third of the United States in 1938 and increased military spending to 76 percent in 1943, a very significant effort of resource mobilization in wartime (Table 3.7).[25]

---

[25] The details of how the internal economy in these countries adjusted to accommodate such large defense ratios are provided in the country studies in Harrison (1998a).

Table 3.7. *Military expenditure as a percentage of net national product at factor cost (select countries, 1937–1950)*

	United Kingdom	United States	Russia/USSR	Germany	Japan	Italy[a]
1937	—	—	9	—	13	11
1938	7	—	—	17	—	10
1939	16	2	—	25	—	8
1940	49	2	21	44	17	12
1941	55	12	—	56	25	23
1942	54	34	75	69	36	22
1943	57	44	76	76	47	21
1944	56	45	69	—	64	17
1945	47	38	—	—	—	23
1946	19	10	—	—	—	6
1947	11	5	—	—	—	3
1948	8	5	18	—	—	—
1949	8	6	17	—	—	—
1950	8	5	16	—	—	—

[a] Zamagni, V. (1998).

Source: Author's elaboration based on data from Feinstein, Temin & Toniolo (2008) and Zamagni (1998).

The American economy experienced a very significant expansion during World War II: its GDP per capita increased by 88 percent between 1939 and 1944 (Table 3.8). It is important to note that most of this expansion took place before the United States entered the conflict. The purchase of food, raw materials, inputs (intermediate parts used in production), and military equipment by Europe were important in stimulating the US economy. In addition, there was a sharp rise in military spending from 2 percent of GDP in 1939–1940 to 45 percent in 1944.[26] As in World War I, the US economy was helped by the fact that the war did not take place on American soil, preventing the destruction of US physical infrastructure and productive assets. In 1939–1942, there was still idle labor and unused productive capacities in the United States. Thus, an expansion in the civil and defense economy could

---

[26] War-led economic recoveries and growth accelerations in the US economy were also present during the Korean War in the 1950s, the Vietnam War in the 1960s, and the various wars that had some US involvement in the 1980s (in Nicaragua, El Salvador, and Afghanistan) and in the Balkans in the 1990s.

Table 3.8. *World War II-related change in real GDP per capita by country (1914–1918, 1939 = 100)*

	France	Germany	United Kingdom	United States	Italy	USSR[a]	Japan
1939	100.00	100.00	100.00	100.00	100.00		100.00
1940	84.33	99.93	109.48	106.84	97.19	100.00	102.07
1941	69.04	105.64	119.47	125.07	94.68	86.14	102.01
1942	62.20	106.17	121.98	148.48	88.84	65.70	100.08
1943	59.67	108.94	123.65	175.56	74.94	73.02	100.20
1944	50.52	112.53	118.25	187.99	60.29	86.77	94.42
1945	53.68	83.50	112.67	178.47	53.97	82.36	47.80
1946	80.43	41.01	107.71	140.18	72.52		51.29
1947	86.33	45.06	105.46	135.44	85.73		54.72
1948	91.66	52.42	107.72	138.16	91.76		61.27
1949	103.19	60.72	111.07	136.32	98.91		63.91

[a] Gross National Product (1940 = 100).

Source: Author's elaboration based on data from Maddison (2013) and for USSR from Harrison (1998b).

take place more or less simultaneously. Thereafter, "guns and butter" had to compete with each other along the production possibilities frontier, as the United States had already reached full employment (Rockoff, 1998). Once the economy was at full capacity, the trade-off between civilian-oriented output and war-oriented production showed in shortages of housing, deterioration in the quality of civilian clothing, and transformation of car-making industries (such as Ford Motor Company) into producers of tanks.

The British economy expanded from 1939 to 1943 but then it fell into recession (between 1944 and 1947). In wartime, the economy had to undergo a transition from civilian to military production that initially stimulated aggregate economic activity but later strained the economy. World War II had a devastating effect on the French economy, as France was occupied early in the war by Germany that extracted food and raw materials to support its war economy. As a consequence of this strain, French GDP per capita declined by roughly 50 percent between 1939 and 1944 (Table 3.8). World War II also had very detrimental effects on the Italian economy with GDP per capita contracting by 46 percent between 1939 and 1945. Foreign occupation and internal political disarray contributed to this outcome.

In Germany during the 1930s, the Nazi regime had followed active policies of demand stimulus to recover from the effects of the Great Depression. A critical step was the massive job creation from 1932 to 1936 based upon public infrastructure, such as road construction. This program managed to create near 6 million jobs reverting most of the employment losses of the 1930–1932 period. This plan was led by Hjalmar Schacht, who became an economic confidant of Adolf Hitler. Hitler apparently was lured by Schacht's reputation as an architect of the stabilization of the mark in 1923, besides his good connections with industrialists, bankers, and the international financial community. Schacht was head of the German central bank from 1933 to 1939.[27]

The rapid recovery of employment in Germany in the second half of the 1930s contrasted with the situation of the labor market in Britain and the United States. While in Britain unemployment was 10 percent and near 20 percent in the United States, the unemployment rate in Germany was below 5 percent (Abelshauser, 2005). Then a second four-year plan (1936–1940) was launched, oriented toward rearmament, which further stimulated economic activity. Between 1939 and 1944, the German GDP per capita increased by 12.5 percent, an expansion short of that of the United States and Britain in the same period.

In Japan, the defense sector helped to launch a recovery after the Great Depression. However, this was not a consensus position. In fact, Finance Minister Korekiyo Takahashi, who following the onset of the Great Depression took Japan out of the gold standard and favored a reduction in interest rates and more export-led growth, urged restraining military spending. In February 1936 he was assassinated (Hara, 2005). After his death, armament took priority, coinciding with the Second Sino-Japanese War that escalated in 1937. GDP expanded rapidly between 1937 and 1941, the year that Japan entered World War II with the attack on Pearl Harbor; thereafter, output more or less stagnated before collapsing in 1944 and 1945, with per capita GDP falling by near half in those two years (Table 3.8 and Figure 3.6).

Another theater of war took place on the Eastern Front, specifically in the Soviet Union. The situation was now different from World War I, when imperial Russia could not cope with the war effort, and the empire finally disintegrated, giving rise to the first socialist regime on earth. The industrialization process in the late 1920s and the institutions of central planning apparently helped rapid resource mobilization for war after the German invasion of 1941. In fact, Stalin was conscious that "socialism

---

[27] Later during World War II, he was suspected to have knowledge of the attempt to assassinate Hitler and was interned in a detention center.

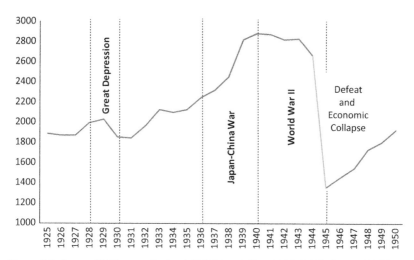

Figure 3.6. Japan: GDP per capita level, (1990 int. dollars, 1925–1950). *Source:* Maddison (2013).

in one country" exposed the country to external risks and foreign invasion was a concern for the Communist ruling elite. The Soviet Union was helped by its large territory, a sizable population, and by its ability to produce machinery and equipment domestically. Although food, certainly, was not plentiful, at the end of the day, it reached the frontlines and the civilian population. In turn, required inputs and machinery were available for the armament sector. These two features were largely absent in World War I under the Tsar's Russia (Gatrell and Harrison, 1993).[28] On the other hand, in spite of their favorable capacity to fight war, the level of economic development of the USSR was behind that of Germany, Britain, and the United States, with the practical consequence of a more limited available surplus over subsistence levels that could be redirected to the defense sector, forcing a sharper adjustment in consumption.

The evaluation of the effects on economic activity of World War II, based on Western recalculation of Soviet Gross National Product (GNP) (Gatrell, 2005) shows that the level of GNP in 1945 was 17.5 percent below its level of 1940. The sharpest contraction took place between 1940 and 1942, with GNP falling by a cumulative 34 percent in those three years. However, aggregate figures mask important differences at sector level (manufacturing,

---

[28] Gatrell and Harrison (1993).

Table 3.9. *Soviet GNP by sector of origin (1940–1945, 1940 = 100)*

	1940	1941	1942	1943	1944	1945
Agriculture	100.0	63.1	39.2	43.6	64.5	67.7
Industry	100.0	97.6	86.3	100.8	113.0	95.7
Defense	100.0	160.0	368.6	455.2	498.1	349.5
Civilian	100.0	87.6	40.5	43.1	50.5	54.6
Construction	100.0	65.1	30.2	32.1	41.5	42.5
Gross National Product	100.0	86.1	65.7	73.0	86.8	82.4

Source: Elaboration based on Harrison (1998b).

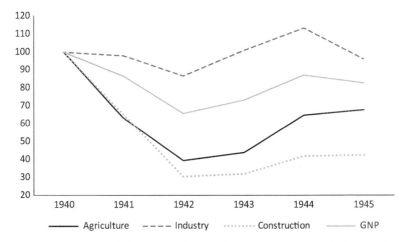

Figure 3.7a. Soviet GNP by sector of origin (1940–1945, 1940 = 100). *Source:* Own elaboration based on Harrison (1998b).

construction, agricultural, defense). Three civilian sectors sharply contacted in 1940–1942: agricultural output fell by 60 percent, construction by nearly 70 percent and industry by 13.7 percent (see Table 3.9 and Figure 3.7a). In contrast, the defense industry *increased production* by 268 percent between 1940 and 1942. If we consider 1944 as a reference year, the level of production of defense industry was near 400 percent higher than in 1940 (Table 3.9) showing the overriding priority given by the Soviet leadership to the defense sector over agriculture, construction, and civilian industry. The trade-off among these economic activities strongly suggests that the USSR was on its production possibility frontier between 1940 and 1944 (Figure 3.7b).[29]

[29] Production in the agriculture, civilian industry and construction sectors started a rebound in 1942.

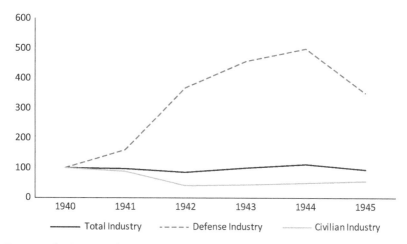

Figure 3.7b. Soviet industry, output index (1940–1945, 1940 = 100). *Source:* Own elaboration based on Harrison (1998b).

3.10 The Aftermath of World War II

The end of World War II led to an economic slump in the United States and the United Kingdom that had previously expanded, in the period 1940–1945. In the United States, GDP per capita declined by 28 percent between 1944 and 1947. In the United Kingdom, the fall in per capita GDP from 1943 to 1947 was half of the US decline, (14 percent; Table 3.10).

The end of the conflict was followed, in the second half of the 1940s, by very strong recoveries in France and Italy (1945–1949) and significant rebounds by Germany and Japan (see Table 3.10 and Figure 3.8). The Soviet Union also experienced a recovery in the second half of the 1940s when per capita GDP increased by 49 percent between 1946 and 1950 (see Table 3.11).

We have stressed the role played by military spending in generating boom and bust cycles during war-related periods. In this perspective, the American post-war bust coincided with a sharp decline in the ratio of military spending from 45 percent of GDP in 1944 to 5 percent in 1947. In Britain military spending was cut from 56 percent of GDP in 1944 to 11 percent in 1947. The recovery of household consumption and private investment after the end of the hostilities apparently was not enough to compensate for the retrenchment of the defense industries.

Table 3.10. *World War II-related expansions and contractions (percentage change in GDP per capita, 1939–1949)*

	Expansion (trough/peak)		Contraction (peak/trough)	
	Years	Percentage change	Years	Percentage change
France	1944–1949	104.25	1939–1944	−49.48
Germany	1939–1944	12.53	1944–1946	−63.56
	1946–1949	48.07		
United Kingdom	1939–1943	23.65	1943–1947	−14.71
	1947–1949	5.32		
United States	1939–1944	87.99	1944–1947	−27.95
	1947–1948	2.01	1948–1949	−1.33
Italy	1945–1949	83.28	1939–1945	−46.03
USSR[a]	1942–1944	32.07	1940–1942	−34.30
			1944–1945	−5.08
Japan	1939–1943	0.20	1943–1945	−52.29
	1945–1949	33.70		

[a] The data is expressed in GNP, Harrison (1998b), 1940 = 100.
Source: Author's elaboration based on Table 3.8 and Maddison (2013).

Table 3.11. *Growth in the USSR in the postwar period (1946–1950)*

	GDP per capita (1990 int. Dollars)	Change in GDP per capita (percent)
1946	1,913	
1947	2,126	11.13
1948	2,402	12.98
1949	2,623	9.20
1950	2,841	8.31

Source: Maddison (2013).

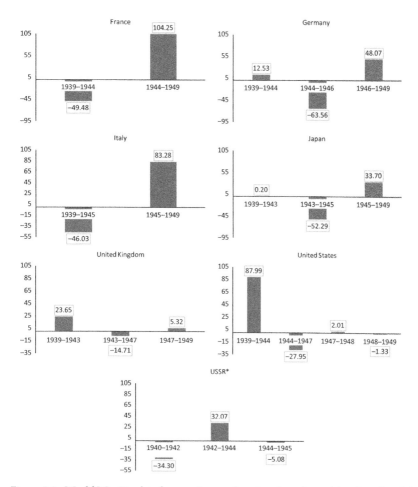

Figure 3.8. World War II-related expansions and contractions (trough/peak and peak/trough, percentage change in GDP per capita, 1939–1949). *Source:* Own elaboration based on Maddison (2013).
* The data is expressed in GNP, Harrison (1998b), 1940 = 100.

3.11 Concluding Remarks

The first half of the twentieth century was an extremely eventful period encompassing two world wars, hyperinflation, and depression, and then hyperinflation again in Greece and Hungary in the 1940s (not examined in this chapter). The twentieth century opened with the first wave of globalization under strong British influence. Before 1914, trade and capital inflows were largely unrestricted, and international migration reached unprecedented levels. However, the conflicts between empires (British, Russian, German, Ottoman, Austro-Hungarian), political intrigues, and uneven distribution of the benefits and costs of globalization eventually led to World War I. This war had different macroeconomic impacts on real economic activity among the warring countries. The United States, which only joined the conflict in 1917, benefitted from increased demand for military equipment, raw material, and foodstuff from Europe, and experienced an acceleration in GDP output growth. Great Britain also experienced an expansionary cycle during most of World War I. In contrast, the war had devastating effects on the declining Austro-Hungarian and Russian empires that experienced big economic slumps and were hit with food shortages, lack of raw material, and a difficult adjustment to a war economy centered upon defense-oriented production and imports. Germany's GDP output sank in 1914–1918, but the magnitude varies across different estimates. France and Italy experienced cycles of boom and bust. After World War I, the economies that expanded during wartime contracted, and those that had experienced big slumps started to recover, although in an uneven way. The early 1920s was a period of serious economic difficulty in Central Europe. Austria, Hungary, Poland, and Germany suffered acute monetary instability, accompanied by continuous exchange-rate depreciation and explosive inflation. Stabilization required important monetary and fiscal reforms and the process was overseen by the League of Nations, except in Poland and Soviet Russia. Economic activity often suffered during hyperinflation and recovered afterwards with the timing and magnitude varying across countries.

World War II led to a strong economic expansion in the United States and a more moderate boom in Britain. Conversely, output contracted in France and Italy. Germany and Japan started preparation for the war in the second half of the 1930s and increased military spending accordingly. In wartime, economic activity moderately expanded in Germany but stagnated in Japan. For war resource mobilization purposes, the Soviet Union benefitted from socialist industrialization and centralization of economic management adopted in the late 1920s and 1930s. We have documented very steep increases in defense spending ratios accompanying World War I and World War II with varying impacts (positive or negative) on the domestic economies. In turn, the retrenchment of military spending after the wars coexisted with some deep recessions but also with strong recoveries.

4

The Great Depression of the 1930s

4.1 Introduction

The precise causes of the Great Depression of the early 1930s, the worst slump of the twentieth century, remain somewhat of an unresolved mystery in economic analysis and history. It is apparent that while there is not a single cause of the Great Depression – or a single country responsible for the big international slump – we can make the following list of factors that did contribute to the Great Depression: (i) the stock market crash of 1929 in the United States; (ii) the decline in terms of trade and capital inflow for exporters of primary products in Latin America and Australia that started in 1928 or before; (iii) bankruptcies of banks in the early 1930s in America, Austria, and Germany; (iv) deflationary policies pursued by central banks in the context of the gold standard; (v) the timing of abandonment of the gold standard (the evidence shows that early-exit countries started their recovery sooner); (vi) the fall in domestic prices that increased the real value of debt held by consumers and firms with a negative effect on consumption and investment; and (vii) the lack of a decisive fiscal policy stance to face recessions and depressions by governments at that time.

The Great Depression was an international slump rather than a contraction affecting only a few isolated countries. However, the exact timing of the start and end of the Depression varied for the core, the European periphery, and primary exporters into Latin America, Asia, and Australia. It is important to recognize the international context that preceded the Great Depression. It is perhaps not a coincidence that the onset of the Great Depression occurred at the end of a particularly complex decade: the 1920s. The economic and political settlement following World War I had serious consequences for Europe and the global economy. A central role in that settlement was played by the treaty of

Versailles and the return to the gold standard. As discussed in Chapter 3, the economic sanctions of the treaty harmed German national pride, deteriorated the fiscal budget and the balance of payments, and reduced the resources available for investment and consumption, thereby diminishing the standard of living of the German population. The Paris treaty and the hyperinflation of 1923 fueled resentment and encouraged the surge of virulent nationalism embedded in the National Socialist party of Adolf Hitler. The restoration of the gold standard in the mid-1920s – in its "gold exchange standard" variety – was problematic in a world that had changed substantially in many respects. Before 1913, the operation of the (classic) gold standard contributed to ensure price stability, policy predictability, and orderly capital movements across nations, although this rosy view is not always consistent with the occurrence of financial crises such as the Baring crisis that affected Great Britain and Argentina. Also, the US economy suffered a "long depression" from the 1880s to the 1890s.

The *classic gold standard* was an international monetary system based upon certain rules obeyed by member countries: deficit countries attracted foreign capital/gold inflows and surplus countries exported capital/gold more or less without interference from governments and monetary authorities. The classic gold standard rested on two main pillars: (i) clear British leadership – through the Bank of England – in international monetary and financial matters; and (ii) international cooperation among member countries that were on the gold standard that, most generally, played by the rules of the standard. Other prerequisites for the success of the system were price and wage flexibility, limited influence of labor unions, and the relative isolation of monetary decisions from political considerations.

In the first wave of globalization before World War I under the gold standard, monetary and financial policies could be defined by central banks and governments without much concern for consequences on the working classes. These background conditions changed after World War I. The labor movement gained considerable strength after the war, there was rising influence of socialist parties, and universal suffrage was adopted. In addition, the irruption and gradual consolidation of the Bolshevik government in Russia in the 1920s and 1930s was also a challenge to the capitalist system. On the other hand, the establishment of nationalist right-wing regimes, notably in Germany and Italy, also affected international political and economic decisions.

As examined in Chapter 3, the aftermath of World War I brought severe currency instability and high inflation, as well as recession in the late 1910s and the first half of the 1920s. France was affected by fiscal and price instability and, more dramatically, Germany, Hungary, Poland, and Soviet Russia experienced hyperinflation in 1922 and 1923. On the other side of the Atlantic, the slump of 1921 in the United States was not without its consequences. After the war, policymakers in Europe and the United States were in search of a framework to ensure macroeconomic stability that would enable growth. The memory of the prosperity of the years under the gold standard was present with policymakers but the attempt at restoring the gold standard – or a reconstructed version of it – in the mid-1920s was accompanied by many difficulties. As stated in Keynes (1927), and then re-examined in Eichengreen (1992) and Feinstein et al. in (2008), one key difficulty was the choices of the exchange-rate parity between national currencies and gold in the mid-1920s. That was a crucial choice, and exchange rates that could be judged as misaligned in some important countries led to balance of payment imbalances, inflationary or deflationary pressures, and adverse (or too favorable) incentives for exports, import competing sectors, and industrial production.

Great Britain decided in 1926 to restore the same 1913 parity (pound sterling price of a unit of gold) in spite of the fact that, between those years, there was accumulated inflation, and productivity shifts had taken place that affected the competitiveness of the British economy. A result of returning to the parity of 1913 was that the pound became overvalued, making exports and investment in Britain more expensive. John Maynard Keynes, in *The Economic Consequences of Mr. Churchill* (1925), noted, vividly, that the new parity was inadequate and would entail a loss of competitiveness for British industry and lead to further economic decline in Britain. In turn, France returned to the gold standard in 1926 under the leadership of President Raymond Poincaré but at what is considered an *undervalued* French franc (just the opposite situation of Great Britain that *overvalued* the pound).[1] External payment imbalances developed in various countries, and it became clear that the way to correcting these imbalances was now different from the hallmark of the classic gold standard prevailing until 1913. The old system was based, at least in theory, on an automatic adjustment mechanism that entailed free and unrestricted flows of gold from surplus economies to deficit countries accompanied by rising interest rates (for the deficit country) and falling interest rates (for the surplus country).

---

[1] See discussions in Feinstein et al. (2008) and Eichengreen (1992).

This mechanism was largely absent, however, in the reconstructed gold standard. France, for example, in the mid- to late 1920s, pursued a policy of building-up large reserves of gold that created international deflationary effects as it took away available gold reserves in other nations.

There were several reasons for the lack of a smooth adjustment mechanism between deficit and surplus countries. Deflationary adjustment through cuts in wages and transient unemployment became very difficult to accomplish in the environment of stronger labor unions and labor militancy that emerged after World War I. On the other hand, the traditional dominance of the United Kingdom as the main economic power, capital exporter, and holder of the global reserve currency, the sterling pound, was eroded after World War I (the US per capita income had surpassed the United Kingdom's level before the onset of the war, see Chapter 3). The critical role played by the Bank of England in steering the impact of the gold standard in the pre-1913 world was clearly diminished. In turn, the United States was not yet prepared, nor willing, to take a strong global leadership in economic affairs. So, when the cloud of global recession emerged in the late 1920s, one that eventually led to an international depression, the world was caught within a vacuum of leadership. No clear hegemonic power was in place that could have steered a recovery or, at least, arrested an impending financial bust and a subsequent depression.[2]

In the absence of international leadership, it was difficult to achieve effective cooperation in areas such as exchange rate management, orderly capital flows, and the adoption of countercyclical demand-management policies. International investors were frightened by the lack of clear rules for international adjustment and searched for safe havens in countries such as the United States. However, between 1930 and 1932, the United States suffered a series of bank failures, showing that the country was not such a financial haven. Nonetheless, as the political situation in Europe was worsening – Hitler's takeover in Germany and the instability of other Central European countries – capital inflows from Europe into the United States increased in the mid-1930s.

Until around 1931, governments still maintained a strong faith in the gold standard and the need to defend exchange-rate parities, the free convertibility of gold, balanced fiscal budgets, and sound money (monetary policy oriented to price stability). The objectives of high employment and

---

[2] Kindleberger (1973 [2013]) attributed the absence of a hegemony to the combination of British decay and the still unconsolidated emergence of the United States as a top economic power (see Chapter 2).

sustained growth were less important than the stability of gold parities (remember that this was before the Keynesian revolution).

In the United States, the Great Depression followed a strong housing boom in the first half of the 1920s in several states, and the stock market was bulling from 1926 to 1928 (Solimano, 2017). However, leveraged speculation in stocks could not last forever, and an abrupt price correction in the stock market price index took place in October, 1929. That financial meltdown destroyed financial wealth, made consumers feel poorer, and induced them to cut purchases of durable and nondurable goods. In turn, several waves of bank failure took place between 1930 and 1932. This generated panic among depositors, who started withdrawing their deposits, leading to a contraction in the supply of credit and inducing a fall in investment and output.[3]

In France, in part due to its policy of maintaining an undervalued franc that stimulated exports and import competing industries, economic activity was strong before the Great Depression (which, in turn, had a less severe impact upon the French economy). In Britain, unlike in France and the United States, there was no previous boom before the Great Depression, confirming Keynes's apprehensions that an overvalued pound was bad for the British economy.

Some Central European nations such as Austria, Poland, and Czechoslovakia were badly affected by the Great Depression, with long and severe contractions in economic activity and increases in unemployment. In primary-goods exporting countries in the periphery of the world economy (Latin America, Africa, Asia) that were very dependent upon external markets for their internal dynamism, the effects of falling agricultural products and mineral commodity prices, and a fall in capital inflows in the late 1920s, gave rise to a complex balance of payment situations. Gold reserves were dwindling and this affected the ability to serve their external debts, creating serious pressures to devalue their currencies.

According to Kindleberger there was an "agricultural depression" in the late 1920s affecting the price of wheat, cotton, sugar, milk, and other agricultural goods. This could have been initiated as early as 1927 in countries such as Australia and Argentina. In turn, the agricultural sector in the United States was not immune to developments in the international prices

---

[3] Romer (1992) documents various mechanisms through which the stock market crash of 1929 and the bank failures of the early 1930s were critical in triggering the collapse of real activity in 1930–1932.

of primary products, thereby affecting agricultural output and introducing financial problems for commercial banks that held a significant proportion of loans to farmers.

4.2 Magnitude and Incidence of the Great Depression

The timing and severity of the economic contraction of the early 1930s differed across nations. The three countries that suffered the largest overall decline in per capita GDP (peak to trough) between 1929 and 1933, were Canada, Chile, and the United States. The League of Nations noted in its *World Economic Survey* that, in particular, the Chilean economy was *most affected* by the global slump (the per capita GDP of Chile declined by 46.6 percent between 1929 and 1933).

In terms of the benchmark of Chapter 1, the three countries were affected by a *mega-depression* (cumulative fall in per capita GDP above 30 percent, see Table 4.1). A second group of countries for which GDP per head declined, from peak to trough, in a range between 20 and 30 percent, included Austria, Poland, Australia, Mexico, and Venezuela. It is interesting to note that these two groups of economies most affected by depression include five net exporters of primary goods (Australia, Canada, Chile, Venezuela, and Mexico), the United States, and two Central-Eastern European countries (Austria and Poland).

Countries that experienced per capita output contractions of nearly 20 percent in the period under analysis were Argentina, Germany, and Czechoslovakia, whose economic slumps were very protracted. In turn, cumulative contractions in per capita GDP below 10 percent occurred in the United Kingdom (where the Great Depression was milder than in the United States), and in the countries of southern and northern Europe. Colombia was the least affected economy within the Latin American group. In the USSR, there was only one year of mild decline (1.5 percent) in GDP per head, in 1932.

The start of the contractionary cycle (slump), measured as the year of the peak of GDP per head, varied across countries. The peak was as early as 1928 in Canada, Germany, Bulgaria, Romania (affected mildly), Mexico, and Finland. In other countries, the peak year for total output was 1929, the year of the "Great Crash" in the US economy. For the 1930s, the bottom (trough) of the contraction ranged from 1931 in the United Kingdom to 1935 in Czechoslovakia (in Romania, the bottom was 1929). In France, the economic contraction followed a double-dip pattern with the first decline taking place between 1929 and 1932 with a second drop in 1934–1935.

Table 4.1. *The Great Depression around the world (level and percentage change in GDP per capita)*

	Peak	Trough	% change between peak and trough	Year of recovery (to reach peak)
Western Europe and North America				
Canada	100 (1928)	65.2 (1933)	−34.8	1940 (12 years)
France	100 (1929)	84.1 (1932)	−15.9	1939 (10 years)
Germany	100 (1928)	82.2 (1932)	−17.8	1935 (7 years)
United Kingdom	100 (1929)	93.4 (1931)	−6.6	1934 (5 years)
United States	100 (1929)	69.2 (1933)	−30.8	1940 (11 years)
Southern Europe				
Greece	100 (1929)	91.1 (1931)	−8.9	1933 (4 years)
Italy	100 (1929)	92.8 (1931)	−7.2	1938 (9 years)
Portugal	100 (1929)	97.6 (1930)	−2.4	1931 (2 years)
Spain	100 (1929)	92.3 (1931)	−7.7	1955 (26 years)
Central-Eastern Europe and the USSR				
Austria	100 (1929)	76.6 (1933)	−23.4	1939 (10 years)
Bulgaria	100 (1931)	94.8 (1932)	−5.2	1933 (2 years)
Czechoslovakia	100 (1929)	79.2 (1935)	−20.8	1948 (19 years)[a]
Hungary	100 (1929)	88.6 (1932)	−11.5	1936 (7 years)
Poland[b]	100 (1929)	75.1 (1933)	−24.9	1938 (9 years)
Romania	100 (1926)	91.6 (1929)	−8.4	1952 (26 years)[c]
The USSR	100 (1931)	98.5 (1932)	−1.5	1933 (2 years)
Northern Europe				
Denmark	100 (1931)	96.5 (1932)	−3.5	1934 (3 years)
Finland	100 (1929)	93.9 (1932)	−6.1	1934 (5 years)
Norway	100 (1930)	91.6 (1931)	−8.4	1934 (4 years)
Sweden	100 (1930)	93.6 (1932)	−6.4	1934 (4 years)
Primary-Goods Producers				
Argentina	100 (1929)	80.6 (1932)	−19.4	1944 (15 years)
Australia	100 (1926)	78.1 (1931)	−20.9	1937 (11 years)
Brazil	100 (1928)	86.7 (1931)	−13.3	1936 (8 years)
Chile	100 (1929)	53.4 (1932)	−46.6	1945 (16 years)
Colombia	100 (1929)	96.2 (1931)	−3.8	1932 (3 years)
Mexico	100 (1926)	68.9 (1932)	−31.1	1942 (16 years)
The Philippines	100 (1929)	96.3 (1931)	−3.7	1937 (8 years)
Turkey	100 (1931)	92.5 (1932)	−7.5	1933 (2 years)
Venezuela	100 (1930)	75.9 (1932)	−24.1	1936 (6 years)

[a] Data gap between 1938 and 1947.

[b] Level of GDP per capita in 1928 not available.

[c] Data gap for 1939–1947 and 1949.

Source: Prepared on the basis of data from Maddison (2013).

In Britain, GDP per person declined by 6 percent between 1929 and 1932, although industrial production fell by 11 percent (see Table 4.2). In southern Europe, the Great Depression was more moderate than in Austria, Germany, and the United States, three countries that suffered failures in their banking systems. Banking crises played a significant role in the worsening of the slump. In Vienna, in 1929, the Bodencreditanstal, the second most important bank in Austria, went under. In 1931, the turn to failure was of Creditanstalt, a main commercial bank in which the Rothschild family held a large stake. The entity failed and had to reorganize with the help of other European banks. This set off a wave of instability for the shilling (Austria's currency) with tremors and affecting also the British pound.[4] In the summer of 1931, a twin banking and currency crisis developed in Germany, which resembled the banking crisis in Austria. German banks had not been very prudent in the 1920s, overextending loans to different sectors in an economy affected by large foreign debt obligations (including war reparations), various shocks to industry, and overall financial fragility.

The impact of the international slump on the southern European economies of Greece, Italy, Portugal, and Spain (a group badly hit eight decades later at the time of the great financial crisis of 2008–2009) was only of moderate intensity (low in Portugal) and of relatively short duration, mostly concentrated between 1929 and 1931.

We can use other economic variables in addition to GDP per capita to measure the intensity of the Great Depression in Europe and Latin America. Table 4.2 presents the declines in industrial output and exports for several European economies. Between 1929 and 1932, the sharpest decline in industrial output took place in Poland (42 percent), followed by Germany (39 percent), then Austria (38 percent). In France, the reduction in industrial output was 26 percent, in Czechoslovakia 25 percent, and in the United Kingdom 11 percent. Smaller declines in industrial production occurred in Norway. In Greece, production in the industrial sector increased slightly during that period. The average decline in industrial production for Europe was 28 percent but the average decline in exports for Europe between 1929 and 1932 was 60 percent, underlying the sharp collapse of foreign trade during that period. In the United States, industrial output fell by 25 percent

---

[4] Good descriptions of these banking crises can be found in Feinstein et al. (2008), James (2002), and Eichengreen (1992).

Table 4.2. *Declines in industrial production and exports in Europe and Latin America, 1929–1932 (percentage change)*

	Industrial production	Value of exports
Poland	−42	−62
Germany	−39	−55
Austria	−38	−68
Belgium	−37	−53
France	−26	−61
Czechoslovakia	−25	−64
Yugoslavia	−24	−65
Finland	−16	−56 (−28)
Netherlands	−16	−58
Hungary	−14	−68
Italy	−14	−56
Romania	−12	−42
Spain	−12	−65
Sweden	−11	−64 (−48)
United Kingdom	−11	−64 (−50)
Denmark	−10	−53 (−33)
Norway	−6	−49 (−25)
Greece	1	−61
Switzerland	—	−62
Total Europe	−28	−60
Argentina	−33	−41
Brazil	−3	−62
Chile	−15	−88
Colombia	−7[a]	−34[a]
Honduras	−13[b]	−24
Mexico	−9	−57

[a] 1929–1931.

[b] 1929–1934.

Source: Adaptation from Feinstein et al. (2008). Data of Industrial production in Argentina, Brazil, Chile, Colombia, Honduras, and Mexico from Twoney (1983); data for exports from Argentina, Colombia, Honduras, and Mexico from Twoney (1983) and data for exports from Brazil and Chile from *League of Nations Statistical Year Book* (1934–1935).

Note: Export values are measured in US gold dollars; the changes in the values of national currencies are shown in parentheses for those countries that had devalued by 1932. Devaluation reduced the foreign exchange proceeds of a given quantity of exports but made the exports more competitive in foreign prices and so increased the volume of sales.

between 1929 and 1933.[5] Chile suffered the most severe reduction in the value of its exports (88 percent between 1929 and 1932) and Argentina experienced the largest contraction in industrial output, 33 percent. In general, industrial production, and exports, suffered badly in the Latin American region due to the contraction of the market in core economies (US and Europe) that were their main export markets and sources of external financing.

4.3 Price Deflation and Terms of Trade Effects

The Great Depression was accompanied by a process of *domestic price deflation*. The overall norm in different countries was a *decline* in the overall price level (see Table 4.3). Chile was an exception, as it recorded positive, but low, inflation in the years of the Depression. However, the combination of output contraction and deflation of prices (a downward shift in aggregate demand over an aggregate supply schedule) during the Great Depression was not often present in other recessionary episodes of the second half of the twentieth century. In those later episodes of economic contraction, slumps were often accompanied by inflation (increases in the price level) and not by deflation. A case in hand is the "stagflation" (stagnation with inflation) of the 1970s, in which output decline (or growth slowdown) in industrial economies accompanied an acceleration in inflation, along with several inflationary crises in emerging economies and developing countries from the 1950s onwards.

The decline in the domestic price level in countries during the Great Depression was significant: in the United States, the Consumer Price Index (CPI) fell by 24 percent between 1929 and 1933; in Canada by 22 percent; in the United Kingdom by 12 percent; and in Germany prices fell by 29 percent (between 1928 and 1932).

In the periphery, between 1929 and 1932, the price level declined by 22 percent in Argentina, by 21 percent in Mexico and in Australia, prices fell by 17 percent between 1929 and 1931;[6] and in Chile, the price level increased by 4 percent between 1929 and 1932.

The macroeconomic effects of price deflation were a subject of controversy and debate among theoretical economists in the era of the Great Depression. Two schools of thought can be identified here. One is the "debt-deflation theory of depressions" identified by the American economist Irving Fisher. He explained that a fall in the level of prices tends to *aggravate* a depression,

---

[5] Twoney (1983).
[6] Twoney (1983).

Table 4.3. *The decline in the price level during the Great Depression (percentage)*

	Peak	Trough	Percentage change (peak to trough)
Canada	1929	1933	−22
United States	1929	1933	−24
Germany	1928	1932	−29
France	1929	1934	−18
United Kingdom	1929	1932	−12
Spain	1929	1933	−5
Italy	1929	1931	−22
Greece	1930	1931	−11
Austria	1929	1933	−17
Hungary	1930	1933	−21
Sweden	1930	1932	−10
Norway	1929	1931	−8
Australia	1929	1931	−17
Argentina	1929	1932	−22
Chile	1929	1932	+4
Mexico	1929	1932	−21

Source: Adaptation from Twoney (1983).

as the *real value of debt* held by consumers and firms increases when prices fall. American household debt increased quite substantially during the speculative bubble of the late 1920s. The purchase of stocks was often financed by loans. In the first half of the 1920s, borrowing also increased significantly during the housing market boom but, in this case, loans were oriented toward financing the acquisition of housing and land.

Another school of thought predicts that price deflation, (a decline in the price level), *increases* the purchasing power of real balances (money); this creates a *positive net wealth effect*. In this situation, price deflation increases the real value of an asset (money) offsetting the effect of falling prices on the real value of liabilities and debt, (net wealth = assets minus liabilities). This "real balance effect" was stressed by the British economist Arthur Cecil Pigou. He argued that an increase in real balances due to a fall in the price level should stimulate consumption and help to restore aggregate demand, eventually bringing the economy back to full employment (Pigou, 1943).[7] The Israeli economist Don Patinkin, in an article on "price flexibility and full employment" published in the *American Economic Review* (Patinkin, 1948), tried to clarify the different channels through which the price level

---

[7] Pigou (1943).

would affect economic activity made by economists Fisher, Keynes, and Pigou. In his article , Patinkin coined the term "Pigou effect," referring to the real balance effect stressed by Arthur C. Pigou.[8]

The Pigou effect, however, was largely dismissed by both John Maynard Keynes and Michael Kalecki.[9] Keynes doubted its empirical relevance as an automatic mechanism to restore full employment in a depressed economy. In turn, Kalecki (in line with Fisher's theory) pointed to the negative impact on the real value of debt servicing of price deflation compressing consumption and investment and thus worsening a depression.

4.4 Terms of Trade Effects, Primary Goods-Producing Countries, and the Periphery

The Great Depression brought about changes in relative prices, for example between domestic and foreign goods and also between agricultural and industrial commodities. The phenomenon was not only deflation in the absolute price level but also changes in *relative prices*. As shown in Table 4.4, in the early 1930s, the price of manufacturing goods fell less than both the price of raw material and the price of food. This created adverse trade effects for countries producing primary goods, typically net exporters of raw materials and food that were also net importers of manufacturing goods from the core countries. In fact, between 1929 and 1932, the price of food declined by 50 percent, the price of raw materials declined by 56 percent, and the price of manufacturing by 37 percent (see Table 4.4).

Between 1932 and 1929, world industrial production fell by 36 percent, with a greater decline (46 percent) in North America (panel 1). This is not surprising, as Canada and the United States were two of the three countries most affected by the Great Depression. In turn, world food production was largely unaffected by the slump (panel 2). However, between 1929 and 1932, the worldwide production of raw materials fell by 25 percent (36 percent in North America). The value of world export prices declined by 61 percent between 1929 and 1932, with export volumes falling by 26 percent, and export prices by 48 percent (see Table 4.5). The contraction of world trade in the Depression had staggering proportions. Trade was affected by the protectionist measures adopted in industrial countries (chiefly in the United States) along with the depressive effect of a simultaneous cut in import demand for consumer and investment goods, and raw materials,

---

[8] See Patinkin (1948).
[9] Kalecki (1944).

Table 4.4. *World production and prices, 1929–1932 (index numbers, 1929 = 100)*

	1929	1930	1931	1932
1. Industrial production				
a. World[a]	100	87	75	64
b. Europe[a]	100	92	81	72
c. North America	100	81	68	54
2. Primary production-food				
a. World	100	102	100	100
b. Europe[a]	100	99	102	104
c. North America	100	102	103	100
3. Primary production-raw materials				
a. World	100	94	85	75
b. Europe[a]	100	90	82	73
c. North America	100	90	80	64
4. World prices				
a. Food	100	84	66	50
b. Raw materials	100	82	59	44
c. Manufactures	100	94	78	63

[a] Excluding the USSR.
Source: Feinstein et al. (2008).

Table 4.5. *World trade, 1929–1932 (index numbers, 1929 = 100)*

	1929	1930	1931	1932
1. Value at current prices[a]	100	80	57	39
2. Export volume	100	93	85	74
3. Export price	100	86	67	52

[a] Index of the value of exports from seventy-five countries measured in US gold dollars.
Source: Feinstein et al. (2008).

following the cut in industrial production and overall GDP, adversely affecting exports both in terms of volume and value.

4.5 The Complex Transition from Depression to Recovery in the United States

A main event leading to the Great Depression in the United States was the sharp decline in stock market prices in October, 1929, that – induced a cut in consumption and investment that lasted several years. A negative wealth effect (affecting consumption) and a squeeze in the supply of credit (affecting investment) provide two linkages between the financial crash and the cut in aggregate demand. In addition, the state of the banking system was far from robust. Between 1930 and 1932, there were four waves of panic in which depositors started to withdraw their funds: in the fall of 1930; in the spring of 1931; in the fall of 1931; and in the fall of 1932 (Romer, 1992). By 1933, 20 percent of the banks that were in operation in 1930 had closed operations. Bank runs (people rushing to withdraw their deposits from the banks) led these institutions to recall loans, reducing the supply of credit to the real sector (production, investment, employment) of the economy. The Federal Reserve Bank was inactive in providing liquidity when it was needed to avert a banking crisis. The logic of the gold standard prevailed among American policymakers during Herbert Hoover's administration. In moments of uncertainty that could undermine the exchange rate and the reserves of gold, the money supply was tightened. For example, in response to the sterling crisis of 1931, the Federal Reserve Bank *increased* interest rates at home. Moreover, fiscal authorities, following a policy of balanced fiscal budgets, increased taxes and reduced fiscal spending, which cut domestic absorption, aggravating the decline in output and the increase in unemployment. In *A Monetary History of the United States, 1867–1960*, Milton Friedman and Anna Schwarz identified indecisiveness by and errors of the monetary authority as a main cause of the Great Depression. Their monetary explanation for the slump was mono-causal in the sense of focusing mostly on the money supply (e.g.: errors in monetary policy) and it focused on the United States, albeit the slump was international in scope.

The prevailing economic ideas in the period of the reconstructed gold standard in the 1920s in several European countries and the United States were the doctrines of a strong currency, balanced fiscal budgets, and reliance on wage and price flexibility to restore full employment. The Keynesian revolution, at an analytical level, appeared with the publication of *The General Theory of Employment, Interest and Money* in 1936. Keynes's theory offered a new framework for interpreting macroeconomics. It emphasized as a main cause of the Depression a massive failure of aggregate demand that required active fiscal expansion and monetary stimulus (the latter would not work, however, as the economy was stuck in a "liquidity trap" in which extra money supply is absorbed by an elastic demand, thereby keeping interest rates unchanged, with no impact upon effective demand).

Keynes, observing the actual behavior of people, emphasized that at times of high uncertainty, individuals increase their demand for money or *preference for liquidity* (this could be manifested, for example, through a rising ratio of currency relative to deposits). This is intuitive: real assets such as houses, land, and machinery are *illiquid,* and therefore cannot be easily transformed into cash. Between 1929 and 1933, the money stock fell by 31 percent and did not accommodate an increase in the demand for money (e.g., fall in money velocity) with the predictable effect of depressing nominal spending.

A similar mechanism can be identified with the help of a money-quantity framework. The monetary authorities reduce the money supply (M) (gold standard logic) with money velocity (V), falling due to an increase in the demand for money (uncertainty effect). On the supply side of the economy, there is a fall in the real quantity of production (Q) and in the price level (P). The reduction in MV (value of spending) equates to the cut in PQ, (value of output). This was the depressive environment of the early 1930s in the United States.

President Hoover defended the gold standard parity until the end of his administration, undertook contractionary monetary policies, and pursued a policy of balanced fiscal budgets. Nevertheless, this orthodox policy stance was abandoned by Franklin Delano Roosevelt in early 1933 (Roosevelt was elected in December, 1932, and inaugurated in March, 1933). Given the fragile situation of many commercial banks at the time, Roosevelt declared a nationwide "bank holiday" on March 6, 1933, closed all banks, and allowed only those considered solvent by federal inspectors to reopen. In addition, Roosevelt became convinced that the fixed parity of the gold standard was a straightjacket. After abandoning the cherished gold standard, he pursued a "reflationary" policy of money creation to raise prices and stimulate economic activity.

Roosevelt decided, in March, 1933, to start a devaluation of the dollar relative to gold and other major world currencies. As a preparation for the devaluation that was envisaged to take place throughout 1933, Roosevelt imposed a ban on the sale of gold by the private sector (Feinstein et al., 2008; Edwards, 2018). In January, 1934, after a policy of floating the dollar, the price of an ounce of gold reached $35.00 and stabilized. This was a 41 percent depreciation from its pre-March, 1933 parity.[10] The depreciation against other European currencies was in the range of 30–40 percent and the devaluation against the Canadian dollar was between 10–15 percent (Canada was the main US trading partner at the time).

It is important to recognize that devaluing the exchange rate gave Roosevelt room to experiment with active demand management policies, something that was not feasible under the parity of the gold standard. The policies of the New Deal included the launching of the National Industrial

---

[10] Eichengreen and Sachs (1985).

Recovery Act (NIRA) and the Agricultural Adjustment Act (AAA), created to support prices of agricultural goods to help farming to recover. To strengthen confidence in the banking system, the Federal Deposit Insurance Corporation (FDIC) was created. Policies oriented to boost economic recovery and financial stability were supplemented by the creation of a nationwide social security system to help alleviate the social consequences of unemployment and provide old age security.

These reforms represented a major reorientation for the economic policy priorities in the United States aiming toward the objectives of economic growth, full employment, and social security. It was a true "regime change" from the priorities of the Hoover administration, oriented toward defending the value of the dollar and balancing the budget (although fiscal policy under Roosevelt, properly measured, was not truly counter-cyclical to expand fiscal spending/cut taxes to speed-up recovery).

As shown in Figure 4.1, after four years of economic contraction (negative growth rates in GDP per capita) from 1930 to 1933, a recovery (positive growth) took place between 1934 and 1936, interrupted by a new recession in 1938. The whole cycle of depression and recovery (lasting eleven years) was completed in 1940, when the per capita GDP peak of 1929 was again achieved.

There are various interpretations about the causes of the recovery in the US economy and the turnaround that started in 1933. One interpretation is provided by Temin and Wigmore (1990), who emphasize the positive effects of "regime change," say, a change in objectives and rules of economic policy rather than isolated actions within a pre-existing framework, that informed President Roosevelt's decision to leave the gold standard and abandon the policy of President Hoover in favor of a resumption of growth and employment.[11] It is interesting to note that, at the time of the devaluation of the dollar (criticized internationally as a "beggar-thy-neighbor" policy), the US balance of payments was in a favorable position, running a foreign trade surplus based in exporting modern manufactured goods such as automobiles, refrigerators, and sewing machines; in addition, Roosevelt imposed some foreign exchange controls on speculative capital flows (Edwards, 2018). Further, in 1933, the United States held nearly one-third of the world's gold reserves.[12] So, the United States did not devalue out of a dire need for stopping a drain on gold reserves, and/or because of an unsustainable pressure on the exchange rate, as a classic balance of payment crisis would predict.

---

[11] The authors, in turn, were inspired by the theory of regime change used by Thomas Sargent to explain the abrupt end of four episodes of severe inflation in Central Europe in the early 1920s.

[12] Temin and Wigmore (1990).

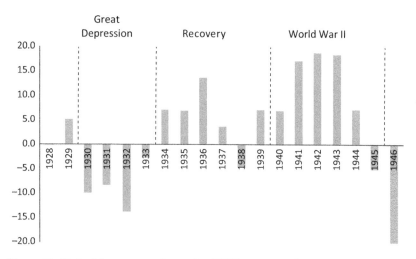

Figure 4.1. United States: rate of growth of GDP per capita (percentage, 1928–1946). *Source:* Own elaboration based on Maddison (2013).

Economic historian Christine Romer investigated the role of aggregate demand stimulus in ending the Great Depression in the United States (Romer, 1992). Her study showed that nearly all of the sources of economic recovery up to 1942 resulted from *monetary expansion*. The money supply (M1) grew at an annual rate of 10 percent between 1933 and 1937, and at even higher rates in the early 1940s (these rates were well above historical rates for money growth in the US economy). Using simulation analysis based upon various macroeconomic models, Romer showed that GDP in 1937 would have been about 25 percent *lower* without the monetary stimulus. Causality tests discard the presence in that period of reverse causality going from output growth to money growth.

The money supply grew fast due to increased gold inflows to the US following the devaluation of 1933, augmented by capital inflows coming to the United States from the other side of the Atlantic, escaping the political and economic instability in Europe.[13]

Cary Brown, an economics professor at the Massachusetts Institute of Technology, contributed an influential analysis of the role of US fiscal policy in the 1930s (Brown, 1940). He noted a complex picture in the overall orientation of US fiscal policy that precluded a clear and effective expansionary

[13] Romer (1992).

role after 1933. Brown shows clear differences in the direction of US fiscal policy at two levels: (i) between spending by local and state governments on one side and federal spending on the other; and (ii) between the expansionary direction of federal spending (except in 1937) and the policy of increased tax rates at different levels of government. During the Depression years, while local and state governments were relatively expansionary in their spending patterns (particularly in 1930 and 1931), the federal government was contracting spending in line with the fiscal orthodoxy of the Hoover administration. The main shift in federal public spending, towards an expansive stance, took place between 1933 and 1936 under Roosevelt. This trend was reversed in 1937, leading to the slump of 1938 noted in Figure 4.1.[14] When taking a comprehensive look at both taxation and public spending (at all government levels), it cannot be said that fiscal policy was, on average, really expansionary between 1933 and 1939. In fact, the US government pursued a policy of a roughly balanced fiscal budget evaluated at full employment (a measure that controls the feedback effects of the business cycle on the levels of tax revenues and spending). There was a fiscal expansion from 1933 to 1936, particularly at the federal level, but increased taxation rates adopted during the same period partially contributed to offsetting its expansionary impact. So, as Brown noted, the actual contribution of fiscal expansion to the overall recovery of the US economy since 1933 to the end of the decade was modest. He added that this was not because fiscal policy was ineffective to stimulate aggregate demand (low fiscal policy multipliers), but because the policy was not really implemented in a consistent and comprehensive way. In the end, it was the fiscal expansion associated with World War II that realized the potentialities of fiscal policy (for details on the economics of World War II, see Chapter 3).[15]

4.6 Depression in Europe and the Role of Exiting the Gold Standard in Bolstering Recovery

The economic slump in Britain, was less severe and of shorter duration than the contraction in the United States, Germany, Canada, and Austria. However, it was far from costless. Employment contracted in coal mining activities, in the steel sector, cotton production, and shipyard building, and the working classes underwent serious human suffering. The social

---

[14] Spending by local and state governments was relatively neutral since 1934.

[15] Alvin Hansen (1938) provided another interpretation for the erratic recovery post 1933 and called attention that the US economy along the lines of the "secular stagnation" hypothesis discussed in Chapter 2.

reality of the British at times of economic hardship was depicted vividly by George Orwell in his book *The Road to Wigan Pier* (1937). Unemployment reached nearly 20 percent of the workforce during the slump, and export values contracted by near 50 percent.

The depression affecting Great Britain had domestic causes but it was also related to the slump in the United States and the banking crises in Austria and Germany in 1931, which affected the value of the British pound. As in the United States under President Hoover, Britain tried first orthodox policies of balancing the fiscal budget, raising taxes, and spending cuts in the midst of depression but this added additional contractionary pressures to the economy. In September of 1931, the United Kingdom abandoned the gold standard and devalued the sterling. This was near *two years before the United States* did so. Depreciation of the pound allowed Britain the implementation of expansive monetary policies to spur economic growth and reduce unemployment. In 1932, Neville Chamberlain – who had become chancellor after the elections of 1931 – introduced tariffs on agricultural and industrial goods, but exempted imports from the countries within the British Empire. It is unclear, however, that protectionism was really expansionary when international effects on the export side are taken into consideration. In any case, the recovery of economic activity started in 1932 and from 1937 to 1939 output was 18 percent above the 1929 level (output in the United States from the same period was only 3 percent above the level of 1929; see Figure 4.2).

Two other countries that also abandoned the gold standard and devalued their currencies in September of 1931 were Sweden and Norway. Moreover, in November, 1931, Denmark devalued its currency, as did Finland in December, 1931. The Nordic countries followed the lead of Britain and opted out of the gold standard.

Leaving the gold standard earlier facilitated the economic recovery after the slump of 1929–1933, and this was the case in the United Kingdom and the Nordic countries. The United States remained on the gold standard until early 1933, and the "gold block countries" (France, Belgium, and Switzerland) until 1935–1936. Germany and Italy introduced foreign exchange controls in 1931, and used the controls to defend their parities relative to gold for a while, in a sort of disguised membership in the gold standard regime. Of course, this was a false or fake allegiance, as the gold standard was incompatible, in spirit, with practices of currency inconvertibility.

In the 1920s, France was busy trying to obtain war reparations from Germany. France managed to grow at a respectable average annual 3.5 percent per capita between 1919 and 1929 but GDP per capita contracted, on average, between 1930 and 1939. The country suffered from exchange-rate

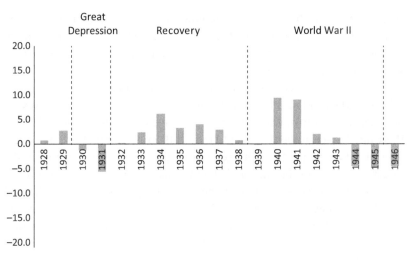

Figure 4.2. United Kingdom: rate of growth of GDP per capita (percentage, 1928–1946). *Source:* Own elaboration based on Maddison (2013).

instability and inflation in the first half of the 1920s, but, the franc was stabilized in 1926 by President Raymond Poincaré. In France, unlike in other countries, there was no financial crisis accompanying output contraction in the first half of the 1930s. Still, economic troubles were not absent and ultimately triggered political effects favoring the *Front populaire* (Popular Front) of the socialist leader Leon Blum, who was elected in 1936. Economic growth was modest from 1936 to 1939, and as shown in Chapter 3, World War II had a devastating effect on the French economy.

Macroeconomic and political development in Germany in the 1920s were driven, largely, by the need to make a foreign resource transfer abroad (war reparations sanctioned by the London Schedule of Payments in 1921). A country that plans to undertake a net resource transfer abroad needs to generate a trade surplus, as well as a fiscal surplus, if private investment exceeds private savings. This transfer often squeezes real wages and forces governments to adopt spending cuts along with increases in taxation. None of these policies are popular, and in a society with serious distributive conflicts and political disarray, as was Germany after World War I, this was exceedingly difficult to accomplish. Then the Weimar Republic decided to refinance foreign reparations and payment obligations by taking loans issued mainly by New York-based banks, avoiding internal adjustment. One type of foreign debt (war reparation to the victorious powers of World War I) was replaced by another type of debt (mainly to United States financial institutions).

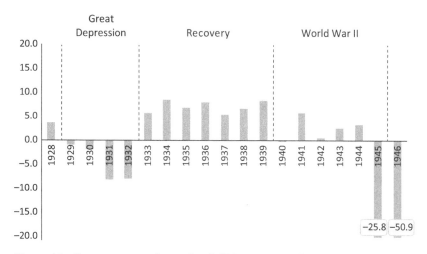

Figure 4.3. Germany: rate of growth of GDP per capita (percentage, 1928–1946). *Source:* Own elaboration based on Maddison (2013).

The US government wanted a stabilization of the German economy and supported the Dawes Plan of 1924 and the Young Plan of 1929. However, things became complicated in 1928 when the Federal Reserve Bank increased interest rates to cool off speculation in the stock market and reduced international lending. This shattered market confidence in the German economy that was crucially dependent on US loans to serve its foreign obligations. In addition, German exports were affected by the Smoot-Hawley Tariff Act levied upon imports by the United States in 1930. The economic crisis led to a sharp rise in unemployment from around 650,000 people in 1928 to over 3 million in 1930, climbing further to 6 million in early 1933.

In 1931, a banking crisis affected the German currency, the Reichsmark. Like the United States under Hoover, Germany followed an orthodox policy of balancing the budget, reduced spending and salaries and increased interest rates. The internally polarized political situation left little room for consensus on a stabilization program that could deal realistically with Germany's overhanging debt problems. When Hitler took power, he suspended all reparation payments and controlled labor unions, but increased public spending, particularly military spending (see Chapter 3). These policies allowed Germany to experience a steady economic recovery from 1933 to 1939 (see Figure 4.3) along with a substantial decline in unemployment under the guidance of Hjalmar Schacht, placed in charge of the German economy by Hitler. Schacht abandoned his previous orthodox beliefs and undertook policies of state intervention, delinking from international markets and massive public works to pull Germany out of the depression. Economic nationalism and autarchy formed the cornerstone of Nazi economic policies, forwarded by Schacht due to his good connections with the business community inside and outside of Germany, along with his prestige in stabilizing the Reichsmark in the 1920s.[16]

4.7 The Great Depression in Latin America and Southern Europe

The Latin American economies experienced adverse shocks in the late 1920s. The terms of trade in countries producing sugar (Cuba), coffee (Brazil, Colombia), copper (Chile, Peru), meat (Argentina), and oil (Venezuela) all deteriorated in the late 1920s. This led to a severe drop in export revenues, affecting the countries' balance of payments position. Their fiscal budgets also worsened, as public revenues tied to taxes on exports and imports fell following the contraction in foreign trade. In addition, the policy of higher interest rates in 1928–1929 in the United States reduced capital inflows to Latin America. The imposition of tariffs on imports in core economies that constituted Latin America's main export markets was another blow to the region's balance of payments position. Most of the Latin American countries abandoned the gold standard between 1929 and 1930. Chile suffered the most from the conjunction of negative external shocks. In addition to the cut in copper prices, Chile was hit by a development in Germany in the 1920s: synthetic nitrate that could be produced at lower cost than natural nitrate. This innovation destroyed the privileged Chilean position in the natural nitrate world market, increasing Chile's difficulties during the Great Depression. As shown in Figure 4.4, Chile's GDP per capita fell sharply between 1930 and 1932, although there was a strong recovery in 1933–1934 that continued with declining force until 1937, with per capita GDP to fall again in both 1938 and 1941.

Argentina also suffered an output contraction between 1930 and 1932 but recovered in 1933–1935. Then, a pattern of irregular growth was followed by years of positive growth, alternating with other periods of negative growth in the second half of the 1930s. Mexico suffered an early contraction from 1928 to 1930 and then fell into a severe slump in 1932, though recovering between 1933 and 1937 (Figure 4.5). The US recession in 1938 also affected Mexico, Chile, Argentina, and other Latin American countries. In Venezuela, the effects of the Great Depression were dire and GDP per capita contracted sharply in 1931, and then more mildly in 1932, followed by a recovery between 1933 and 1939.

---

[16] See Frieden (2007, Chapter 9) and Chapter 3.

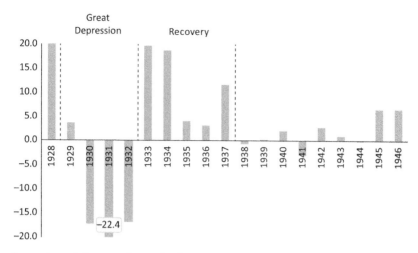

Figure 4.4. Chile: rate of growth of GDP per capita (percentage, 1928–1946). *Source:* Own elaboration based on Maddison (2013).

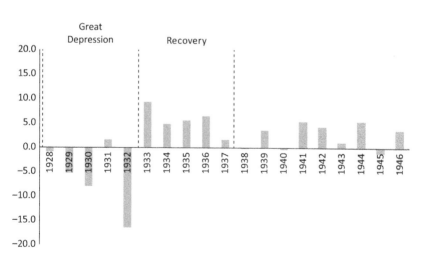

Figure 4.5. Mexico: rate of growth of GDP per capita (percentage, 1928–1946). *Source:* Own elaboration based on Maddison (2013).

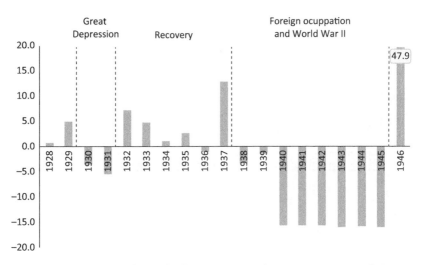

Figure 4.6. Greece: rate of growth of GDP per capita (percentage, 1928–1946). *Source:* Own elaboration based on Maddison (2013).

The effects of the Great Depression on southern European countries was less severe than its impact on Central European economies (particularly Austria, Poland, and Czechoslovakia), and core western European nations (Germany, France and, the United Kingdom). Spain had negative per capita growth in 1930–1931, and again in 1934, but the real contraction took place at the time of the civil war between republicans and nationalists from 1936 through 1939. GDP per capita fell sharply in 1936 and 1937, then more mildly in 1938. Greece suffered relatively mild contractions in economic activity in 1930 and 1931, followed by irregular recovery until 1937. However, the real blow was in 1938–1945, when the economy underwent an eight-year economic contraction of great proportions (Figure 4.6).

Poland experienced a four-year contraction from 1930 to 1933, followed by stagnation in 1934 and 1935, and then recovery in 1936–1939. Czechoslovakia experienced a six-year contraction from 1930 to 1935, followed by recovery in 1936 and 1937 (Figure 4.7). The effects of the Great Depression on the USSR's economy in the 1930s were minimal. As the Soviet economy was largely delinked from international private capital markets and the gold standard, it was not as affected by the Great Depression as the capitalist nations (see Figure 4.8).

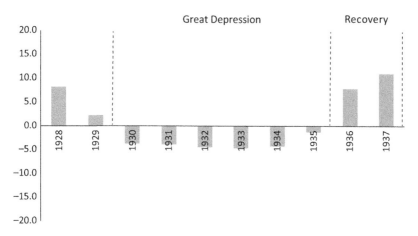

Figure 4.7. Czechoslovakia: rate of growth of GDP per capita (percentage, 1928–1937). *Source:* Own elaboration based on Maddison (2013). *Note:* Data gap between 1938 and 1948.

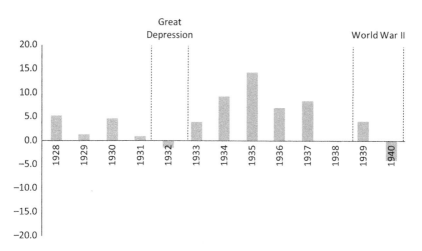

Figure 4.8. The Soviet Union: rate of growth of GDP per capita (percentage, 1928–1939). *Source:* Own elaboration based on Maddison (2013). *Note:* Data gap between 1941 and 1945.

4.8 Concluding Remarks

The Great Depression was an international crisis with multiple causes and ramifications. The financial crash of 1929; the "agricultural depression"; falling commodity prices; insolvencies in the banking system; the lack of coordination between main economic powers; and the strictures of the gold standard all contributed to create the worst economic depression of the twentieth century.

The rules of the gold standard forced the United States, Germany, France, Britain, and other countries to implement restrictive monetary and fiscal policies in the early 1930s, at a time of financial uncertainty, bank fragility, and recession. The need for currency stabilization and balanced fiscal budgets needed at a time of monetary instability and hyperinflation as in the first half of the 1920s became counterproductive when pursued in the midst of a big slump accompanied by declining prices as in the early 1930s.

Economic and social hardship forced governments to abandon the gold standard, devalue their currencies, and adopt a new pragmatic approach to economic policy. This was the case in Britain, Sweden, and Norway in September, 1931; Latin American countries and Australia had amended their parities with gold in 1929 and 1930. Other countries, such as Germany and Italy, introduced foreign exchange controls in 1931 to contain the pressure against their exchange rates. In the United States, a change of administration (President Roosevelt was inaugurated in March, 1933) brought a departure from the orthodox policies of Herbert Hoover and devalued the dollar against gold and other currencies. The evidence shows that countries leaving the gold standard earlier (the United Kingdom, Sweden, and Norway) also started their economic recovery earlier. In the United States, rapid rates of growth of the money supply, rather than a comprehensive fiscal expansion, were the main impulse toward economic recovery in the second half of the 1930s. The full employment budget deficit was nearly on balance, on average, between 1933 and 1940.

In retrospect, it becomes apparent that it was World War II that brought a definite impulse to the US and British economy. "Military Keynesianism" (stimulation of the economy through increases in military spending) did indeed succeed in increasing aggregate demand and output in the early 1940s, in countries such as the US and Germany.

Price deflation was another feature of the Great Depression. There were cumulative drops in the price level of 20–30 percent in several countries in the period 1929–1932/1933 (the Unites States, Canada, Germany, and others). This reality spurred theoretical disputes over the effect of price deflation in correcting or aggravating an economic slump. British economist Arthur Cecil Pigou argued that, in principle, a positive real balance effect could restore the equality between aggregate demand and aggregate supply at full employment. However, Irving Fisher, Michael Kalecki, and John Maynard Keynes pointed to the effects of price deflation on increasing the real value of loan servicing for debtors that often aggravated depression. Keynes, in particular, stressed the practical irrelevance of a downward price spiral as an automatic mechanism to restore full capacity and high employment. Moreover, President Roosevelt sought "reflation" – rather than deflation – to bolster agricultural activity, industrial production, and the construction sector to pull the economy out of depression. The Great Depression also led to shifts in electorate preferences in the United States (the election of Roosevelt), Germany (the rise of Hitler), France (the advent of the Popular Front), and spurred a change in economic paradigms moving toward Keynesian macroeconomics.

Stagflation in the 1970s, Globalization, and the Financial Crisis of 2008–2009

5.1 Introduction

The end of World War II led to a new postwar settlement in the capitalist world led forcefully by the United States. The emerging economic order excluded the socialist block that had emerged after the war; entailed a new international monetary system (the Bretton Woods system); supported global political institutions, including the United Nations; and entered into more balanced social contract between capital and labor. The Bretton Woods system, based on fixed-exchange rates among main currencies, a fixed dollar to gold parity, and controlled capital inflows across nations, would help to manage external imbalances in a more orderly fashion than in the inter-war period. The US-led Marshall Plan would channel a net resource transfer to support the economic reconstruction of Europe. At internal level, policies revolved around objectives of full employment pursued through countercyclical fiscal policies. This new settlement was followed by a period of strong growth, from around 1950 to 1973, absence of global financial crises, and reasonable social peace in advanced capitalist countries. This period was labelled the *golden age of capitalism* that came to an end in the 1970s, triggered by the abandonment of the parities of Bretton Woods as the US "walked away from gold" in 1971 under the presidency of Republican Richard Nixon. In contrast to the broad-based prosperity and reasonable stability of the 1950s and 1960s, the 1970s witnessed the simultaneous surge of inflation, slower growth, and higher unemployment, known as "stagflation." The abandonment of the free convertibility of dollar to gold and the end of fixed-exchange rates between the dollar and the main European currencies (the British pound, the Italian lira, German marks, and the Spanish peseta) opened the door to a period of exchange rate and stock market instability. In addition, industrial economies were hit by two oil price shocks in 1973 and 1979.

At the geopolitical level, the United States' defeat in Vietnam and the Iran crisis were two important events that challenged US hegemony. The 1970s also witnessed heightened labor activism in Italy, Britain, Germany, and other nations, and a slowdown in productivity growth in North America and western Europe.

This chapter examines how the rapid growth phase of the golden age was eventually interrupted by the stagflation of the 1970s, giving rise to subsequent decades, since the 1980s, of neoliberal globalization accompanied by a greater frequency of financial crises and recessionary cycles than during the golden age. We document various recessions in the 1970s and 1980s. In the late 1990s/early 2000s, after a long boom that started in the 1980s in the stock market, US growth fell following the dot.com bubble burst in the high-tech sector.

A main crisis of neoliberal globalization took place in 2008–2009 and was originated in the sub-prime crisis (real estate and financial sector) in the United States and spreading to Europe. This was followed by a period of sluggish growth in advanced (center) economies and serious contraction of economic activity in the European periphery. The most affected countries were Greece, Portugal, Spain, and the Baltic countries.

This instability and volatility is increasingly becoming a more structural feature of neoliberal capitalism. The empirical part of the chapter covers advanced capitalist countries and the European periphery in the period 1950–2015 and examines cycles of output and investment decline and recovery, noting an increase in the intensity and duration of these cycles since the 1970s compared with the golden age with more adverse effects upon the countries of the European periphery.[1]

5.2 American Hegemony: The Post-World War II Settlement

In 1944, an important international monetary conference was held at Bretton Woods, located in New Hampshire, in the northeast of the United States. Its purpose was to establish new monetary and exchange rules that would govern the global economy. The conference, that lasted around three weeks, was attended by representatives of the main European nations, the United States, the Soviet Union, China, and Latin American and Asian

---

[1] Some authors talk of the "glorious thirty" as a period between the mid-1940s and mid-1970s to refer to the golden age of capitalism. However, the second half of the 1940s and the first half of the 1970s were still transitional, unstable periods (reconstruction, the end of the Bretton Woods system, oil price shock).

countries. Disputes developed on a number of issues, but at the end it was clear that the new system was to rest on the supremacy of the American dollar as the global reserve currency, that would keep a fixed parity of USD 35 per one ounce of gold backed by a sufficient stock of gold held by the United States.

In the new system, exchange rates would be adjusted if a country faced a "fundamental disequilibrium," say an external imbalance that could not be financed by borrowing on a more permanent basis. In addition, private controls on international capital flows were introduced to prevent financial speculation, which happened to be a destabilizing feature of the interwar period. To support the new financial architecture, two key international financial institutions were created: the International Monetary Fund, (IMF) and the International Bank for Reconstruction and Development (IBRD), known as the World Bank. The mission of the IMF was to promote an orderly balance of payments adjustment by member countries, through the provision of financing, surveillance, and technical assistance. In theory, the IMF could induce adjustment in surplus nations, but this function largely failed to materialize as the Fund would not have enough political leverage to do so on its main stockholders, running balance of payments surpluses.

Deficit countries, in turn, could borrow from the IMF and other external sources to cover external imbalances that were considered as transitory; otherwise, the correction of the disequilibrium called for currency devaluation and the reduction of internal spending. The original mission of the World Bank was to lend for the reconstruction in Europe but thereafter, this was extended to provide loans and technical assistance to developing countries and decolonizing nations.

IMF-led adjustment programs avoided the recourse to imposing tariffs and other restrictions to international trade of the sort used in the 1930s by center economies, a practice that aggravated the world depression. For this the General Agreement on Tariffs and Trade (GATT) established rules for multilateralism and promoted gradual trade liberalization. As a sign of the dominant US influence in the postwar settlement, the headquarters of the IMF and the World Bank were established in Washington DC, near the US Department of the Treasury. In turn, the United Nations replaced the League of Nations in 1944–1945 – an organization formed in 1919 that the United States refused to join, with established headquarters in New York City.

At the time of the Marshall Plan, Europe faced various political challenges. Italy and France had important Communist parties and in Britain, a labor government headed by Clement Richard Attlee, nationalized an important part of the British industry within a framework of regulated capitalism. In addition, a block of socialist countries in Central and Eastern Europe emerged after World War II. A race between two economic and political systems developed: the capitalist block under US leadership and the socialist block under Soviet guidance. Later the Cold War led to the North Atlantic Treaty Organization (NATO), the Council for Mutual Economic Assistance (COMECON), and the Warsaw Pact.

Following the growing influence of Keynes's ideas, governments appreciated the potential of fiscal policy to ensure a high level of economic activity and full employment. The Employment Act of 1946 passed by the US Congress, for example, stated explicitly the need for the federal government to use all of its instruments to "promote maximum employment, production and purchasing power in a system of free competitive enterprise and general welfare." This represented an important departure from the doctrine of balanced budgets prevailing until the Great Depression and created a role for federal government's *automatic stabilizers*. The public sector, to stabilize economic activity, will run fiscal deficits during downturns and recessions along with fiscal surpluses during times of high economic activity and employment. A similar philosophy of fiscal policy was adopted in several European countries and elsewhere to the extent they could finance concomitant fiscal deficits with government debt and/or external borrowing.

5.3 Golden Age, Stagflation, and Globalization

Besides initial slumps that accompanied the end of World War II (see Chapter 3), the United States and western Europe engaged in an expansionary cycle through the 1950s and most of the 1960s. Economic historian Charles P. Kindleberger (Kindleberger, 1967) coined the phrase "European Super-Growth" to describe the dynamism after World War II. The postwar boom was supported by active demand policies, a protective welfare state, and a concern on inequality.

5.4 Core Economies: The United States, the United Kingdom, France, and Germany

The growth record of the United States and western Europe (core and periphery) in the 1950s and 1960s is depicted in Table 5.1a and Figures 5.1 and 5.2.

Table 5.1a. *Growth in GDP per capita, core economies and European periphery (annual average change, percentage, 1950–2015)*

	France	Greece	Ireland	Italy	Portugal	Spain	United Kingdom	United States	Germany
1950s	3.7	5.0	1.7	5.6	3.1	3.5	1.7	2.36	8.20
1960s	4.6	6.6	4.2	5.4	6.0	7.1	2.5	3.07	3.84
1970s	3.0	4.4	3.2	2.9	4.5	4.2	2.2	2.18	2.98
1980s	1.7	1.3	2.7	2.3	3.0	2.5	2.2	2.10	1.70
1990s	1.61	1.41	6.36	1.44	2.70	2.25	1.82	1.97	1.79
2000s	0.73	2.45	1.90	0.16	0.60	1.36	1.19	0.86	0.85
2010–2015	0.65	–3.74	5.70	–0.69	–0.10	–0.20	1.23	1.38	2.06

Source: Author's elaboration. Data for 1950–1989 period from Maddison (2013); and for 1990–2015 period from World Development Indicators, The World Bank 2017.

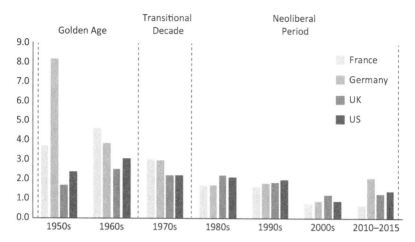

Figure 5.1. Core economies: GDP per capita, average change (percentage) by decade (or half-decade), 1950–2015. *Source:* Data for France and UK 1950–1989 period from Kornai (2006); for Germany and US from Maddison (2013), and for 1990–2015 period from World Development Indicators, The World Bank 2017.

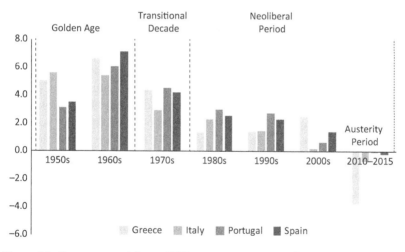

Figure 5.2. European periphery: GDP per capita, average change (percentage) by decade (or half-decade), 1950–2015. *Source:* Data for 1950–1989 period from Kornai (2006), and for 1990–2015 period from World Development Indicators, The World Bank 2017.

Table 5.1b. *Growth in GDP per capita, core economies (annual average change, percentage)*

Average	France	Germany	United States	United Kingdom
Golden Age (1950–1969)	4.0	6.0	2.7	2.1
Neoliberal period (1980–2015)	1.2	1.2	1.6	1.7

Source: Author's elaboration. Data for 1950–1989 period from Maddison (2013); and for 1990–2015 period from World Development Indicators, The World Bank 2017.

The fastest growing economy in the 1950s was Germany's (over 8 percent in per capita GDP) and in the 1960s, France's (over 4 percent in GDP per capita). Growth dynamism stalled in the 1970s and per capita GDP growth decelerated in both core economies and the European periphery. It is interesting to note, however, that after the 1970s, there was no return (i.e., "mean-reversion" in statistical jargon) to the rapid growth of GDP per capita rates of the 1950s and 1960s. On the contrary, as shown in Table 5.1b, there is a *permanent deceleration* in GDP per capita growth starting in the transitional decade of the 1970s. A more pronounced deceleration took place in Germany that reduced its average annual per capita growth from an average of 6 percent in 1950–1969 to 1.2 percent in 1980–2015 (Table 5.1b). In the United States and the United Kingdom, per capita growth deceleration between 1950–1969 and 1980–2015 is in the range of 0.5 percent and 1 percent per annum.

At least three factors contributed to the growth slowdown in the 1970s and 1980s: (i) the oil price hikes were supply-side disturbances, equivalent to a *negative productivity shock* (Bruno and Sachs, 1985); (ii) inflation and exchange-rate instability contributed to price/profitability volatility, affecting investment decisions and the quality of resource allocation; and (iii) a drift to higher wages in the 1970s, a period of strong labor militancy in Europe, squeezed profits, features that also acted as a deterrent to capital formation, creating uneasiness to the owners of capital.

The 1980s was not generally a period of high growth in the United States, and in Europe, which also experienced persistently higher unemployment. The 1990s was a decade of renewed faith in the benefits of free markets coinciding with the collapse of socialist regimes in the USSR and Central and Eastern Europe. Although this was also a decade of abundant capital flows, the statistics do not show a systematic upsurge in growth rates in advanced capitalist countries (Table 5.1a). In the 2000s, after a boom between 2003 and 2007, came the global financial crisis of 2008 and 2009 followed by sluggish recovery.

5.5 The Southern European Periphery

The economies of the southern European periphery, like the center economies, grew relatively fast in the 1950s and 1960s, with high growth rates in
Greece, Italy, and Spain. This probably reflected an upward adjustment in
GDP (catch-up effect) that took place after the destruction of the capital
stock, and losses of lives and economic assets in World War II that affected
Greece and Italy more severely (see Table A.1 Chapter 9). In turn, Spain
suffered a devastating civil war in 1936–1939 that was followed by some
economy recovery afterwards.

The overall growth deceleration between the golden age and the neoliberal
period was pronounced in Greece, Italy, Portugal, and Spain. In these economies, annual GDP per capita fell between 2 and 3 percent in the neoliberal
era (the averages, of course, are affected by the contractions in 2008–2009
and its aftermath that was particularly serious in Greece). An exception to
this trend was Ireland, where average GDP per capita accelerated by 1 percent between the two eras, see Table 5.1c) It is worth noting that in Ireland,
GDP per capita grew at an average annual 6.4 percent in the 1990s, following
the adoption of aggressive policies of reducing corporate tax rates oriented
to attract multinational corporations and foreign direct investment.

The great recession of 2008–2009 and its aftermath hit hard in Portugal,
Spain, Italy, and in Greece, which experienced average negative growth during the austerity period, 2010–2015. Again, the exception was that Ireland
experienced positive growth, on average, between 2010 and 2015.

In contrast, the four core economies (United States, United Kingdom,
France, and Germany) experienced, on average, positive growth in 2010–2015.

5.6 The Onset of the Free-market Policies
and Economic Turbulence

The combination of higher inflation and unemployment of the 1970s
started to show the limits of Keynesian demand policies to restore full
employment and maintain price stability. At the same time, new academic
fashions such as the rational expectations school, monetarism, the efficient market hypothesis, and supply-side economics became dominant
paradigms at universities. Milton Friedman and Friedrich Hayek, cham-
pions of free-market economics, started to wield an influence on academia
and policymakers that they did not have before and provided practical policy advice to the governments of Ronald Reagan, Margaret Thatcher, and

Table 5.1c. *Growth in GDP per capita, European periphery (annual average change, percentage)*

Average	Greece	Ireland	Italy	Portugal	Spain
Golden Age (1950–1969)	5.8	3.0	5.7	4.6	5.4
Neoliberal period (1980–2015)	0.8	4.0	1.0	1.7	1.7

Source: Author's elaboration. Data for 1950–1989 period from Maddison (2013); and for 1990–2015 period from World Development Indicators, The World Bank 2017.

dictator Augusto Pinochet in their free-market revolutions (earlier, Hayek had approached the authoritarian leader Oliveira Salazar in Portugal).

Based on the prescriptions of privatization, market deregulation, tax cuts, squeezing of labor unions, and shifts in wealth and income to capital and financialization, a new accumulation regime supported neoliberal capitalism. Technological breakthroughs in information technology and computer science were other important developments that more or less coincided with these new policies. Also, the economic geography of investment changed: international corporations moved parts of their operations to low–wage countries such as China, Indonesia, Vietnam, and others. Several factors facilitated the shift towards a more pro-capital policy environment in the neoliberal era: (i) the use of harsh tactics against the labor movement in the United Kingdom and the United States (under Thatcher and Reagan, respectively) and open labor repression in Pinochet's Chile;[2] (ii) the change in priorities in macroeconomic policy towards a primacy of lower inflation over steady growth and high employment since the 1980s; (iii) the use of protracted unemployment for debilitating the bargaining power of labor; (iv) a decline in union membership; (v) higher movement of corporations to low-wage countries, which reduced the demand for labor in advanced capitalist economies; and (vi) labor-saving technological change replacing machinery, equipment, and computers for workers. As a result of these interrelated changes, the evidence shows that *functional income distribution* turned in favor of capital and against labor. In fact, labor shares in national income have declined since the 1970s and 1980s in economies such as the United States, Germany, and China, as well as in a host of developing nations (Atkinson, 2015, Solimano, 2017).

[2] See Solimano (2012).

The changes ongoing in economic policies and paradigms took place at a time of geopolitical crises affecting the United States and western Europe. The United States was engaged in an increasingly difficult military and political situation in Vietnam (the war ended in 1975, forcing a hasty withdrawal that year). Then, a few years later, in 1979, a crisis developed in Iran with the overthrowing of the pro-US regime of Mohammed Reza Shah Pahlevi and the hostage crisis, which added another blow to US global hegemony. The election of Ronald Reagan in 1980 can be, in part, interpreted as an aspiration by political and economic elites to revert the geopolitical setbacks and economic maladies of the 1970s. In the United Kingdom, Thatcher also started a neoliberal agenda oriented to stop what was perceived as an inexorable process of national decline and loss of global status. The new engine of growth would be the private sector encouraged by higher profit rates and a debilitated working class.

In the southern European periphery, the 1970s witnessed political transitions from authoritarian regimes to democracy in Portugal, Greece, and Spain. In Portugal, on April 25, 1974, the authoritarian regime of Marcelo Caetano (who succeeded the civilian dictator António de Oliviera Salazar in 1968) was overthrown by a group of progressive young colonels with ample popular support from dissatisfied citizens, social movements, and left-wing parties (see Box 5.1). This opened the door for democratization and led to the dismembering of Portuguese colonial enclaves in Africa. In Greece, the "colonel's junta," a right-wing authoritarian regime ruled from 1968 to 1974, backed by the United States under the logic of the Cold War. In 1974, the Greek regime had to leave after its mishandling of a political crisis in Cyprus (the junta wanted the unification of the northern and southern part of Cyprus under Greek rule).[3]

In Spain, General Francisco Franco died in 1975. He had been at the helm of the country for nearly four decades since the end of a bloody civil war in 1939. After his death, a brief transitional period led to the

---

[3] On July 15, 1974 a coup d'état on the island of Cyprus overthrew Archbishop Makarios III, the Cypriot president. This move was sponsored by Greek junta strongman Brigadier Dimitrios Ioannidis. Turkey replied to Greek intervention by invading Cyprus and occupying the northern part of the island, after heavy fighting with the Cypriot and Greek Hellenic Force in Cyprus (ELDYK) forces. The Cyprus fiasco led senior Greek military officers to withdraw their support for Ioannidis. The junta-appointed President Phaedon Gizikis (a military man) called a meeting of old guard politicians for a national unity government that would lead the country to elections. New Democracy (a political party in Greece) won the November, 1974 general election, and parliamentary democracy was thus restored in Greece. The Greek legislative elections of 1974 were the first free elections held in a decade, opening the door on the start of redemocratization of Greece.

establishment of "normal," democratic institutions and a new constitution was adopted in 1978, leaving behind four decades of nondemocratic rule. Economically, Portugal, Greece, and Spain had, in the 1950s and 1960s, an industrial base, agriculture was still important, and there were considerable labor surpluses that encouraged emigration toward more affluent economies such as Germany, France, and Britain. Spain and Portugal were also former imperial powers, with Portugal retaining colonial outposts until 1974. Greece, in turn, had a very distinguished past as the cradle of Western Civilization, modern democracy, mathematics, and philosophy.

Definitely, the 1970s was not a tranquil decade neither for the most advanced capitalist economies of North America and western Europe nor for the less developed European periphery. Several western European countries were affected by social conflicts between labor and capital showing up in frequent strikes, active labor militancy, and the ascendancy of left-wing parties. Moreover, there was also active political violence in Northern Ireland and England related to actions of the Irish Republican Army (IRA) and the responses of the British army. Terrorist groups included the Baader-Meinhof in Germany and the Red Brigades in Italy, to cite the most prominent cases. The combination of social unrest and politically motivated violence frightened economic elites and created an atmosphere of uncertainty that affected private investment and growth.

5.7 The Fall of Communism and the Rise of the Market Economy

Another very important event of the late 1980s and early 1990s, with global consequences, was the end of communist regimes in Central and Eastern Europe following the fall of the Berlin wall in 1989 and the demise of the Soviet Union as a political entity in 1991.[4]

The collapse of centrally planned economies, long affected by microeconomic inefficiencies, excessive centralization, ideological rigidity, and technological backwardness gave new impetus to the project of an integrated global economy, led by the United States. The hope was that a combination of free markets and liberal democracy (the "end of history" in the words of

---

[4] Since the Bolshevik Revolution in 1917, and the creation of socialist regimes after 1944–1945, a permanent competition (tense and dangerous at the time of the "Cold War") developed between the capitalist world (the US, Western Europe, Japan, Australia, and other countries) and the communist block led by the Soviet Union comprised socialist nations in East and Central Europe. Moreover, since 1949, China provided the communist world with a giant country of several hundred million people.

Rand Corporation's academic Francis Fukuyama) would bring about lasting material prosperity, market economies, and political freedom for the world. However, things in reality do not always proceed in the way envisaged by theoreticians. In fact, the experience of the last two to three decades has shown that the failure of communism does not imply, per se, that global capitalism will work as a smooth machine of wealth creation free of crisis and major disruptions in economic activity. Mainstream macroeconomists declared that advanced economies had entered a new era of "Great Moderation" in which the secrets of taming the business cycle and ensuring stability were in the hands of central bankers and ministers of finance, several of them trained in top departments of economics at prestigious universities in the United States and Europe. Financial markets were confident that governments had the best people available to avert systemic crises. This unwarranted confidence masked both failures of training[5] and of judgment by a new brand of policymakers. This was particularly evident in their unrealistic views of financial markets coupled with inadequate regulation, in generating financial crisis and economic depression. Memories of the 1930s were too distant and the experience of repeated financial and debt crises since the 1970s in Latin America, Asia was, apparently, discarded as of little relevance for the advanced capitalist countries at the center of the world economy. Nevertheless, financial excesses and misadventures by reckless financiers were incubating a crisis in the United States and other main economies before 2008–2009. The symptoms were clear: overvalued stock prices, expensive real estate property, overlending, high personal debt, and risky portfolios held by commercial banks and other financial intermediaries.

The wake-up to a reality of multiple crises was sharp. Episodes of financial fragility and crises were not in short supply both in the global north and the global south: the banking crisis in Scandinavian countries in the early 1990s; the speculative attacks against the British pound, the Italian lira and the Spanish peseta in 1992; the Mexican crisis of 1994; the Asian crisis of 1997; the Russian crisis of 1998; and the bursting of the bubble in the price of information technology (IT)'s share prices in the United States in 1999–2000 confirmed a fragile financial situation that could not be ignored anymore. Global capitalism, freed from the threat of socialism and operating under the new mantra of free-market economics and

---

[5] Many students of economics nowadays have a high exposure to theories of market fundamentalism and are less familiar with the ideas of Keynes and other "big thinkers" (Marx; Schumpeter) who stressed the crisis-propensity of unregulated capitalism and its self-destructive tendencies.

deregulation became a system very prone to financial crises, currency instability, and sharp cycles of economic activity.

5.8 The Global Financial Crisis of 2008–2009

The crisis of 2008–2009 was the most severe since the 1930s and originated in the world's most economically powerful economy, the United States. It came after a succession of price bubbles, first in the stock market (in the second half of the 1990s) and then in the real estate market, mostly residential property, that brewed in 2003–2007. The real estate boom of the early twenty-first century was reminiscent of the real estate boom of the early to mid-1920s in the states of Florida and New York that also spread to the city of Chicago and others. The 2008–2009 crisis was labeled the "sub-prime crisis" due to the fact that residential credit was largely oriented to serve a segment of borrowers with low incomes and limited financial capacity to acquire residential property. By around 2006, it was apparent that these borrowers faced serious problems to serve their housing loans granted by banks and other financial intermediaries taking advantage of a period of low interest rates and ample liquidity following the policy of easy money pursued by the Federal Reserve to counteract the bursting of the IT bubble in the early 2000s.

The sequence of asset price bubbles of the 1990s and 2000s in the United States was different from the bubbles of the 1920s. Speculation in the 1990s–2000s *started in the stock market* and then moved to the real estate market. In contrast, in the 1920s, speculation *started in the real estate market* and lasted until 1925–1926; then a second bubble in the stock market followed that ended with the crash of October 1929, followed by a large-scale banking crisis and massive output contraction and unemployment (see Chapter 4 and Solimano, 2017).

Besides, the US economy in the run-up to the crisis of 2008–2009 had significant external current account deficits with the rest of the world that served the purpose of absorbing the "saving glut" (excess savings relative to investment opportunities) originated in countries such as China, Germany, and other high savings nations, as well as oil-exporting economies. The US was seen as a safe destination for foreign investors seeking a place to deposit their savings. Nevertheless, reckless lending in the real estate market and the existence of an unregulated derivative market showed that this assumption was unsafe.[6] Nevertheless, financial fragility did not only pertain to

---

[6] The existence of mortgage serving problems in the US real estate market, a result of hasty lending practices to risky borrowers, was noted as early as 2006. The reduction of the down payment required when buying a house increased the risk profile and

the US and a dynamic of financial contagion was triggered by the failure of Lehman Brothers in September 2008. A crisis that originated in the US morphed into an international crisis affecting other core capitalist economies in Europe.

The syndrome of overvalued asset prices, leveraged borrowers, easy credit, poor regulation, and macroeconomic imbalances were also present, in different degrees and shapes, in the United Kingdom, Ireland, Spain, and Iceland in 2007–2008. In the United Kingdom, there was a run on the North Rock Bank, which –after facing financial troubles – requested, on September 14, 2007, liquidity support from the Bank of England. This move led to a decline in its share price by 30 percent. On September 15, 2007, clients started to withdraw deposits from the bank and two days later the government decreed a guarantee of deposits to stop the run. On February 2008, the British government took over the bank and then legislation was passed that nationalized Northern Rock Bank. During 2011, the bank was privatized again, and the government sold its shares of Northern Rock Bank to Virgin Money for near 747 million British pounds in cash.[7]

Another country seriously affected by the crisis is Iceland where its three main banks Glitnir, Landsbankinn, and Kaupthing were rescued by the government in the last quarter of 2008. There were banking problems also in Ireland, Spain, and other European nations.

The financial cycle leading to the 2008–2009 crash hit, among other countries, the United States and Iceland featured elements highlighted by both Irving Fisher and Hyman Minsky as typical in a financial crisis. This involved, in the booming phase, credit expansion and inflated asset prices in equity and real estate markets with the financial system funding the speculation spree. Debt acquired by households, corporations, and governments in the booming phase introduced vulnerability into the system. Then as the boom ran its course, distress borrowing, a fall in asset prices, the appearance of nonperforming loans, and deteriorated balance sheets all occurred. The origin of the financial crisis, in turn, was intermingled with macroeconomic imbalances such as current account deficits and fiscal deficits. A main difference, however, between the Great Recession (2008–2009) and the Great Depression (early 1930s) was the response of central

---

vulnerabilities of balance sheets of the financial sector, tilting the risk of mortgages not being repaid to lenders. Nevertheless, after the crisis exploded the number of foreclosures (borrowers losing their homes) skyrocketed to the millions.

[7] BBC News, November 17, 2011.

banks. As shown in Chapter 4, in the early 1930s, central banks adopted *restrictive* monetary policies whereas in the Great Recession of 2008–2009 central banks and treasuries *expanded* liquidity and bought bad assets from financial institutions in trouble. There were also other similarities between the Great Depression and the Great Recession. In the crisis of 2008–2009, massive bank bankruptcies were avoided; but depressed asset prices, weak demand, and diminished expectations destroyed net financial wealth of consumers and brought financial fragility to firms affecting both consumption and investment in the productive sector. An empirical study, carried out by Romer (1990), of the connections between the Great Crash of 1929 and the Great Depression for the United States shows that the destruction of financial wealth after the financial crash of 1929 along with a credit squeeze triggered a drop in aggregate demand that led to the big output slump in the early 1930s.

5.9 Growth and Investment Cycles in Core Economies

The shocks of the 1970s, the rise of globalization, and the crisis of 2008–2009 had various impacts on investment and growth in core economies. Tables 5.2a–5.2c) present a list of episodes of recessions (annual growth in per capita GDP) and investment declines along with their duration in the United States, the United Kingdom, France, and Germany from 1970 to 2015.

The United Kingdom experienced a recession in 1974–1975 (GDP per capita fell by 1.5 percent). The recession was not that deep, but the economy had incubated external imbalances, debt problems, inflationary pressures, labor conflicts, and a slowdown in productivity. In an unprecedented move, for a former imperial power and advanced Western economy, Labor Prime Minister James Callaghan applied for financial support, with austerity measures included, to the International Monetary Fund in 1976.[8]

France, Germany, and the United States also experienced recessions in 1975, with the most severe fall of GDP per capita taking place in the United States. These countries were affected by hikes in oil prices, internal wage-push pressures, inflation, currency volatility, and fiscal deficits. These events had an adverse impact on economic growth in these countries. As can be seen from Table 5.2a, there were also years of negative per capita growth in the early 1980s, early 1990s, and early 2000s. However, the most severe blow was the financial crisis of 2008–2009, leading to negative growth in those years in the four countries.

[8] See Burk and Caincross (1992).

Table 5.2a. *Recessions (negative GDP per capita growth) in the United States, the United Kingdom, France, and Germany since 1970*

Country	Period	Cumulative decline in GDP per capita (%)	Years of decline	N° of years for GDP pc to reach pre-recession levels	Percent (and number) of years of negative growth over sample
France	1975	−1.18	1	2	10.64% (5 years)
	1993	−1.04	1	2	
	2008–2009	−3.79	2	9	
	2012	−0.3	1	3	
Germany	1975	−0.19	1	3	12.77% (6 years)
	1982	−0.77	1	2	
	1993	−1.61	1	2	
	2002–2003	−0.93	2	3	
	2009	−5.38	1	3	
United Kingdom	1974–1975	−1.48	2	3	14.89% (7 years)
	1980–1981	−3.19	2	4	
	1991	−1.42	1	3	
	2008–2009	−6.38	2	8	
United States	1970	−0.99	1	2	19.15% (9 years)
	1974–1975	−2.43	2	3	
	1980	−1.13	1	2	
	1982	−2.81	1	2	
	1991	−1.4	1	2	
	2001	−0.02	1	2	
	2008–2009	−4.81	2	7	

Source: Author's elaboration. Data for 1970–1989 period from Maddison (2013); and for 1990–2015 period from World Development Indicators, The World Bank 2017.

The United Kingdom reached a cumulative decline in per capita GDP of 6.4 percent in 2008–2009. In the United States, per capita GDP accumulated a decline of 4.8 percent in 2008–09 followed by a rebound in 2010 and then a recovery of output (more robust for investment) in 2011–2015 (see Figure 5.3). A milder contraction of economic activity took place in France with per capita GDP falling by 3.8 percent in 2008–2009. In Germany, per capita output fell (5.4 percent) only in 2009.

Looking at the adjustment in physical investment across episodes of output contraction in the period 1970–2015, it is apparent that the *magnitude* of the decline of investment is often much larger than the decline in GDP per person (Tables 5.2b and 5.2c). For example, in France during the recession

Table 5.2b. *Episodes of investment decline in the United States, the United Kingdom, France, and Germany (percentage change in total investment, 1970–2015)*

Country	Period	Cumulative decline in Investment (%)	Consecutive years/ decline	Change in real investment 3 years after recession (cumulative)	N° of years for Investment to reach pre-recession levels
France[a]	1975	−4.91	1	4.36	5
	1977	−0.67	1	8.85	2
	1981–1984	−5.61	4	11.65	6
	1991–1993	−7.34	3	3.64	8
	2002	−0.92	1	8.3	2
	2009	−9.07	1	4.38	
	2013–2014	−1.14	2		
Germany[a]	1974–1975	−12.75	2	12.83	6
	1981–1982	−9.02	2	3.83	8
	1993	−4.2	1	3.11	6
	1995–1996	−0.53	2	9.32	3
	2001–2003	−9.38	3	8.31	7
	2009	−10.08	1	11.9	3
	2012	−1.8	2		3
United States	1974–1975	−10.94	2	28.95	4
	1980	−4.28	1	3.83	5
	1982	−5.38	1	29.36	2
	1990–1991	−4.23	2	15.36	4
	2001–2002	−2.29	2	15.33	3
	2007–2009	−18.31	3	11.09	9
United Kingdom[a]	1972	−0.04	1	2.7	2
	1974–1975	−3.81	2	2.71	6
	1977	−1.53	1	0.38	2
	1980–1981	−13.07	2	20.15	5
	1990–1991	−8.40	2	8.85	6
	1997	−1.57	1	14.04	2
	2008–2009	−20.73	2	9.19	

[a] Data from 1971–2015.
Source: Author's elaboration based on World Development Indicators, The World Bank 2017.

of 1975, per capita GDP fell by 1.2 percent, but investment declined by close to 5 percent. In turn, in 2009 investment fell by 9.1 percent near three times the cut in per capita GDP in 2008–2009. In the United States, GDP fell by 2.5 percent in the recession of 1974–1975 and investment declined by 11 percent in these two years. In turn, in the recession of 2008–2009 the

Table 5.2c. *Number of years of decline in GDP per capita and investment in core economies, 1970–2016*

	GDP per Capita	Investment
France	5	13
Germany	6	13
United Kingdom	7	11
United States	9	11
Average	6.8	12

Source: Author's elaboration based on data in Tables 5.2a and 5.2b.

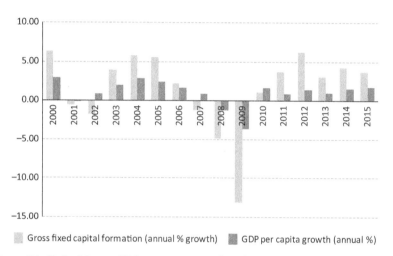

■ Gross fixed capital formation (annual % growth)   ■ GDP per capita growth (annual %)

Figure 5.3. United States: GDP per capita growth and investment growth (percentage change, 2000–2015). *Source:* World Development Indicators, The World Bank 2017.

drop in GDP was 4.8 percent while investment declined by 18.3 percent (2007–2009). For the United Kingdom and Germany, the fall in investment was also larger than the decline in GDP in years of recession.

In the 1970–2015 period, the average number of years in which GDP per capita fell was 6.8 years and the number of years in which investment declined was 12 years for the whole period (see Table 5.2c).

On the other hand, in the recovery phase (after the contraction) the growth of investment typically *exceeds* the growth of GDP (see Figures 5.3–5.6). In some countries, a cut in investment may *precede* the decline in GDP, but this is not always the case (in the United States, the drop in investment preceded the fall in GDP per person before 2008–2009, Figure 5.3). In the United Kingdom, both investment and GDP declined in 2008 and 2009 but (unlike

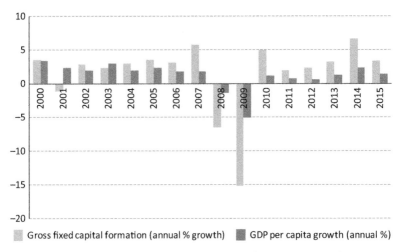

Figure 5.4. United Kingdom: GDP per capita growth and investment growth (percentage change, 2000–2015). *Source:* World Development Indicators, The World Bank 2017.

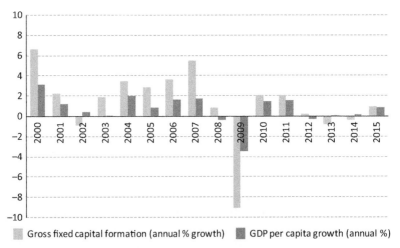

Figure 5.5. France: GDP per capita growth and investment growth (percentage change, 2000–2015). *Source:* World Development Indicators, The World Bank 2017.

in the United States) investment growth was positive in 2007 (Figure 5.4). In France, investment growth was positive in 2008 (GDP per capita fell slightly that year) but investment fell in 2009, 2013, and 2014 (Figure 5.5). In Germany, both investment and GDP declined in 2009 (investment fell more); and investment fell again in 2012 and 2013 (Figure 5.6).

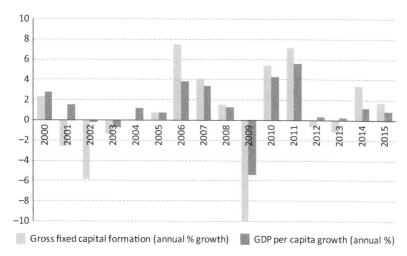

Figure 5.6. Germany: GDP per capita growth and investment growth (percentage change, 2000–2015). *Source:* World Development Indicators, The World Bank 2017.

5.10 Recession and Investment Adjustment in Southern Europe and Ireland

The recessions of the 1970s in Portugal, Spain, Italy, Greece, and Ireland were associated with country-specific factors and international disturbances. The end of authoritarian regimes in Portugal and Greece in 1974 was associated with *declines* in GDP and investment in both countries. In Greece, GDP per capita fell by nearly 7 percent in 1974, the year that the government of the "colonel's junta" had to leave power. In Portugal, in 1974 – the year of the April 25th revolution – GDP per capita fell, slightly, 0.2 percent but in 1975 the decline was more severe: 7.5 percent. The oil price shock, the effect of a massive return of emigrates from Angola and Mozambique, the effects of nationalization policies undertook by the new Portuguese government, and increased social activism (strikes and factory occupations) all took a toll on private investment (see Box 5.1).[9] A recession also took place in Italy in 1975 where GDP per capita declined by 2.7 percent.

In the first half of the 1980s, there was at least one year of negative growth in GDP per person in Greece, Ireland, Portugal, and Spain (Table 5.3a).

In the mid-1980s, Greece, Portugal, and Spain entered the EEC which imposed new conditions upon their fiscal and regulatory policies and in labor and environmental standards. Entering the EEC enabled the

---

[9] It is estimated that 244 private enterprises were nationalized between March, 1975 and July, 1976 by the Portuguese government.

Box 5.1. Portugal: The Revolution of April 25, 1974, European Integration, and the Crisis of 2008–2009

The revolution of April 25, 1974 in Portugal, led by the progressive *Movimento das Forcas Armadas* (Armed Forces Movement; MFA) led to the demise of a four decade long dictatorial regime, comprising the *Estado Novo* of Oliveira Salazar (1932–1968) and the government of Marcello Caetano (1968–1974). Importantly, the revolution led also to the breakdown of Portugal's African colonial system comprised of Angola, Mozambique, Guinea-Bissau, São Tomé and Principe, and Cape Verde.

The colonial regime became increasingly costly to maintain. Estimates for the early 1970s are that Portugal was spending nearly half of its GDP in sustaining the presence of over 150,000 military personnel in Africa. The breakdown of the colonial system after the revolution led to the massive return of Portuguese emigrates living in the former African colonies (the *retornados*). Economic policy after the revolution strengthened the state sector through policies of nationalization and regulation of the private sector. The MFA also pursued a policy of redistribution of income from property owners and high-income groups to workers, small agricultural-ists, the lower middle-class, and peasants. These policies created alarm in the economic elites and also led to fiscal imbalances. With the arrival of the Socialist Party under the leadership of Prime Minister Mário Soares, economic policies changed course and Portugal engaged in stabilization programs with the IMF in 1977–1978 and again in 1983–1985. The sec-ond IMF program coincided with negative per capita GDP growth in 1983–1984 (−2.3 percent) and came along with a collapse of investment of −28 percent between 1983 and 1985. The decline in investment was a costly mechanism to reduce the external current account deficit, follow-ing a pattern that is common in many IMF-sponsored adjustment pro-grams (see Chapter 6). In 1986, Portugal entered the European Economic Community (EEC) and in the early 2000s adopted the euro as the legal tender phasing out the escudo (the national currency).

The country suffered the effect of the 2008–2009 global financial crisis, which destabilized two main banks: Banco Português de Negócios (BPN) and Banco Privado Portugês (BPP). BNP was nationalized in October, 2008 to avoid a large-scale financial crisis. In 2011, following instability in bond markets and fears about the solvency of the Portuguese econ-omy, the government requested an adjustment package from the IMF, the European Central Bank (ECB), and the European Commission (EC). Several years of harsh austerity followed.

Table 5.3a. *Recessions (negative GDP per capita growth) in southern Europe and Ireland, 1970–2015*

Country	Period	Cumulative decline in GDP per capita (%)	Consecutive years/decline	N° of years for GDP pc to reach pre-recession levels	Percent (and number) of years of negative growth over sample
Greece	1974	−3.99	1	2	29.8%
	1981–1983	−1.18	3	4	(14 years)
	1987	−0.69	1	2	
	1990	−1.05	1	2	
	1992–1993	−2.24	2	4	
	2008–2013	−25.96	6		
Italy	1975	−2.70	1	2	17.0%
	1993	−0.91	1	2	(8 years)
	2003	−0.29	1	2	
	2008–2009	−7.51	2		
	2012–2014	−6.61	3		
Portugal	1974–1975	−7.73	2	4	21.3%
	1983–1984	−2.30	2	3	(10 years)
	1993	−2.16	1	3	
	2003	−1.31	1	2	
	2009	−3.07	1		
	2011–2013	−5.81	3		
Spain	1981	−0.18	1	2	17.0%
	1993	−1.54	1	2	(8 years)
	2008–2013	−10.63	6		
Ireland	1976	−0.19	1	2	12.8%
	1983	−0.92	1	2	(6 years)
	1986	−0.44	1	2	
	2008–2009	−11.14	2	7	
	2012	−0.39	1	2	

Source: Author's elaboration. Data for 1970–1989 period from Maddison (2013); and for 1990–2015 period from World Development Indicators, The World Bank 2017.

ascending countries to access structural and cohesion funds (oriented to help countries with lower per capita incomes in Europe). These funds, along with economic integration, boosted economic convergence with more developed nations in Europe.

In addition, in the period 1970–2015, the incidence of episodes of economic contraction (drops in investment and GDP) in the European periphery was

Table 5.3b. *Episodes of investment decline in southern Europe and Ireland since 1970*

Country	Period	Cumulative decline in Investment (%)	Consecutive years/decline	Change in real investment 3 years after recession (cumulative)	N° of years for Investment to reach pre-recession levels
Greece	1970	−1.38	1	42.15	2
	1974	−33.51	1	30.85	5
	1980–1982	−26.52	3	−0.53	19
	1984	−16.24	1	3.82	8
	1987	−5.63	1	13.14	3
	1992–1994	−10.2	3	16.69	5
	2002	−0.33	1	6.19	2
	2005	−11.88	1	28.08	2
	2008–2015	−65.84	8		
Spain[a]	1971	−3	1	33.4	2
	1975–1979	−12.67	5	0.06	13
	1981	−1.65	1	−5.01	6
	1983–1984	−5.96	2	29.36	3
	1992–1993	−12.67	2	12.06	6
	2008–2013	−35.92	6		
Italy	1975	−6.26	1	4.77	5
	1981–1983	−6.25	3	7.8	6
	1992–1993	−12.49	2	9.81	7
	2003	−0.3	1	6.94	2
	2008–2014	−30.05	7		
Portugal[a]	1974–1975	−17.47	2	19.04	7
	1979	−1.34	1	16.3	2
	1983–1985	−26.00	3	43.7	6
	1993	−5.54	1	14.39	3
	2002–2003	−10.45	2	−0.61	
	2006	−0.85	1	−4.1	2
	2009–2013	−36.59	5		
Ireland[a]	1974–1975	−14.81	2	36.49	4
	1980	−4.72	1	−3.17	2
	1982–1987	−24.25	6	28.77	14
	1991–1993	−11.74	3	44.06	5
	2008–2010	−37.59	3	9.86	8
	2013	−5.67	1		2

[a] Data start in 1971.

Source: Own Elaboration. Data for 1970–1989 period from Maddison (2013); and for 1990–2015 period from World Development Indicators, The World Bank 2017.

Table 5.3c. *Numbers of years of GDP per capita and investment decline in the European periphery, 1970–2016*

	GDP per Capita	Investment
Greece	14	20
Spain	8	17
Ireland	6	16
Italy	8	14
Portugal	10	15
Average	9.2	16.4

Source: Own elaboration based on data in Tables 5.3a and 5.3b.

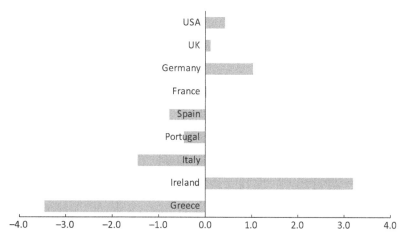

Figure 5.7. Average GDP per capita growth in core economies and European periphery (annual percentage change, 2008–2015). *Source:* Own elaboration based on WDI, World Bank.

higher than in the mature economies of western Europe and the United States. For Greece, Spain, Ireland, Italy, and Portugal, the average number of years of negative growth in GDP per capita was 9.2 years (6.8 years for core economies) and there were, on average, 16.4 years (12 years in core countries) of decline in investment (Tables 5.2c and 5.3c).

The countries with the highest frequency of GDP and investment contractions in the period were Greece followed by Portugal. Finally, as shown in Figure 5.7, the crisis of 2008–2009 and its aftermath hit the economies of the south of Europe (Portugal, Spain, Italy, and Greece) much harder than the core economies of the United States, the United Kingdom, France, and Germany. On average, in the period 2008–2015, there was negative growth in GDP per capita in the four economies of southern Europe. In the core economies, France and the United Kingdom suffered more than Germany and the United States.

5.11 Conclusion

In the second half of the twentieth century, the United States and western European (core and periphery) economies experienced a transition from the regime of high economic growth in the 1950s and 1960s, so-called golden age to the neoliberal era of frequent financial crises and more intense investment and growth cycles. After World War II, there was also a consolidation of US hegemony and the building of global institutions shaped by the United States. Divides between the advanced capitalist countries of North America, European core economies, and the European periphery also were preserved.

The evidence presented in this chapter shows that in the period 1970–2015, countries in the southern periphery of Europe (in particular Greece and Portugal) had a much higher frequency and severity of recession/depression than the core economies of Europe and the United States. In turn, investment cycles were of longer duration and more intense than cycles in GDP per capita. It is apparent that the impact of the global financial crisis on core western European countries and the United States was less severe than on the countries of southern Europe. Although the first group of countries experienced output contractions in 2008–2009, they had *positive* (albeit modest) *average* growth in the period 2008–2015. In contrast, Greece, Portugal, Spain, and Italy all experienced *negative average growth* in that period, with several years of output and investment contractions. There is a clear difference between the *stagnation* (slow growth) that affected core economies and the protracted *contraction* (or depression) that affected countries in the southern European periphery.

This disparity in economic performance between core and European periphery may also reflect structural differences between the set of economies. Although economic integration brought a degree of convergence between the European core and its periphery, still countries such as Greece, Portugal, and Spain clearly lagged behind the most advanced European economies in their levels of economic development and institutional strength. In addition, these countries had, at the onset of the global financial crisis, significant levels of sovereign and private debt that rendered them particularly vulnerable to changes in confidence levels in international capital markets, making them prone to "sudden stops" that often have devastating effects on real economic activity. In addition, in spite of being "euro countries" the countries in the European periphery underwent austerity policies more similar to those traditionally imposed on developing nations by the IMF and other international bodies.

6

Two Depressions in the Early
Twenty-First Century

The Cases of Latvia and Greece

6.1 Introduction

We can identify at least two depressions in the European periphery follow-ing the global financial crisis of 2008–2009: in Latvia and in Greece. Both episodes were surrounded by the direct conditionality in economic policies by the IMF, the European Commission and the European Central Bank. In Greece, the contraction started in 2008 and continued for six consecu-tive years, while in Latvia the contraction was shorter (2008–2010) and the recovery faster. The boom prior to the crisis in the two countries came after admission into the European Union (EU) that reduced country risk and stimulated large capital inflows to them. Latvia (also Estonia and Lithuania) had a large presence of commercial banks from Nordic nations, mainly Swedish banks.

The intensity of the depression was severe in the two countries: in Latvia, GDP declined by 22 percent in 2008–2010 and in Greece, GDP declined by 29 percent between 2008 and 2013. The Greek depression was more severe and lasted longer, resembling an L-shape while the cycle in Latvia was closer to a V-shape. Both episodes can qualify as *depressions* if we use the criteria of classification of chapter 1.

This chapter examines the main features of the contractive cycles in Latvia and Greece during and after the 2008–2009 crisis and discusses the causes and consequences, similarities and differences in the severity and duration of the slumps in the two economies. It also discusses the role played by international organizations such as the IMF, the ECB, and the EC –the so-called Troika – that were actively involved in the design and supervision of austerity programs in the two countries. The chapter also highlights main internal economic and political economy developments pertaining to each country.

Interestingly, while the Latvia adjustment was presented as a "success story" by the IMF and Latvia's authorities handling the crisis of 2008–2010, the Greek protracted contraction in the 2008–2015 period has been an embarrassment for the Troika and the European Union.

The political economy of implementing austerity policies can be tricky. In the case of Greece, external creditors did not meet with sympathy the two referendums in 2011 and 2015, in which the Greek people was asked about the continuation of austerity. Under strong external pressure from creditors, Prime Minister George Andreas Papandreu who had called the first referendum was compelled to leave office in 2011. In the second case, it was Alexis Tzipras, the left-wing prime minister who initiated the second referendum, whose result provided a mandate to renegotiate with foreign creditors a relaxation of austerity; however, at the end, Alexis Tzipras retreated in his initial quest for more economic autonomy and less foreign-imposed austerity and, the prime minister ended up leading the adoption of strict conditionality including policies of denationalization of the Greek economy through massive sales of public assets.

6.2 Latvia

Latvia is a small country with a population of little more than 2 million people and a GDP of USD 27 billion (2015). In 1940, the country was annexed by the former Soviet Union and the circulation of the national currency at the time, the lats, was stopped and replaced by the soviet ruble.[1] Latvia recovered its independence in 1991.

In 2004, the country became a member of the EU and NATO; in January 2014, it adopted the euro as its legal currency replacing its previous currency, the lats.

As mentioned before, EU admission and financial integration into the Union led to an internal boom accompanied by a rapid expansion of domestic credit to finance consumption, investment, and production for exports. The capital inflow, in turn, induced a boom in the construction sector with rising housing prices and positive wealth effects for property owners. Also, a portion of the capital inflow went to the stock market, pushing up equity prices and generating a positive wealth effect for stockholders.

In 2008, it was apparent that the private sector (household debt plus corporate debt) was highly indebted (a large proportion of it in euros). Signs of vulnerability started to appear in the final years of the boom (2006 and 2007), the external creditors of Latvia's debt became increasingly uneasy

---

[1] The last was reintroduced in 1992 and pegged to a basket of foreign currencies.

with the level of the current account deficit of the balance of payments: 20 percent of GDP (average for 2006–2007). A currency run developed in February of 2007 and, again, in 2008. The confidence shock was amplified by the downgrading by Standard & Poor of Latvia's external debt. This contributed a worsening economic outlook for the country and financial conditions became very fragile. Latvia's second most important bank, Parex Banka, with a market share of 20 percent, suffered the outflow of deposits held by nonresidents that could, eventually, precipitate the failure of the bank. In October 2008, to prevent a panic affecting other financial institutions, the Latvian government intervened: a partial deposit freeze was imposed upon Parex-Banka and the government acquired a majority share position in the capital of the bank. A cutoff in foreign and domestic credit triggered a drop in asset prices (stocks and real estate), reducing the value of collaterals held by indebted agents and augmenting the degree of fragility in the financial system. We have to remember that this came only one month after the failure of Lehman Brothers in the United States, which shocked market confidence worldwide.

Given the drying up of international capital markets in the last quarter of 2008, and the difficulties of funding a large current account deficit, the Latvian government asked the IMF, the EU, and Nordic countries for loans to support the balance of payments. The total support package agreed in 2008 was 7.5 billion euros.[2] The financial package ended the drain on international reserves.

The request to the IMF was approved by its board of directors before Christmas 2008. In January, 2009, the EU's Economic and Financial Affairs Council (ECOFIN) also approved funding to Latvia. The loans targeted financial help to support Parex Banka meet its obligations with external creditors. Money also went to finance the fiscal deficit and support the currency peg considered as an important "nominal anchor" to stabilize expectations.

The Swedish Riksbank provided a bridge loan while negotiations between Latvia and international creditors proceeded. The active and prompt financial support from Sweden to Latvia was probably motivated by the important presence of Swedish banks and companies in the country that could have been exposed in the event a full blown financial crisis exploded.

---

[2] The IMF's part of the package amounted to €1.7 billion, the EU contributed €3.1 billion; the Nordic countries contributed €1.8 billion; the World Bank contributed €400 million; the Czech Republic contributed €200 million; the European Bank for Reconstruction and Development, Estonia, and Poland contributed €100 million each. IMF Survey: After Severe Recession, Stabilization in Latvia, *IMF News*, February 18, 2010.

At the root of the output contraction of 2008–2010 was the need to engineer a *swift reversal* in the current account deficit in a short period of time, as foreign creditors were unwilling to provide funding to Latvia at the levels before 2008. The magnitude of the reversal was daunting: the current account went from a deficit of 20.8 percent of GDP in 2007 and 12.6 percent in 2008 to a *surplus* of 7.9 percent of GDP in 2009 and 2.1 percent in 2010 (Table 6.1a).

Then, the current account stabilized at a more modest level, (–2.5 percent of GDP, average, during the recovery phase 2011–2015, Table 6.1b). The average fiscal deficit *increased* sharply from 1.4 percent of GDP in the pre-crisis period 2000–2007 to 7.2 percent of GDP in 2008–2010, stabilizing at 1.6 percent in 2011–2015 (Table 6.1b and Figure 6.1).

The worsening of the fiscal deficit during the crisis was due to a reduction in the level of tax revenues associated with the drop-in output, along with increases in some countercyclical spending items. As a consequence of the widening fiscal deficit, the ratio of government debt to GDP rose by 25 points between 2000–2007 and 2011–2015. Household debt as a proportion of income also increased during the crisis years (Table 6.1b and Figure 6.2).

The reduction in the current account deficit was accomplished through protracted *cuts in the investment rate*, a main determinant of economic growth.

A very important feature of the crisis phase and the subsequent adjustment process in Latvia is that it took place *without* abandoning its pegged exchange-rate regime, an exchange-rate band tied to the euro adopted in 2005.

It is well known in standard open-economy macroeconomics that maintaining a fixed nominal exchange rate during the correction (reduction) of an external imbalance shifts the burden of deflationary adjustment to domestic wages, output, and employment. Adopting the route of the so-called "internal devaluation" can be very costly in terms of losses of output, investment, and employment compared with a more balanced policy mix that would have depreciated the lats to boost exports and reduce imports.[3]

The macroeconomic policies followed in Latvia during the period under analysis were subject to controversy. Weisbrot and Reiss (2011) compare the size of output expansion three years after episodes of devaluation in

---

[3] This amounts to *expenditure-switching* policies complemented by *expenditure-reducing* policies.

Table 6.1a. *Latvia: yearly macrofinancial indicators, 2000–2015*

Year	GDP growth (annual % Change)	Current account balance (% of GDP)	Inflation, consumer prices (annual % Change)	General government deficit (% GDP)	Gross fixed capital formation (% of GDP)	Gross domestic savings (% of GDP)	General government gross debt (% of GDP)	Household debt, total (% of net disposable income)
2000	5.41	-3.66	2.65	-2.73	25.22	16.74	12.11	—
2001	6.46	-6.00	2.48	-1.97	27.36	17.80	13.93	—
2002	7.10	-5.47	1.92	-2.23	24.55	18.11	13.15	—
2003	8.43	-7.22	2.96	-1.55	24.78	17.64	13.93	—
2004	8.34	-11.68	6.22	-1.03	28.88	17.49	13.82	36.66
2005	10.70	-11.74	6.72	-0.43	31.27	20.72	11.17	54.69
2006	11.89	-21.07	6.50	-0.61	34.16	18.56	9.18	74.63
2007	9.95	-20.80	10.14	-0.66	36.39	22.52	7.24	85.82
2008	-3.61	-12.59	15.43	-4.12	32.05	22.17	16.19	76.89
2009	-14.33	7.90	3.47	-9.05	22.54	20.37	32.49	84.97
2010	-3.79	2.08	-1.07	-8.48	19.39	17.84	40.34	89.19
2011	6.21	-3.16	4.40	-3.37	22.21	20.06	37.59	84.03
2012	4.00	-3.64	2.21	-0.83	25.41	21.60	36.86	70.95
2013	2.90	-2.72	0.00	-0.91	23.23	20.70	35.91	63.70
2014	2.10	-1.99	0.61	-1.56	22.61	21.20	38.59	56.64
2015	2.74	-0.78	0.20	-1.27	22.58	20.90	34.94	52.00

Source: Author's elaboration based on World Economic Outlook Database, World Development Indicators and OECD (2017a, b).

Table 6.1b. *Crisis phases in Latvia: economic indicators,*
average by sub-period, 2000–2015

	Before crisis, 2000–2007	Crisis stage, 2008–2010	Recovery phase, 2011–2015	2008–2015
GDP growth (annual %)	8.53	−7.24	3.59	−0.47
General government balance (% GDP)	−1.40	−7.22	−1.59	−3.70
Current account balance (% of GDP)	−10.96	−0.87	−2.46	−1.86
Inflation, consumer prices (annual %)	4.95	5.94	1.48	3.16
Gross fixed capital formation (% of GDP)	29.08	24.66	23.21	23.75
Gross domestic savings (% of GDP)	18.70	20.13	20.89	20.61
General government gross debt (% of GDP)	11.82	29.67	36.78	34.11
Household debt, Total (% of net disposable income)	62.95[a]	83.69	65.46	72.30

[a] From 2004 to 2007.

Source: Author's elaboration based on World Economic Outlook Database, World Development Indicators and OECD (2017a, b).

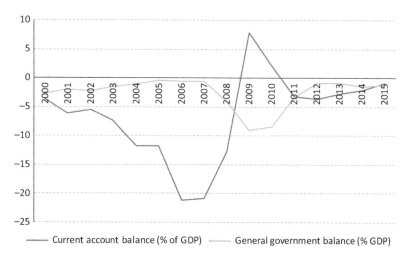

Figure 6.1. Latvia: current account balance and central government balance (percentage of GDP, 2000–2015). *Source:* Data for current account balance from World Development Indicators, The World Bank 2017, and for General government balance from OECD (2017a).

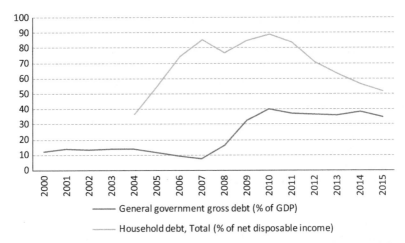

- General government gross debt (% of GDP)

- Household debt, Total (% of net disposable income)

Figure 6.2. Latvia: central government debt (percentage of GDP) and household debt (percentage of NDI), 2000–2015. *Source:* Data for central government gross debt from International Monetary Fund, World Economic Outlook Database, October, 2016, and for Household debt from OECD (2017b).

Argentina, Indonesia, Mexico, Korea, Sweden, and the United Kingdom in the 1990s and 2000s, with the costs of pursuing "internal devaluation" adopted by Latvia in the late 2000s. The study concludes that policies of "internal devaluation" are more costly than adjustment policies that devalue the national currency in real terms to facilitate the adjustment process.

The rationale for *not* devaluing the currency[4] in Latvia is presented in an IMF report (Purfield and Rosenberg, 2013). The authors highlight three main reasons for avoiding a devaluation:

(i)   The high proportion of bank loans to households and corporations denominated in euros;

(ii) A high pass-through coefficient to domestic prices from the exchange rate in which a nominal devaluation would have only a limited effect on real competitiveness; and

(iii) the role played by an exchange-rate peg as the anchor for macroeconomic stability.

In this context, the IMF report argues that a devaluation of the currency in Latvia at the time of the 2008–2009 crisis would have increased the real

---

[4] It is rather obvious that the decision of avoiding a devaluation was taken in consultation with the IMF.

value of liabilities (in local currency) of indebted households and firms, increasing also the stock of nonperforming loans held by banks. In addition, a *real* depreciation would have been difficult to accomplish in an economy whose productive structure is very dependent upon imports of intermediate inputs, raw materials, and foreign capital goods, as in the case of Latvia. Finally, a devaluation would have further shaken confidence in the health of the economy. Interestingly, some of these arguments (particularly that of confidence) were given in the 1930s to argue against devaluing the national currency (the US dollar, the British pound) in the midst of output contraction and rising unemployment (Chapter 4). Also, in countries with an inelastic short-run supply of tradable goods, a high reliance on imported inputs, and capital goods and consumption depending on real wages, a devaluation can be contractionary.[5]

The adverse effects of a currency devaluation in Latvia could have been managed. In several countries, a clean up of liabilities of the productive enterprise sector was done by the treasury with help from the central bank, through buying low-quality loans denominated in foreign currency (of course at a fiscal cost).[6] In turn, pass-through coefficients (from the exchange rate to domestic prices), estimated by econometric methods in "normal" times, may not apply to an economy in a depression that lowers this coefficient.

The authors of the IMF report recognize that the policy choice of keeping the exchange-rate peg shifted the bulk of adjustment to restrictive fiscal and wage policies with negative effects on real economic activity.

An interesting exchange developed during the adjustment period between Latvian Prime Minister Valdis Dombrovskis, defending the course of action adopted by the government (with backing from the IMF), and Nobel Prize winner in economics Paul Krugman, who argued that the Latvia story of severe recession, followed by recovery, can hardly be considered a "success story."[7]

We can delineate the pros and cons of Latvia's adjustment strategy. On the pro side, the strategy of nondevaluation has been credited as avoiding a full-blown banking crisis, including possible bankruptcies of firms, along with an increase in the domestic value of government and household debt in local currency in the event of a sharp depreciation of the lats.

---

[5] See Solimano (1987) and Krugman and Taylor (1978).
[6] Chile did so in 1982–1983 when faced a large scale financial crisis after a three-year fixed-exchange rate-based stabilization program in which borrowing in foreign currency (US dollars) skyrocketed.
[7] See, Blanchard et al. (2012).

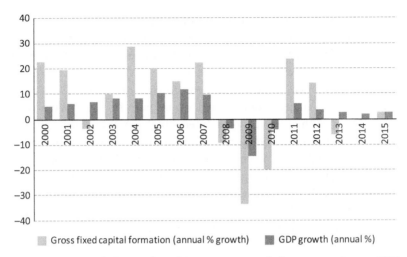

Figure 6.3. Latvia: GDP growth and investment growth (percentage change, 2000–2015). *Source:* World Development Indicators, The World Bank 2017.

On the con side, the economic policies adopted by the Latvian government did not prevent a dramatic fall in output and investment and an increase in public debt ratios. Probably, the nondevaluation policy *amplified* the contraction, with unemployment reaching 30 percent in 2010, if involuntary part-time and discouraged workers effects are included.[8] However, the severe contraction of 2008–2010 was *not* followed by a *stagnation trap* as in Greece. Latvia's growth after adjustment stabilized at around 3.5 percent per annum in 2011–2015.[9] The full costs of the depression are not only output contraction and higher unemployment. A valve of escape from the crisis was large-scale emigration from Latvia to other nations where workers and professionals could obtain employment lacking at home. In fact, it is estimated that the economic crisis led to *a decline of nearly 8 percent of Latvia's population* with the emotional and social costs implied by such large scale migration (Figure 6.3).[10]

Summing up, Latvia's case can be viewed as a "sudden stop" with a drastic reduction in the current account deficit leading to massive cuts economic activity and large emigration flows escaping economic hardship.

---

[8] Weisbrot and Reiss (2011).
[9] See Table 6.1 and Figure 6.3.
[10] On the pecuniary and emotional costs of international migration, see Solimano (2010).

This adjustment was probably exacerbated by the decision *not* to devalue the local currency to facilitate resource reallocation to the tradable goods sector and reduce the trade deficit.

6.3 Greece

Greece had a population of around 10 million people and a GDP of 250 billion euros in 2015. Ancient Greece was a leading place for the development of arts, science, and humanities, as well as the invention of democracy. In 1974, Greece overthrew the Colonel's junta and applied to join the EC in 1975, obtaining full admission in 1981. In 2001, Greece joined the euro area and euros started circulating in Greece in early 2002. Greek elites were lured by the possibility of adopting the euro as a symbol of status and a guarantee of price stability. The euro also would lower transaction costs in foreign trade and borrowing costs in international financial markets.

The demise of the drachma, the Greek national currency since 1833[11] with its, at times, turbulent monetary history, would inaugurate a new era of monetary stability and prosperity for Greece, of course, this proved to be illusory. A dramatic period in Greek monetary history was between 1941 and 1946, when the country experienced bouts of hyperinflation[12] associated with: (i) large government deficits financed by money creation and (ii) military spending to finance resistance to German occupation.

The virulence of Greek hyperinflation in the 1940s is comparable to the German case in 1923 and the Hungary case in 1946, along with the Austrian, Polish, and Soviet Russian cases in the early 1920s. After several unsuccessful stabilization plans at the end of Greek civil war, domestic prices were stabilized, and a new drachma was introduced with monetary reform supported by fiscal reform and external financing.

A second monetary reform took place in 1954, after Greece joined the Bretton Woods system in an effort to halt a new round of high inflation; the old drachma was converted into a new drachma at a 1,000 to 1.[13] As discussed in Chapter 5, Greece was not immune to the shocks of the 1970s (i.e., the end of Bretton Woods parities, the oil price shocks, and monetary instability). In the 1980s, in spite of its recent membership to the EEC, the economy developed fiscal and balance of payments deficits and went into higher debt

[11] The first modern drachma, a silver currency supplemented by gold coins, replaced the Phoenix.
[12] See Palairet (2000). Inflation reached a peak of near 14 percent *per day* in October of 1944. See also Lazaretou (2003).
[13] Lazaretou (2003).

levels. Attempts at income redistribution to the middle and working class were accompanied by inflation higher than the average European levels. There was a series of devaluations of the drachma in 1983, 1985, and 1987.

In the 1990s, Greece put more emphasis on stabilizing inflation and started deregulating the domestic economy. Macroeconomic policy was steered to meet the Maastricht criteria on fiscal deficits and inflation, and started to prepare for membership in the Economic and Monetary Union (EMU) and the adoption of the euro.[14] Between 2001 and 2007, GDP grew at an average of 4 percent per year.

6.4 Boom, Crisis, and Austerity

During the crisis and austerity period, the current account deficit went down from a high of 14.5 percent of GDP in 2008 to almost balance in 2015 (Table 6.2a).[15] In the precrisis period (2000–2007), Greece was spending more than its total production covering the gap with external borrowing. In turn, three-fourths of the average current deficit of the precrisis period was explained by the *fiscal imbalance* (negative saving of the public sector).

In the initial years of the crisis (2008–2010), the current account deficit averaged 11.8 percent of GDP but it was reduced to 3.2 percent of GDP in 2011–2015 (Table 6.2b).

As in Latvia, the counterpart of the reduction in the current account deficit was a *sharp cut in gross capital formation,* in this case from 26 percent of GDP in 2007 to 11.5 percent in 2015 (Table 6.2a).

Nonetheless, at the same time, there was a *decline* in domestic savings of around 6 percent of GDP between 2000–2007 and 2011–2015, largely associated with an increase in the deficit of the central government budget (see Table 6.2b and Figure 6.4).

As a consequence of crisis and austerity between 2008 and 2015, there was a devastating decline in GDP of nearly 30 percent with six years of consecutive negative growth starting in 2008 (see Figure 6.5). It is worth noting that the most severe decline in GDP took place in 2012, which coincided with the third year of implementation of the austerity program. As shown in Figure 6.5, the declines in GDP and investment in 2008–2009

---

[14] In 1998, the drachma was devalued again to compensate for accumulated inflation differentials between Greece, the United States, and Europe.

[15] In the precrisis period (2000–2007), the average current account deficit had reached 8.1 percent of GDP.

Table 6.2a. *Greece: yearly macroeconomic indicators, 2000–2015*

Year	GDP growth (annual % change)	General government deficit (% GDP)	Current account balance (% of GDP)	Inflation, consumer prices (annual % change)	Gross fixed capital formation (% of GDP)	Gross domestic savings (% of GDP)	General government gross debt (% of GDP)	Household debt, Total (% of net disposable income)
2000	3.92	−4.06	−7.55	3.17	24.64	14.85	104.94	30.36
2001	4.13	−5.47	−6.90	3.37	24.74	15.13	107.08	37.38
2002	3.92	−6.02	−6.23	3.63	23.60	14.63	104.86	43.77
2003	5.79	−7.83	−6.34	3.53	25.32	16.27	101.46	47.80
2004	5.06	−8.83	−5.60	2.90	24.40	16.82	102.87	55.50
2005	0.60	−6.19	−7.36	3.55	20.83	13.82	107.39	67.60
2006	5.65	−5.95	−10.82	3.20	23.69	15.65	103.57	74.12
2007	3.27	−6.71	−14.00	2.90	26.01	14.65	103.10	82.69
2008	−0.34	−10.18	−14.48	4.15	23.81	11.90	109.42	86.87
2009	−4.30	−15.14	−10.88	1.21	20.79	8.56	126.75	87.64
2010	−5.48	−11.20	−10.11	4.71	17.56	8.42	146.25	105.15
2011	−9.13	−10.28	−9.93	3.33	15.27	8.33	172.10	111.91
2012	−7.30	−8.84	−2.51	1.50	12.63	8.35	159.57	119.85
2013	−3.24	−13.15	−2.06	−0.92	12.16	8.79	177.68	122.23
2014	0.35	−3.60	−1.58	−1.31	11.59	9.39	180.06	117.69
2015	−0.22	−7.53	0.11	−1.74	11.55	9.97	176.94	118.48

Table 6.2b. *Crisis phases in Greece: economic indicators,*
average by sub-period, 2000–2015

	Precrisis, 2000–2007	Crisis stage, 2008–2010	Austerity period, 2011–2015	2008–2015
GDP growth (annual %)	4.04	−3.37	−3.91	−3.71
General government balance (% GDP)	−6.38	−12.17	−8.68	−9.99
Current account balance (% of GDP)	−8.10	−11.82	−3.19	−6.43
Inflation, consumer prices (annual %)	3.28	3.36	0.17	1.37
Gross fixed capital formation (% of GDP)	24.15	20.72	12.64	15.67
Gross domestic savings (% of GDP)	15.23	9.63	8.97	9.22
General government gross debt (% of GDP)	104.41	127.47	173.27	156.09
Household debt, Total (% of net disposable income)	45.96	93.22	118.03	108.73

Source: Author's elaboration based on World Economic Outlook Database, World Development Indicators and OECD (2017).

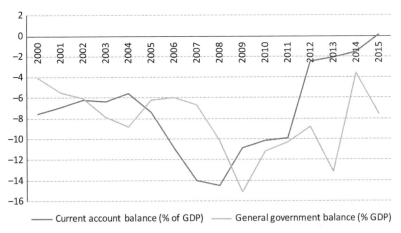

Figure 6.4. Greece: current account balance and central government deficit (percentage of GDP, 2000–2015). *Source:* Data for current account balance from World Development Indicators, The World Bank 2017, and for General government deficit from OECD (2017a).

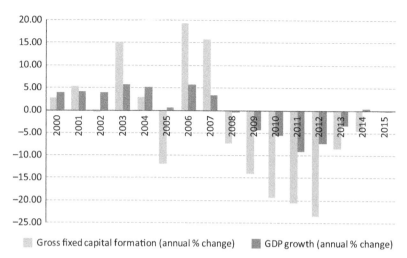

Figure 6.5. Greece: GDP growth and investment (percentage change, 2000–2016). *Source:* World Development Indicators, The World Bank 2017.

were of *smaller* magnitude than the contraction that took place under the austerity program supervised by the Troika.[16]

6.5 The Program with the International Monetary Fund (IMF)

A key player in the Greek drama was the IMF. In 2010, affected by the global financial crisis, and overburdened by its own fiscal and external imbalances and external debt, Greece requested a three-year standby program of financial support from the IMF. The size of the loan provided to Greece and approved by the Fund's board was exceptionally large: 30 billion euros, representing 32 times Greece's quota of 2010 at the IMF. The total loan in 2010 from the Troika was USD 110 billion, with 80 billion provided by European creditors and 30 billion coming from the IMF. A second adjustment program was approved in 2012 and a third in 2015.[17]

The willingness of main stockholders in the IMF, such as the United States, the United Kingdom, France, and Germany, to grant such a large loan to Greece (well above the standard criteria for the size of a loan relative to a country's quota) deserves some comment. It is very likely that they perceived an economic and financial meltdown in Greece would inflict a

---

[16] The duration of the slump in Greece was longer than in Latvia and the cumulative decline in GDP larger.

[17] See Wyplosz and Sgherri (2016).

severe blow to the euro project, affecting the financial position of creditor banks, mainly German and French, that had lent heavily to Greece during the boom years after admission into the EU.

It is interesting to note that the IMF program with Greece involved a country using a main international reserve currency, the euro. However, precedents exist. In 1976, Great Britain signed an austerity agreement with the IMF and the pound was still an international reserve currency, although of somewhat diminished importance. Of course, there are important differences between the two countries, as the United Kingdom was a former imperial power and Greece a middle-sized economy located on the periphery of Europe.

6.6   The IMF Underestimates Gross Domestic Product (GDP) Contraction, Neglects Distributive Impacts of Austerity, but Flags the Need for Debt Reduction

Analyzing the data for IMF programs, it is apparent that the Fund systematically *overestimated* economic growth in its projections – made at the outset of the crisis – with regard to Greece. This can be seen from the 2019 Article IV consultation document[18] that made GDP growth projections far removed from what actually occurred between 2009 and 2014 (Table 6.3).

It is apparent that the *severity and duration of the slump* in GDP that would take place in the years of implementation of the program were underestimated.

A decade later, since the onset of the crisis in 2017, the IMF started to indicate that fiscal stringency was probably excessive and that the targeted primary fiscal surplus (the budget before interest payments) needed to be reduced to leave more space for fiscal impulse to support a recovery of the economy. On the other hand, the IMF signaled that Greece needed some *debt reduction*.

From a social perspective, a main concern of IMF staff was the "excessive generosity" of the Greek pension system; the IMF recommended reduced pensions and salaries for public sector employees as a mechanism to improve the budgetary position of the government. Nonetheless, it is

---

[18] Article IV consultations are reports presented by the staff of the IMF to the board of executive directors on the monetary, fiscal, financial, balance of payments of member countries. These reports reflect the evaluation by the staff and guide surveillance and program design for member nations. See also IMF (2009).

Table 6.3. *GDP growth in Greece: baseline IMF's projection (Article IV -2009) and actual (average change, percentage)*

	2008	2009	2010	2011	2012	2013	2014
Projected (IMF)	2.9	−1.7	−0.4	0.6	1.2	1.6	1.8
Actual GDP growth	−0.34	−4.3	−5.5	−9.1	−7.3	−3.2	0.35

Source: Author's elaboration based on IMF (2009).

clear that reducing pensions and wages during a period of serious economic hardship can lead to an increase in old-age poverty.

The elderly were not the only ones vulnerable to austerity; the young were, as well. In fact, the unemployment rate in Greece for the workforce in the age range 18–28 years old was above 50 percent during several years since 2008 (Solimano, 2017). In this context, one strategy for the young to cope with the lack of jobs and income – besides emigrating to other countries – was to live with their parents, since they were at least receiving relatively decent pensions.[19]

What about the situation of economic elites and the rich during the austerity period? The *Global Wealth Report* prepared by the Credit Suisse[20] shows a startling *increase* of 41.5 percent in the *wealth share* of the top ten percent in Greece in the period 2008–2014, compared to 2000–2008, not a trivial result for an economy undergoing massive output contraction.[21] Regrettably, no mention is made in the 2017 IMF's Article IV report of the *rising* wealth concentration at the top of the distribution in Greece during austerity.[22]

6.7 Credibility of Economic Statistics and the Size of the Fiscal Deficit

The interplay between the accuracy of economic statistics, market perceptions, and crisis dynamics in the Greek crisis is worth mentioning. Already in the early 2000s, there were doubts about the extent official

---

[19] In addition, cutting public sector salaries has squeezed the living standards of the middle class, creating perverse incentive effects on motivation and commitment among employees in the public sector.
[20] This report is prepared by recognized world experts in wealth distribution, Professors A. Shorrocks, J. Davis, and R. Lluberas.
[21] Solimano (2017), Ch. 9.
[22] The IMF has an Independent Evaluation Office (IEO) that reports directly to the board of executive directors comprised of representatives of the governments of member

fiscal statistics reflected the true state of Greek public finances. In 2009, Prime Minister Papandreou recognized that the size of the actual fiscal deficit he had inherited from the previous government was substantially larger than what was officially stated: Papandreu's figures for 2009 were closer to 12 percent of GDP rather than the official 7 percent.[23] The recognition that fiscal accounts could have been manipulated to present a more rosy situation to external creditors and the EU was important in triggering market uncertainty about the true situation of the Greek economy at the time of the crisis.

Although initially global market instability in 2008 did not lead to a full confidence crisis about the Greek economy, market perceptions worsened after Papandreou's revelations, leading to higher spreads on Greek sovereign bonds. This was followed by the downgrading of Greek debt by Fitch and Standard & Poor. Analysts of the Greek crisis highlighted that the crash involved at least three factors: (i) a sovereign debt crisis (unwillingness by the market to finance the government deficit); (ii) a banking crisis (difficulty of financing in the interbank market and losses in bank's net worth); and (iii) a sudden stop (the high current account deficit could not be financed by international capital markets).[24]

6.8 Adjustment Within and Outside a Monetary Union

As Greece was in the euro area, the Greek central bank could not – as in the past – resort to a devaluation of the currency (e.g., the drachma) because there was not a *national* currency around to depreciate.

As discussed earlier in the chapter, both Greece and Latvia adopted a strategy of "internal devaluation" during their respective crises, entailing cuts in wages to regain external competitiveness and boost (ideally) a growth recovery. However, the wage compression led rather to a situation of depressed aggregate demand and protracted depression. The export effect of an improvement in competitiveness was not enough to compensate for the decline in domestic absorption stemming from wage compression.

---

countries. IEO is largely staffed by career IMF economists but also relies upon external consultants to carry out evaluations. An IEO assessment of the 2010 standby program for Greece identifies several shortcomings in the design of the operation such as the risks of not requesting a debt reduction strategy, the abnormally large level of the financial support from the IMF (relative to Greece's quota), and other issues. However, the high social cost of the Greek program does not appear significantly in the IEO evaluation.

[23] Wyplosz and Sgherri (2016).
[24] Gourinchas et al. (2016).

The "Grexit" option, say to reintroduce the drachma – or another national currency – to regain the ability to conduct an autonomous monetary and exchange-rate policy was apparently on the cards during the anti-austerity period of the Syriza Government in the first half of 2015, when Yanis Varoufakis was the finance minister.[25]

An indicator of what could have happened if Greece had exited the euro area can be provided by Argentina when, in late 2001, the country abandoned its ten-year-old currency board and devalued the peso, scrapping the fixed one-to-one parity with the US dollar (see chapter 8). The initial period after the devaluation was surrounded by confusion and heightened economic and political uncertainty. Furthermore, Argentina had several Presidents in December of 2001, right after the currency board was discarded. Nevertheless, since 2003, economic growth picked up after the government of Nestor Kirchner stopped paying part of the external debt, distanced itself from IMF policy prescriptions, and maintained a depreciated peso to promote exports.

As said, the exit option for Greece was not an easy course of action: the rules of the EMU do not include the possibility of a country leaving the common currency area. It is very likely the government of Greece considered that a unilateral exit of the euro area could have weakened its overall status as a member country within the EU, with complicated economic and geopolitical repercussions.

6.9 Rising Public and Private Debt Ratios in Spite of Austerity

To the various problems of austerity discussed earlier in the chapter, we should add the failure of debt ratios to decline. On the contrary, as a result of the protracted output contraction in the crisis and austerity periods, the public debt to GDP ratio *increased* from nearly 110 percent in 2008 to 177 percent in 2015 (Table 6.2a).[26] In turn, the household debt ratio also experienced a rapid increase from 30.4 percent in 2000 to 118.5 percent in 2015. So, in that year, the combined debt of the private and public sector represented nearly 300 percent of GDP, a high level by international standards (Figure 6.6).

---

[25] This was a period in which the Greek government pursued an actively independent stance towards the EU and the international financial community (see Galbraith, 2016).

[26] The Greek fiscal deficit was consistently high in the 2000–2015 period. The average general government deficit to GDP ratio was 6.4 percent in 2000–2007, rose to 12.2 percent in 2008–2010, and then declined to 8.7 percent in 2011–2015 (Table 6.2b). IMF programs imposed primary surplus conditions for loan disbursement. A primary fiscal surplus generates public resources to be transferred abroad in the form of debt servicing on external debt.

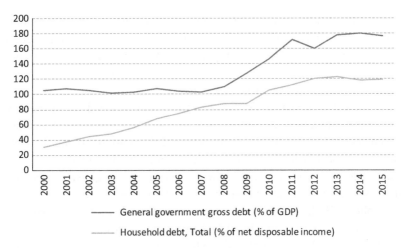

Figure 6.6. Greece: central government debt (percentage of GDP) and household debt (percentage of net disposable income), 2000–2015. *Source:* Data for central government gross debt from International Monetary Fund, World Economic Outlook Database, October, 2016, and for Household debt from OECD (2017b).

6.10 Some Political Economy Considerations

The Greek economy and society suffered severe strains during the period of crisis and austerity. Between 2010 and 2016, Greece had ten finance ministers and seven prime ministers. Their political affiliations ranged from PASOK (social democrats), New Democracy (center-right) and Syriza (left wing). Moreover, the economic crisis and ensuing political volatility led to the surge of far-right, nationalist parties such as Golden Arrow, as more moderate parties lost ground with the electorate due to their poor management of the economic crisis.

It is important to note, as mentioned at the outset of the chapter, that Greece tried a direct consultation with its population twice in the austerity period of 2010–2015, on the convenience – or the lack of it – of implementing foreign-led austerity policies. Incidentally, this exercise of democratic consultation is not very commonly observed in countries implementing austerity measures. The Greek exception may be related to the historical fact that Greece was the cradle of modern democracy.

Democratic consultation on austerity was not well received by external creditors and Papandreou's "unconventional" democratic procedure forced him to resign in November 2011, being replaced by an economic technocrat, Lucas Papademous, former head of the Bank of Greece (the central bank), who became acting prime minister and convened new elections. In the conflict between democracy and finance, the upper hand was on the side of finance.

In the second referendum on austerity of July 5, 2015, the majority of the Greek population rejected prevailing austerity and supported a different approach to deal with the country's debt problems. However, Prime Minister Tzipras decided rather to ignore the results of the referendum, sacked antiausterity Minister Yaroufakis, and signed a third program with the foreign creditors. The exact causes of Tzipras's swift change of position are not entirely clear. Apparently he anticipated a cut in the lifeline of credit from the ECB following a rejection of austerity that would have triggered the collapse of the Greek banking system, a shortage of euros in circulation, panic, capital flight, and possibly a downfall of the government with wider geopolitical consequences.

For these apparent reasons, austerity was continued. In exchange for new external funding, the Syriza government and the Greek parliament approved legislation oriented to increase taxes, cut public spending and regulatory policies that were negotiated in the conditionality agreement. Conditionality also included the creation of a large privatization fund, the Hellenic Corporation for Assets and Participation (EDIS) that could rise up to 50 billion euros in proceeds obtained by the sale (at fire prices?) of assets owned by the Greek state. The list of "valuable assets" identified in the bill submitted to the Greek parliament included airports, highways, ports, urban transport, tourist real estate property, the Hellenic Post Office, the Olympic Stadium, public utilities (water and electricity), state-owned enterprises, and so on. It is well known that German Finance Minister Wolfgang Schäuble, a "hard liner" in the Greek crisis, pressed hard for the creation of this privatization fund that could be used to reduce Greek external debt. EDIS was to be under direct supervision of the IMF, the ECB, and the EC, which would oversee the rapid denationalization of the Greek economy at a time of extreme weakness of the owner of these assets: the indebted and demoralized Greek state. In addition, EDIS's headquarters would be located in Luxembourg and managed by a local entity controlled by the German Finance Ministry.

6.11 Conclusion

The depressions in Latvia and Greece were closely managed by the IMF and the Troika and were preceded by a domestic boom directly associated with their modernization project of joining the EU. In the precrisis period, Greece took advantage of abundant foreign credit to finance its fiscal deficits and stimulate consumption and investment for a while. Latvia also received massive capital inflows in the run-up to the crisis leading to booming equity and property prices. As the boom completed its course, both countries faced difficulties for financial markets to continue financing their high current account deficits and requested large loans from international financial institutions and European governments. Neither a devaluation of the currency (in Latvia) nor the reintroduction of a new currency (in Greece) – at a more depreciated level – were considered as acceptable policies to correct external sector crises.

Austerity policies in both nations were very costly, leading to severe cuts in investment and output, and rising unemployment. Public debt ratios and household debt often grow during their austerity periods. In the two countries, the economic crises led also to massive emigration by the local population to escape from domestic economic hardship.

In Greece, external creditors, interested in getting repaid at all costs, were not tolerant with internal democratic consultation about austerity and encouraged its continuation, complemented by policies of rapid privatization and denationalization of the economy through the selling of public sector assets.

7

Soviet-Type Socialism and the
Postsocialist Transition

7.1 Introduction

The Great Depression of the 1930s and the Great Recession of 2008–2009 are often presented as the two largest instances of economic contraction in global capitalism. Nevertheless, the size of the economic contraction in the former socialist countries of Central-Eastern Europe (CEE) in the initial phase of post-socialist transition (early to mid-1990s) was even larger than in these two episodes.

The return to capitalism in CEE of the world has been affected by two major recessionary and stagnation cycles: (i) the deep contraction in GDP and investment in the early 1990s; and (ii) the recessive economic consequences of the financial crisis of 2008–2009 and its aftermath. During the socialist periods in the CEE and the former Soviet Union, there were also recessionary periods that we will review in this chapter. Some of them were associated with the turbulent period that followed the Bolshevik Revolution of 1917 and, later, World War II, in the Soviet Union. Also, in the late 1970s and 1980s, several socialist economies of Central and Eastern Europe had to undertake adjustment policies to serve their external debts in hard currency acquired in the 1970s and early 1980s.

This chapter takes a longer term look at these trends. First, it provides an overview at the growth performance and cycles of output collapse in imperial Russia, Soviet Russia, and Post-Soviet Russia, covering a period of more than a century. Then, we focus on the growth dynamics of the 1950–1989 period in Central- Eastern Europe (covering most of the socialist period). The data shows a cycle of acceleration in the rates of economic growth per capita in the 1950s and 1960s, a slowdown in the 1970s, and stagnation/contraction of the 1980s, before the ultimate demise of the centrally planned regimes. Then, the chapter focuses on the transition to market economies that led, initially, to deep recessions. In some postsocialist countries, the slump lasted until the second half of the 1990s, although it was of shorter duration (though not necessarily milder) in others (e.g., Poland). Then growth resumed in the framework of capitalist modernization and EU accession (for Central and Eastern Europe) but growth was interrupted by the effects of the global financial crisis of 2008–2009. Although several of the shortcomings of the socialist economic systems were overcome, the new economies became more prone to external shocks and the destabilizing effects of financial crises.

7.2 Brief Historical Overview

Let us start with the case of Russia from the late nineteenth century to the early twenty-first century, highlighting main developments that affected the economy.

7.3 The Russian and Soviet Economies

In the last 120 years, Imperial Russia, the Soviet Union and Post-Soviet Russia combined very distinctive phases of economic development and political regimes. In the late nineteenth century, and before World War I and the Bolshevik Revolution, the ruling Tzar monarchy attempted an uneven capitalist modernization project. This was followed by some positive results in terms of industrial development and overall economic growth, complemented by trade and financial linkages with the West. From the 1880s to 1913, industrial production rose at an annual rate of 5 percent, a higher pace than the growth of industrial production in Germany and the United States on a per capita basis.[1] However, this capitalist modernization also embedded contrasts and contradictions. In spite of the dynamism of the industrial sector, Russia was still a predominantly agrarian society with more than 80 percent of the population living in rural areas and provinces (Nove, 1990). The peasantry (a majority of the population) lived under feudal conditions. The Imperial Russia allowed limited democratic rights and class differences were large. In urban centers, the industrial working class faced rather tough conditions. In 1913, the per capita national income in Russia was only 22 percent of the United Kingdom's (the most advanced economy of the time), 28 percent of France's, and 44 percent of Austro-Hungary's.[2] Russia was still in the periphery of the world capitalist system.

---

[1] Nove (1990).
[2] Nove (1990, chapter 1).

The Bolshevik that launched the October revolution of 1917, managed to remain in power under the difficult conditions of civil war and foreign intervention. After implementing war-communism, at the encouragement of Vladimir Lenin, the Soviet government shifted gears and tried the New Economic Policy (NEP) between 1922 and 1927, which gave autonomy to agricultural industry and used markets and the price mechanism to encourage more food production. The aim of the NEP was to stabilize the economy and improve living standards shattered by rationing and war. A pending issue was the definition of the strategic orientation of the Socialist economy in "one country" (the Soviet Union as the only socialist country on earth, with little access to foreign credit). This was an open question to be reckoned with by the socialist leadership. After charged debates between the "primitive socialist accumulation" school of Yevgeni Preobrazhensky[3] and the NEP approach of Nikolai Bukharin, a project of socialist modernization based on rapid industrialization prevailed.

The theory of socialist growth was largely developed in the 1920s, following the writings of Gregory Feldman (Feldman, 1928, [1964]) and Preobrazhensky (Preobrazhensky, 1926, [1964]) to illuminate Soviet dilemmas about how to ignite and sustain economic growth in a socialist economy. They posited that the growth of aggregate output chiefly depended upon the investment in the industrial sector producing machinery and equipment, and that maintaining overall growth required priority be given to investment in that sector. Feldman wrote about "extended reproduction" and highlighted the need to mobilize savings, and control consumption to allow for this allocation of resources to produce capital goods, helped by planning methods. Preobrazhensky, in turn, spoke of "primary socialist accumulation" drawing on the concept of primary capitalist accumulation stressed by Karl Marx. In addition, this author elaborated on the terms of trade between industry and agriculture (the "scissors problem").

Rapid industrialization required the mobilization of *internal savings* – extraction of the surplus from the agricultural sector – to finance investment in the industrial sector, needed to accelerate GDP growth. The option of relying on foreign savings to finance investment and industrialization was largely irrelevant for Soviet Russia for at least two reasons: (i) Western bankers were not keen to make loans to Soviet Russia in the 1920s after the Bolsheviks had defaulted on Russian foreign debt in early 1918; and (ii) the country was surrounded by capitalist powers rather hostile to the

[3] See Preobrazhesnky (1926[1965]).

new Soviet regime. The need to build "socialism in one country" and facing the eventual threat of foreign invasion, forced the Soviet state to rely on domestic savings. This took the form of collectivization of farms and the "liquidation" of the *kulaks* (as a class, according to Stalin), prosperous peasants who held land and livestock. This process was carried out in the late 1920s and early 1930s at high human and political cost.

In addition, the market mechanism was replaced by planning and centralization in resource allocation. The centralization plan underwent several modifications throughout the life cycle of the Soviet regime, until its final demise in 1991. Main attempts of reform were undertaken by Premier Nikita Khrushchev in the 1950s and 1960s, and by President Mikhail Gorbachev in the second half of the 1980s. These reforms, particularly Gorbachev's, aimed at introducing a degree of decentralization and markets to the process of resource allocation and capital accumulation in the Soviet Union, although always within the framework of a socialist economy. In the early 1990s, the pendulum swung back again. The post-Soviet Russian governments dismantled, swiftly, Soviet institutional and economic structures and embraced unregulated capitalism dominated by rich oligarchies, generating high wealth inequality.

Two main disruptions to economic activity can be identified during the pre-Soviet, Soviet, and post-Soviet regimes. The first big economic contraction took place in the turbulent period 1914–1922. Between the peak of 1913 and the trough of 1922, the per capita GDP of Russia declined by 58.6 percent (Table 7.1). The second main output collapse occurred more than 70 years later, during the initial years of the post-Socialist transition in the 1990s. In addition, there were also (small) recessions in the 1950s, 1960s, and 1970s. In 1989, under Gorbachev, output started to decline. Then under Boris Yeltsin, the application of shock therapy and privatization policies to hasten the return to capitalism, output and investment contraction accelerated. Table 7.1 shows that, between the peak of 1989 and the trough of 1996, Russia's GDP per capita declined by 42.1 percent, an unprecedented decline, since the Great Depression of the 1930s, in economic activity during peace time, with the bulk of the output per capita decline taking place in the initial years after the end of the Soviet regime (between 1991 and 1996, the cumulative drop in GDP per capita was 36.7 percent).

Besides slumps, we can identify also cycles of strong economic expansion in the Soviet Union. A first cycle of growth acceleration took place from 1925 to 1939, when GDP per capita doubled. This period included the final years of the NEP and then, after the triumph of the primitive Socialist accumulation wing within the Soviet Communist Party, the adoption of

Table 7.1. *Two main disruptions of economic activity in Russia: war and revolution (1913–1922) and postsocialist depression (1989–1996) (GDP per capita, 1900 = 100)*

Contraction of 1913–1922 (peak/trough)		Contraction of 1989–1996 (peak/trough)	
Years	GDP pc	Years	GDP pc
1913	118.26	1989	594.83
1922	51.09	1996	344.48
Cumulative decline	58.6		42.1 (percent)

Note: GDP per capita is drawn from Maddison database for Russia.

the first five-year plan encouraged rapid industrialization and collective farming. It is interesting to note that, as discussed in Chapter 4, the Soviet Union avoided the adverse effects of the financial crash in 1929 and the Great Depression in the early 1930s. Of course, there were other problems with the Soviet economic model, as we discuss below.

A second phase of rapid economic expansion took place between 1946 and 1971. In that period, the cumulative increase in per capita GDP was 196 percent, representing a near doubling of Soviet per capita income over a period of 26 years. This second expansionary cycle included a rapid recovery of growth after the destruction of World War II involving large scale mobilization of labor and capital (with a tendency to over–investment and a lack of completion of projects). However, the second expansion phase did not last and was followed by a deceleration from 1972 to 1991, when GDP per capita expanded, cumulatively, by a modest 14.6 percent, reflecting already the undercurrents of stagnation that preceded the terminal years of the Soviet regime.[4]

7.4 Central and Eastern Europe

The growth strategy of socialist countries in Central and Eastern Europe in the 1950s and 1960s was broadly similar to the Soviet model, based upon the mobilization of labor, part of it coming from the agricultural sector, with a priority given to industrialization. However, not all countries needed to industrialize when embarking upon a Socialist economic system.

---

[4] There is a vast literature on Soviet economic growth; see Offer (1987), Easterly and Fischer (1995), Popov (2014).

Table 7.2. *Rates of growth of GDP per capita in Central and Eastern Europe, the USSR, the Russian Federation, and Ukraine, 1950–2015 (annual average, percentage)*

	1950s	1960s	1970s	1980s	1990s	2000s	2010–2015
Hungary	4.0	3.8	2.1	1.0	−0.1	2.7	1.9
Poland	2.4[a]	3.2	3.4	−0.4	2.5	4.1	3.1
Bulgaria	5.8[a]	5.4	3.3	0.0	−1.7	6.0	1.9
Romania	4.7[a]	4.7	4.0	−0.5	−2.6	5.8	2.3
Czechoslovakia	3.9	2.9	2.1	1.2			
Slovak Republic					0.8[b]	4.6	2.8
Czech Republic					0.3[b]	3.3	1.6
USSR	3.4	3.6	2.2	0.9			
Russian Federation					−4.9	5.8	1.5
Ukraine					−8.5	5.5	0.1

[a] The 1950s average growth rate is for the 1951–1959 period.
[b] The 1990s average growth rate is for the 1991–1999 period.

Source: Data for Hungary (1950–1989), Poland (1950–1989), Czechoslovakia and USSR from Kornai (2006); for Bulgaria (1951–1989) and Romania (1951–1989) from Maddison (2013); for Hungary (1990–2015) and Poland (1990–2015) from International Monetary Fund, World Economic Outlook Database, October, 2016; for Bulgaria (1990–2015) and Romania (1990–2015) from OECD (2017); for Slovak Republic from National Accounts Main Aggregates Database (United Nations); and for Czech Republic, Russian Federation and Ukraine from World Development Indicators, The World Bank 2017.

For example, in the 1930s before the advent of socialism, Czechoslovakia already had, a large industrial sector (Solimano, 1991). This helped avoid the "primitive socialist accumulation" phase to extract resources from agriculture and shift them to industry.

As this chapter discusses, there was a life-cycle growth pattern in the socialist economies of Central and Eastern Europe and the Soviet Union, with growth accelerating in the initial decades of socialism but running out of steam later (see Popov, 2014). In Hungary, Czechoslovakia, Bulgaria, and Romania, per capita growth proceeded at respectable rates in the 1950s and 1960s to give way to slowdown in the 1970s and 1980s. Poland accelerated economic growth during most of the 1970s, but it was subject to a sudden stop later in the decade. In the 1980s, average output growth per capita turned negative in Poland and Romania. In Bulgaria per capita GDP stagnated (zero average growth) see Table 7.2 and Figure 7.1. A broadly similar pattern was observed in the former Soviet Union. Average per capita GDP growth was 3.5 percent per year in the 1950–1969 period, 2.2 percent in the 1970s, and 0.9 percent in the 1980s.[5]

[5] See Table 7.1 and Figure 7.3.

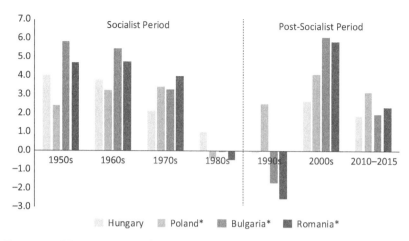

Figure 7.1. GDP per capita in former socialist countries, average rate of change (percentage) by decade, 1950–2015. *Source:* Data for Hungary and Poland 1950–1989 from Kornai (2006); for Bulgaria and Romania 1950–1989 from Maddison (2013), and for 1990–2015 period from International Monetary Fund, World Economic Outlook Database, October, 2016.
* For these countries, the 1950s average growth rate is for the 1951–1959 period.

In addition, CEE socialist nations followed patterns of international specialization of their productive structures according to the guidelines of the COMECON, a trade bloc led by the USSR to coordinate export and import allocations among socialist economies. In that scheme, Poland specialized in shipbuilding and agroindustry; Czechoslovakia in trucks, heavy machinery, armament, and cars; Bulgaria in agricultural products, armament and light industry; and East Germany in machines and cars.

In the 1970s, taking advantage of the abundant and cheap liquidity created after the recycling of surpluses from oil exporting countries, channeled to the European and US capital markets, socialist governments started to borrow in hard currencies. Loans were used to maintain internal consumption and investment levels while their economies were experiencing a decline in factor productivity and GDP growth. This is, in contrast, to the inability of the Soviet Union to receive foreign loans on a significant scale in the 1920s and 1930s. External borrowing, however, postponed adjustment and internal restructuring of the Central European economies. In particular, servicing Western debt in convertible currency presented problems for the socialist economies, since their trade patterns within the socialist block was denominated in "convertible rubles" that were *not* traded in international currency markets. Therefore, earning revenues in convertible currencies to serve Western foreign debt was not easy for socialist countries.[6]

When international interest rates soared in the early 1980s, this exacerbated the debt servicing problems of the economies that had borrowed more heavily, leading to the curtailment of their growth rates in the 1980s. Stagnation, in turn, undermined the legitimacy of these regimes, contributing to their eventual demise.

The dominant view on the cause of the growth slowdown in CEE and the USSR after the "golden age" (1950s and 1960s) centers upon the declining labor and total factor productivity growth. Behind this were poor incentives for work effort, as workers were only earning modest salaries and could buy only a limited range of goods. They faced chronic shortages of food and durable consumer goods, although they received education, housing, and health services, almost for free. Shortages also were compounded by an ineffective allocation of capital by central planning offices (Offer, 1987, Kornai, 1992, Easterly and Fischer, 1995).

In dynamic terms, the socialist economies tended to have meager incentives for innovation and technological improvement applied to the civilian economy. Besides, official ideology stifled private entrepreneurship and limited, to a large extent, the existence of private sector activity in the economy.

Inefficiency as a main driving force behind growth slowdowns was questioned in Vonyo and Klein (2016). The authors, while admitting, of course, inefficiencies in central planning show, using new estimates of investment and labor-hours for the period 1950–1989 for Poland, Hungary, and Czechoslovakia, that the official rates of factor accumulation (labor and capital) seriously *overstate* the actual rates of factor accumulation in these economies. The study claims that insufficient rates of capital formation – below the investment levels of comparable southern European and other eastern European countries – and a persistent decline in hours worked since the 1960s would be more important than a slowdown in productivity growth in explaining the declining growth and socialist stagnation in the 1970s and 1980s. According to these authors, the theory about productivity slowdown prevailing in the literature would not be accurate

---

[6] The external sector deficits co-existed with several features of the socialist economies such as shortages, soft–budget constraints, the hoarding of inputs (raw material, industrial parts) and overcentralized economic planning. For different causes the economy generated stop and go cycles that further contributed to economic growth deterioration beyond the effects of low-factor accumulation and lagging productivity growth.

once correct estimates of capital formation are considered. In addition, the study shows that GDP growth was substantially lower (on the order of 2–3 percent per year) than official figures using NMP (net material product) methodologies that presented growth rates of 6–7 percent per year during most of the socialist period (the net material product excludes the service sector and uses accounting-fixed prices and questionable index-number procedures to aggregate outputs).

It is interesting to note that the evolution of economic growth in the 1950–1970 period in the centrally planned economies of Central and Eastern Europe was not very different from the growth path of the capitalist economies of western Europe and the United States, which also experienced stagflation in the 1970s and irregular growth in the 1980s. In Chapter 5, we argued that the 1970s in capitalist economies was a turning point – a decade of transition – from the golden age of the 1950s and 1960s – based upon Keynesian social-democratic capitalism – to a new neoliberal capitalist regime of accumulation that took off in the 1980s and 1990s. In socialist countries, the 1970s were also a turning point (see Figures 7.2 and 7.3).

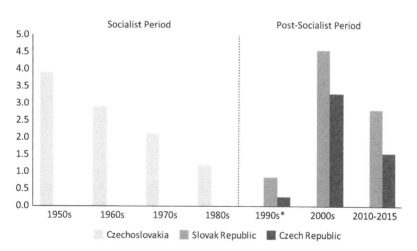

Figure 7.2. Czechoslovakia, Czech Republic, and the Slovak Republic GDP per capita, average rate of change (percentage) by decade, 1950–2015. *Source:* Data for Czechoslovakia from Kornai (2006), for Slovak Republic from National Accounts Main Aggregates Database (United Nations), and for Czech Republic from World Development Indicators, The World Bank 2017.
* The 1990s average growth rate is for the 1991–1999 period.

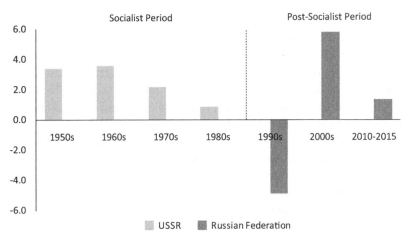

Figure 7.3. GDP per capita, in the USSR and the Russian Federation, average rate of change (percentage) by decade, 1950–2015. *Source:* Data for 1950–1989 period from Kornai (2006), and for 1990–2015 period from World Development Indicators, The World Bank 2017.

7.5 Recessions and Debt Cycles in Socialist Countries

Socialist economic theory claimed that centrally planned economies were free of the typical macroeconomic cycles of boom and recession that often affect capitalist economies. However, in practice, there were also economy-wide recessions in Central-Eastern European countries and the Soviet Union during their socialist period. Some recessionary cycles were severe and protracted, such as those of Poland in 1979–1982 and Romania in 1980–1989 (see Table 7.2). Still, the intensity of the decline in GDP in the cycles of contractions of economic activity during the socialist period was, often, less severe than those experienced by the same countries in the 1990s and 2000s, in their capitalist restoration phase.

Hungary experienced a recession in 1956 (GDP per capita fell by 5.4 percent), the year of the Hungarian revolution and subsequent Soviet occupation. In the 1970s, Hungary experienced several mild recessions and also in the 1980s, before the end of the socialist regime (Table 7.3).

The international debt cycle of the 1970s and early 1980s initially benefited but later adversely affected the economies of Poland, Hungary, Romania, and Yugoslavia. Increased real interest rates in the late 1970s and early 1980s, compounded by higher oil prices, amounted to a combination of negative terms of trade effect plus an interest rate shock. The higher oil prices had negative consequences, provided socialist countries were oil-importing nations and had a high energy-intensive productive structure.

Table 7.3. *Recessions in the socialist period, 1959–1989*

	Years	Decline in GDP per capita (percent)
Hungary	1956	−5.35
	1970	−0.68
	1976	−0.24
	1979	−0.04
	1983	−0.88
	1985	−2.28
	1989	−1.82
Poland	1962	−2.50
	1969	−1.76
	1979	−2.76
	1980	−3.40
	1981	−6.18
	1982	−1.80
	1987	−1.96
	1989	−1.82
Bulgaria	1952	−4.80
	1954	−2.90
	1956	−0.92
	1977	−1.43
	1980	−3.22
	1983	−2.09
	1985	−3.18
	1988	−0.74
	1989	−1.88
Romania	1968	−0.14
	1980	−0.31
	1981	−1.18
	1982	−0.36
	1983	−1.11
	1985	−0.46
	1987	−2.48
	1988	−0.61
	1989	−3.54
USSR	1951	−1.25
	1959	−2.86
	1963	−3.74
	1972	−0.43
	1975	−0.67
	1979	−1.31
	1980	−0.70
	1985	−0.01
	1990	−3.06
	1991	−6.80

Source: Maddison, A. (2013).

There were contrasts between Poland, Bulgaria, and Romania in their patterns of debt accumulation and subsequent adjustment. In Poland, GDP per capita declined by more than 13 percent between 1979 and 1982 (Table 7.3). This was a severe contraction. The Polish economic crisis of the late 1970s was accompanied by higher agricultural and oil prices, investment programs that could not materialize, low real wages, and food shortages: all clear symptoms that the Polish economic system was in trouble.

Besides borrowing with the West, Poland also received economic emergency assistance in 1981 from the USSR and other eastern European countries.[7] At that time, Poland was not a member of the IMF, and Western creditors became hesitant to reschedule Poland's external debt. At the sociopolitical level, those years also coincided with the expansion of the solidarity movement (registering nearly ten million members in the early 1980s) led by the Gdansk shipyard charismatic labor leader Lech Walesa, who became the first elected postcommunist president in 1989. Fearful of the combination of labor unrest and a deepening economic crisis, the communist regime imposed martial law, led by General Wojciech Jaruzelski, in late 1981.

On the economic front, Jaruzelski implemented an austerity program to contain spending and imports, creating a trade surplus with the West to pay interests on external debt. A sustained recovery after adjustment was hampered not only by cuts in aggregate demand but also by negative supply-side conditions such as an obsolete capital stock, the lack of imported inputs, a poorly motivated labor force, and high dependence on imported, more expensive, energy. These problems could not be reverted throughout the 1980s.

Bulgaria had nine episodes of negative GDP per capita growth in the period 1950–1989, concentrated mostly in the 1950s and 1980s (Table 7.3). The country experienced a debt crisis in the early 1960s, with London- and Paris-based Soviet banks. The crisis was solved through large sales of gold by the Bulgaria Central Bank in 1962 and 1964. Another crisis occurred in the late 1970s, again involving the Soviet Union, which intervened through oil reexport agreements with the West at international prices.[8]

---

[7] See Nuti (1981) and CIA (1986).

[8] For an interesting contrast between Bulgaria and Yugoslavia official austerity policies in the 1980s, using now declassified official records from the Bulgarian National Bank (Central/Monobank) and the Yugoslavian central bank, see Avramov and Gnjatovic (2008) and Gregory and Harris (2005).

Between 1981 and 1989, Bulgaria borrowed heavily from Western banks, and its total external debt increased by more than *six times in real terms*. The loans helped Bulgaria to cover its trade deficits, partially originated by the fact that Bulgarian exports (mainly of armament) to highly indebted third world countries were financed with export credits that, ultimately, were only partially repaid by the buyers of Bulgarian armament. In addition, most of Bulgaria's imports came from Western nations and hard currency was in short supply (Solimano, 1990).

The rapid buildup of the Western external debt of Bulgaria during the 1980s, apparently, did not ring open alarms in the international financial community at the time. Two factors may have contributed to that situation: first, the policy of extreme secrecy regarding the level of Bulgaria's external debt adopted by the Todor Zhivkov (communist leader, President of the Republic in Bulgaria for 35 years until 1989) government (according to the Bulgarian constitution external debt was a state secret); and, second, the perception by creditor banks that, in case Bulgaria failed to meet its external obligations, it would be rescued by the Soviet Union.[9]

According to the Madison database, Romania experienced high growth rates in per capita terms – close to an average of 5 percent per year, in the 1950s and 1960s – then average growth declined to 4 percent in the 1970s and turned to –0.5 percent in the 1980s. In that latter decade, growth rates were negative in all years except in 1984 and 1986 before the collapse of the regime of Nicolae Ceausescu, communist leader, president of the Republic of socialist Rumania from 1974 to 1989. In December of 1989 after a popular uprising he and his wife Elena were executed by order of a military tribunal marking the collapse of the Ceausescu regime.

Interestingly, Romania was the first socialist country to join the IMF in 1972. This was considered a reward for its independent stance in foreign policy regarding the Soviet Union, as Romania refused to lend troops to the Warsaw Pact invasion of Czechoslovakia in 1968. Between 1978 and 1982, the level of external debt of Romania increased sharply from near USD 3.5 billion to USD 25 billion. In 1979, the country was hit hard by the second oil price increases agreed by OPEC (organization of oil producing countries) and the rise of international interest rates. In 1982, the Ceausescu regime decided, after failing to reach agreement with the IMF

---

[9] The author of this book, a World Bank economist at the time, visited Bulgaria in 1990 as part of the first World Bank mission ever to the country. One of the most complicated issues in the dialogue with authorities was to get external debt figures that were considered at the time *state secrets*.

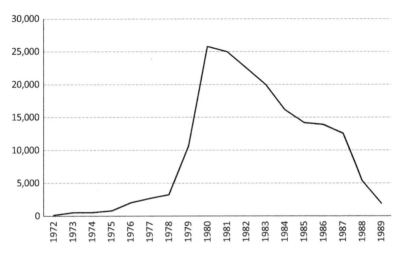

Figure 7.4. Total external debt in Romania (millions 2000 USD, 1972–1989). *Source:* International Debt Statistics, The World Bank 2017.

on debt rescheduling and domestic adjustment policies, to *repay in full* its external debt (including amortization of principal). The policy worked in terms of reducing, by 1989, external debt to a minimal level (Figure 7.4) but it was achieved at a large cost for Romania and its population, as it entailed compression of domestic consumption to minimal levels and led to almost a decade of output contraction in the 1980s.

The austerity policy pursued by Ceausescu sought to generate a series of trade surpluses through export increases and a squeeze on imports. Food that was previously for internal consumption was exported, depressing further domestic living standards. An important role in managing, at a political level, the austerity period was played by Romania's secret service – the infamous *Securitate*. Besides engaging in tasks of political control and repression, the Securitate owned an ample network of foreign trade companies that provided resources and economic autonomy to the secret service, becoming a sort of "state within the state."

The decision of the Ceausescu regime to pay the external debt in full and disengage with international financial markets after the debt crisis of the early 1980s was *atypical* of what highly indebted countries do in these circumstances. In general, highly indebted countries opt for either default or debt restructuring (supported by adjustment) in order to avoid cutting too much domestic growth and investment, and compressing the living standards of their citizens. In contrast, after 1981, when austerity policies started to be applied, Romania opted for an autarkic path of extreme austerity that ultimately delegitimized the communist regime.[10]

The cases of Bulgaria and Romania, two relatively less developed countries of Central and Eastern Europe illustrate how the attempt to counteract the structural problems of macrodisequilibria through external borrowing, outdated technologies, obsolete capital stock, and low labor motivation was a futile endeavor. In turn, austerity policies along with structural economic problems and the lack of political freedom proved to be ultimately fatal for the survival of the socialist regimes.

Recessions occurred in the Soviet Union in 1951, 1959, 1963, 1972, 1975, 1979–1980, 1985, and 1990–1991. The recessions of the late 1970s and early 1980s coincided with the second oil shock (that should have benefitted the Soviet economy as an oil exporting country). Other shocks in the period that posed an extra burden to the Soviet economy were the higher international interest rate following anti-inflationary policies in the United States and the fiscal cost of the invasion of Afghanistan. Soviet authorities also returned to foreign borrowing from the West, particularly in the second half of the 1980s. In fact, between 1985 and 1991 (June), the external debt of the USSR (bank and non-bank trade related debt) went up from $ 31 billion to $ 51 billion.

7.6 The Postsocialist Shock and Depression in the 1990s

In the early 1990s, the United States, the IMF, the World Bank, and the international private sector encouraged postsocialist governments to embrace a market economy.

The dominant blueprint for the transition to market economics was the "Washington Consensus" tailored in Washington, DC. In the context of former socialist countries, the blueprint entailed the following set of measures: (i) abolition of most price controls and use of the market mechanism for resource allocation; (ii) macroeconomic stabilization including control of inflation, reduction of fiscal deficits, and correction of external imbalances; (iii) rapid privatization of state-owned enterprises and sales of other public assets; (iv) external integration in foreign trade and capital account

---

[10] Ban (2012) offers an interesting account of the political economy of austerity policies and regime change in Ceausescu's Romania.

liberalization; and (v) creation of an institutional infrastructure functional to capitalism including private property rights, modernized central banks, budgetary institutions, and the establishment of regulatory agencies.

This strategy of reform was applied more or less uniformly across former socialist economies (and developing market economies), although there were also national variations in policies due to the specific political and institutional conditions of each country. The new policy package was supported by loans and technical assistance from the IMF and the World Bank.

The rapid transition to capitalism after Soviet-type socialism was embraced with an unbridled faith in the merits of the market and with relative disregard for the social and economic costs and institutional features of each economy.[11] The dismantling of the state sector as producer was swift and traumatic for communities whose jobs, working life, and community relations had been developed around public enterprises and the guarantee of permanent job security. Many workers and employees of the state-owned companies had to convert their skills and capabilities to fit into the working requirements of a capitalist economic system, which had been abolished for decades and now was being restored under the new conditions of globalization and active external competition. People had to find new jobs at home or migrate, in the expectation of getting jobs abroad (or ultimately become chronically unemployed). Economic insecurity started to be the "new normal" in postsocialist societies. Life expectancy declined to less than 70 years in Russia. As a result of the new economic realities, and the inability to cope with rapid change, many people developed psychological illnesses such as stress, anxiety, depression, and alcoholism. Similar syndromes were present in the Great Depression of the 1930s in the United States and other countries affected by it.

A gradual and pragmatic approach to introduce market mechanisms and new property relations dominated by private capital and the profit motive, that had given generally good results in China in the 1980s, was discarded as unsuitable for the economies of CEE and Russia.

The dismantling of the trade regime between socialist countries was swift and the adjustment was costly. Industries of former socialist countries, affected by unsuitable technologies and lagging managerial practices, faced stiff competition from Western countries possessing superior technology, skills, marketing strategies, and updated knowledge. After rapid trade liberalization, CEE economies were inundated by imported

---

[11] There is already a vast literature on the topic, see Kornai (2006), Amsden et al. (2004), Gale (2011), and Kodolko (2000).

goods from mature Western economies and newly industrialized countries, mainly from Asia (China, Korea, and others).[12]

No doubt that a degree of restructuring was needed, and many factories and plants were unprofitable at world prices. Nevertheless, the speed of
restructuring was such that many companies had to close operations and
lay off workers. The process of building new production, new brands, and
sales capacities to become competitive in domestic and international markets takes time to develop and this has to be considered in a sensible program of economic restructuring.

In the 1990s, average economic growth per capita was negative in
Hungary, Bulgaria, Romania, the Russian Federation, and Ukraine. The
largest contraction took place in Ukraine followed by Latvia, Lithuania and
Russia (Table 7.4). On the other hand, in the 1990s decade-average GDP
per capita growth was positive only in Poland and the Czech and Slovak
Republics (see Table 7.2).

Public enterprises were divested and capital formation in the public
sector was drastically reduced. In this context, the situation was ripe for
massive *privatization* at fire prices. Foreign corporations arrived to acquire
productive assets at low cost. In several countries, public property was
turned over to private individuals in rather opaque and non-transparent
ways (sales of public assets to politically connected friends and insiders),
and this contributed to the formation of a new capitalist class that grabbed
the assets. New economic oligarchies appeared, composed in part of former directors of state-owned firms that had insight into the privatization
process. International corporations were very interested in acquiring property in former socialist countries given their convenient location in Europe.
These countries, in turn, had an educated labor force but were earning
much lower salaries than their Western counterparts. Another motivation for multinational enterprises to set up operations in former socialist
nations of CEE was the lure of production for potentially growing internal
consumer markets.

The size of the "postsocialist shock" was very large in terms of output
and investment contraction. Its magnitude qualifies in several cases as a
"depression." As shown in Table 7.4, episodes of contraction in GDP per
capita in the first half of the 1990s in CEE were in the range of −12 percent
in the Czech Republic to −48.8 percent in Latvia. In Russia, per capita GDP
fell by 42 percent between 1990 and 1996 and the drop in output per capita in Ukraine was −60 percent and lasted nine years (from 1990 to 1998).

---

[12] See Becker (2016).

Table 7.4. *Postsocialist episodes of recession and depression in the 1990s (cumulative rate of change in GDP per capita)*

Country	Period	Cumulative decline in GDP per capita (%)	Consecutive years/decline
Bulgaria	1988–1993	−22.43	6
	1999	−5.58	1
Czech Republic[a]	1991–1993	−11.98	3
	1997–1998	−0.72	2
Estonia[a]	1991–1993	−28.09	3
Hungary	1989–1993	−19.11	5
Latvia[a]	1991–1993	−48.75	3
Lithuania[a]	1991–1994	−43.13	4
	1999	−0.41	1
Poland	1989–1991	−16.27	3
Romania	1987–1992	−29.61	6
	1997–1999	−10.26	3
Slovak Republic[a]	1991–1992	−20.78	2
	1999	−0.25	1
Slovenia	1987–1992	−25.35	6
Russian Federation	1990–1996	−42.09	7
	1998	−5.14	1
Ukraine	1990–1998	−60.25	9

[a] From 1991 to 1999.

Source: Data for Hungary and Poland from International Monetary Fund, World Economic Outlook Database, October, 2018; for Bulgaria, Czech Republic, Romania, Russian Federation, Slovak Republic, and Ukraine from World Development Indicators, The World Bank 2018; for Slovenia from Maddison (2013); and for Estonia, Latvia, and Lithuania from National Accounts Main Aggregates Database (United Nations).

These contractions in GDP per capita were far more severe than those of the Great Depression of the 1930s.

The *investment contraction* was much larger than the decline in GDP per capita in CEE, in line with the findings of Chapter 5 for core western European countries, the United States, and the southern European periphery. The investment decline in the period 1990–1994 was 20 percent in Hungary, 58 percent in Poland, 67 percent in Romania, 63 percent in Bulgaria, and 108 percent in Latvia (see Table 7.5). There were also *massive declines in real wages* in the initial years of the transition: between 1989 and 1995, the cuts in average real wages were in the range of 20 to 30 percent in Poland, Hungary, Romania, Slovakia, and Slovenia (Table 7.6). For Estonia and Bulgaria, the real wage declines were in the range of 50 to 55 percent.

Table 7.5. *Investment decline in Central and Eastern Europe, the Russian Federation, and Ukraine in the 1990s*

Country	Period	Cumulative decline in Investment (%)	# years/decline
Bulgaria	1990–1993	−63.2	4
	1996–1997	−40.8	2
Czech Rep.	1990–1991	−29.5	2
Estonia		NA	
Hungary	1990–1992	−20	3
Latvia	1991–1993	−108.4	3
Lithuania		NA	
Poland	1990–1992	−57.9	3
Romania	1990–1991	−67.1	2
Slovenia	1991–1992	−24.4	2
Slovakia	1991–1994	−37.5	4
Russian Federation[a]	1991–1998	−84.04	8
Ukraine[a]	1991–1996	−83.13	6

[a] Data from 1991 to 1999.

Source: Own elaboration. Data for Bulgaria, Czech Republic, Estonia, Hungry, Latvia, Lithuania, Poland, Romania, Slovenia, and Slovakia from Podkaminer (2013) and wiiw database; and data for Russian Federation and Ukraine from World Development Indicators, The World Bank 2017.

Table 7.6. *Real wages in Central and Eastern Europe, 1989–2012*

	1989	1995	2000	2005	2012
Bulgaria	100	45.9	42	46.2	72.5
Czech Rep.	100	93.3	110	136.7	154.0
Estonia	100[a]	47.8	63.7	88.0	110.0
Hungary	100	79.8	85.7	118.9	116.4
Latvia	100[b]	105.4	111.1	147.6	195.2
Lithuania	100	34.3	45.1	57.1	74.8
Poland	100	76.5	93.3	102.1	124.5
Romania	100	70.2	62.8	94.5	130.3
Slovenia	100	77.0	87.6	99.2	111.1
Slovakia	100	76.0	82.1	93.7	104.8

[a] 1990 = 100.

[b] 1993 = 100.

Source: Author's elaboration based in Podkaminer (2013), and wiiw database.

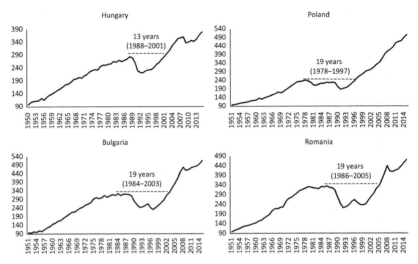

Figure 7.5. GDP per capita level in former socialist countries, 1950–2015 (1950 = 100). *Source:* Data for 1950–1999 period from Maddison (2013); and for 2000–2015 period from World Development Indicators, The World Bank 2017.

The drop in real wages was even higher in Lithuania: 65 percent between 1989 and 1995.[13] Thereafter, real wages started to recover although slowly in several cases.

Summing up, CEE, Russia, and Ukraine suffered in the early 1990s (initial phase of the transition) large contractions of output and investment concentrated, mostly, in state-owned enterprises, which was the dominant sector of the economy. In most countries, it took nearly *two decades* for GDP per capita to reach the last peak prior to 1990 (Figure 7.5). In Hungary, the 1988 peak was attained in 2001 (13 years later); in Poland, the peak of 1978 was attained in 1997 (19 years later); in Bulgaria, the peak of 1984 was reached in 2003 (19 years later); and in Romania, the peak of 1986 was attained in 2005 (19 years later).[14]

---

[13] In contrast, the decline in real wage was milder in Czechoslovakia: –7 percent between 1989 and 1995. In Latvia, real wages increased by 5 percent between 1993 and 1995 (years available for comparison).

[14] In the case of Russia and Ukraine, a precise comparison with the USSR in 1989 is more difficult to establish as the USSR was a different country from these two republics (albeit the two most important republics of the former USSR).

7.7 Causes of the Postsocialist Contraction

There were multiple causes for the big contractions in GDP, investment, real wages, and employment during the initial years of postsocialism. They included adverse demand and supply factors, including slumps in investment, reorganization of production, adjustment to new property relations, the effects of new trade agreements, and the dismantling and overhauling of the dominant sector of state-owned enterprises.

The sharp decline in real wages and the layoffs of workers and employees in the state sector affected consumption and squeezed aggregate demand (see Podkaminer, 2013); in addition, the decline in public investment added an additional negative effect on aggregate spending. The cut in exports to the former socialist block could not be compensated in the short term by exports to Western nations. The effects on the supply side of the postsocialist shock has been the subject of an ample literature (Calvo and Coricelli, 1990, Easterly and Fischer, 1995, Campos and Coricelli, 2002, Popov, 2015).

The dominant assumption of most of this literature is that the transition to a market economy should have entailed static and dynamic *efficiency gains* due to the introduction of market discipline and the creation of new firms and employment opportunities in the private sector. In addition, private investment should pick up to capture new business opportunities. All this should, in principle, lead to higher economic growth in the medium to long run, but this explanation neglects short-term effects that, can last several years and be very severe (Figures 7.6 and 7.7).

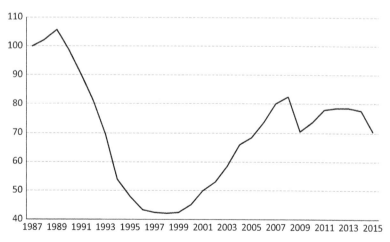

Figure 7.6. Ukraine: GDP per capita level, 1987–2015 (1987 = 100). *Source:* World Development Indicators, The World Bank 2017.

Figure 7.7. GDP per capita level in the USSR and the Russian Federation, 1950–2015 (1990 = 100). *Source:* Data for 1951–1990 period from Maddison (2013); and for 1991–2015 period from World Development Indicators, The World Bank 2017.

7.8 Debt-led Growth and the Recessionary Cycle of 2008–2009

A new cycle of negative growth occurred in 2008–2009 as a consequence of the global financial crisis originating in the United States and extending into Europe (although Poland avoided negative growth in 2008–2009). In the preceding years, 2003–2007 (e.g., in Latvia and Greece) there was a boom of economic activity fueled by foreign credit, low interest rates, and a drop in exchange-rate risk. A similar dynamic was present in postsocialist countries in Europe after entering the EU that led to a surge in capital inflow, which stimulated investment in construction and domestic consumption, and increased stock and real estate prices. In addition, there was a widening in the current account deficits of the balance of payments that depended, crucially, on foreign credit to be funded. External (and fiscal) imbalances and inflated asset prices are typical in the booms previous to economic and financial crises and sudden stops. This occurred in 2008–2009, when a new debt crisis erupted giving rise to sharp output contractions in 2008–2010, followed by generally weak and erratic recoveries.

No doubt, external debt cycles (borrowing followed by sudden stops) accompany macro- and financial cycles of boom/expansion and bust/recession. We can identify two main debt cycles in CEE: (i) one in the 1970s; and (ii) another in the 2002–2007 period.

In the borrowing cycle of the 1970s, countries such as Poland, Hungary, Bulgaria, Romania, and Yugoslavia started from low levels of external debt.

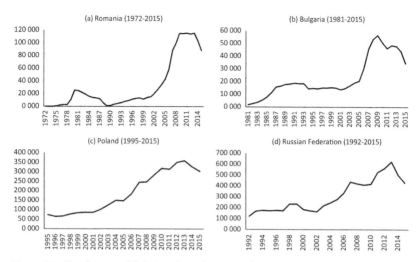

Figure 7.8. Total external debt in selected postsocialist countries (millions 2000 USD). *Source:* Data for Romania, Bulgaria, and Russian Federation from International Debt Statistics, The World Bank 2017 and for Poland from National Bank of Poland.

At the time, several socialist economies were *not* members of the IMF – the exceptions being Romania and Yugoslavia. As the IMF did not include several communist countries, the countries were not subject to regular *surveillance missions* (that perform the important roles of fact finding, data gathering, and regular policy dialogue with the local authorities). This background diagnostic is very relevant for international lenders. As a consequence, the actual fiscal, debt, and balance of payments situation in socialist economies that were no within the IMF was lesser known to the international creditors community (although Romania and Yugoslavia, both IMF members, were not shielded from debt problems in the 1980s).

In contrast, in the debt cycle of the 2000s, former socialist countries had already been members of the Bretton Woods institutions for at least a decade (some of them longer). However, membership to the IMF was *not* a sufficient condition to *prevent* a rapid external debt accumulation in the postsocialist nations after 2000. In addition, the post-2000 dynamics of debt accumulation proceeded at a faster pace than the process of debt accumulation of the late 1970s and early 1980s (see Figure 7.8).

Between 2000 and 2008, the stock of total external debt (private plus public) increased by more than seven times in Ukraine, six times in Romania, four times in Bulgaria and Poland, three times in Russia, and more than twice in Hungary.

Table 7.7. *The Great Recession (2008–2015) in Central and Eastern Europe (percentage change in GDP per capita)*

Country	Period	Cumulative decline in GDP per capita (%)	Consecutive years/decline
Bulgaria	2009	−2.96	1
Czech Republic	2009	−5.34	1
	2012–2013	−1.45	2
Estonia	2008–2009	−18.85	2
Hungary	2009	−6.47	1
	2012	−1.11	1
Latvia	2008–2010	−17.71	3
Lithuania	2009	−13.58	1
Poland[a]	2008–2015	0	0 years
Romania	2009–2010	−7.02	2
Slovak Republic	2009	−5.56	1
Slovenia	2009	−8.63	1
	2012–2013	−4.10	2
Russian Federation	2009	−7.85	1
	2014–2016	−4.44	2
Ukraine	2009	−14.42	1
	2014–2015	−10.48	2

[a] There were no years of negative growth between 2008 and 2015.
Source: Author's elaboration. Data for Hungary and Poland from International Monetary Fund, World Economic Outlook Database, October, 2018; for Estonia, Latvia, Lithuania, and Slovak Republic from National Accounts Main Aggregates Database (United Nations); and for Bulgaria, Czech Republic, Romania, Russian Federation Ukraine, and Slovenia from World Development Indicators, The World Bank 2018.

As shown in Table 7.7, and examined in more detail in Chapter 6, the most severe decline in GDP per capita took place in the Baltic countries.[15,16] Slovenia experienced a double dip recession in 2009 and 2012–2013, Bulgaria had recession in 2009 (3 percent), and Romania's per capita GDP contracted by 7 percent in 2008–2010.

The two republics of the former Soviet Union, Russia and Ukraine, were also hit hard by the global financial crisis of 2008–2009. In 2009, Russia's per capita GDP contracted by 7.9 percent in 2009 and Ukraine by 14.4 percent.

[15] In Latvia, GDP per capita contracted by 17.7 percent (2008–2010), by 18.5 percent in Estonia (2008–2009), and by 13.6 percent in Lithuania in 2009.
[16] The Czech Republic saw its GDP per capita decline by 5.4 percent in 2009 and 1.5 percent in 2012–2013, in Hungary GDP contracted by 6.5 percent in 2009 and 1.1 percent in 2012, and in the Slovak Republic GDP fell by 5.5 percent in 2009.

Later in 2014–2016, these economies again experienced drops in GDP per capita, related to reduced oil prices and the effects of armed conflict (in the case of Ukraine).

7.9 Conclusion

The USSR experienced rapid economic growth in the 1950s and 1960s but this was followed by a slowdown in the 1970s, and stagnation in the 1980s, before the demise of the socialist regime. A similar pattern was observed in the CEE economies. Several centrally planned economies borrowed in convertible currencies from Western capital markets in the 1970s and 1980s, increasing substantially their level of external debt. This provided only temporary relief to these ailing economies. In the late 1970s and early 1980s, countries were hit by higher international interest rates and oil price increases. Poland had to cope with protracted recession between 1979 and 1982, accompanied by the rise of a mass working-class movement – "solidarity" – that challenged both communist rule and economic mismanagement. This led first to martial law in 1981 and later, in 1989, to the first free elections in a communist country. Romania, governed by Nicolae Ceausescu, entered the IMF in 1972, and after a spree of external borrowing it decided, in the early 1980s, to fully repay its external debt to the West at the cost of sustained compression in internal consumption at near subsistence levels and protracted output contraction. This was a case of welfare-reducing, self-imposed austerity.

The external debt of Bulgaria (the data for which was maintained as a state secret until the end of the communist regime) skyrocketed in the 1980s, but foreign borrowers kept financing it in the expectation of a Soviet bailout. After, the travails of the socialist period, countries that had adhered to central planning for decades changed course and embraced a swift but costly transition to capitalism, with the hope of achieving immediate prosperity through market economies, private property, and integration into globalization. This transition entailed, initially, massive output contraction (particularly severe and of long duration in the former Soviet republics) accompanied by very large cuts in investment and sharp declines in real wages. Following EU accession in the early 2000s, former socialist CEE countries experienced an economic boom, followed by a bust in 2008–2009. After more than a quarter-century of capitalist modernization in CEE and Russia, these economies became more prosperous, but also more volatile, and prone to experience recurrent macro- and financial crises.

8

Economic Crises in Latin America and East Asia

8.1 Introduction

This chapter provides an overview of selected episodes of macroeconomic and financial crises that led to output contractions of different intensity and duration in Latin American and Asian economies between 1970 and 2018. This is a broad period encompassing a variety of economic, financial, and sociopolitical shocks and regimes affecting countries with different economic structures, policies, and history.

Latin America is a net exporter of commodities, economic and social inequality is high, and distributive conflicts make policy consensus often difficult to attain.[1] Policy models adopted range from import-substitution industrialization and socialism to free market economics and neoliberalism. In the early 1970s, left-wing governments in periods of growing democratization implemented overexpansive fiscal, credit, and wage policies that, when adopted in Chile and Argentina, led to inflationary and foreign exchange crises. Economic and political destabilization was then followed by military coups and the collapse of democracy.[2] Right-wing military regimes embraced free-market policies and shock treatment (e.g drastic cuts in money supply and large reductions in fiscal deficits to stabilize inflation) with adverse output consequences.[3] The 1980s was the

---

[1] For an overview of the economic history of Latin America see Bertola and Ocampo (2013). A set of country studies of policies of inflation stabilization including Argentina, Brazil and Chile appears in Bruno et al. (1991). Analysis of stabilization policies in Bolivia, Peru, Colombia, Nicaragua and others appear in Ocampo (1987).

[2] Brazil was also under military rule after the Constitutional President Joao Goulart was ousted in 1964.

[3] Venezuela enjoyed a windfall from high oil prices in the 1970s, maintained democracy at a time when other Latin American countries turned to authoritarian regimes, but it experienced output declines between 1978 and 1985.

"lost decade" in Latin America as a consequence of the debt crisis, high inflation, and severe output contraction. There were episodes of hyperinflation in Bolivia in 1985, Nicaragua in 1986–1991, Peru in 1988–1990, and Argentina in 1999–1990. These extreme monetary situations were accompanied by substantial declines in GDP.

In the 1990s, episodes of capital outflow and recession occurred in Mexico in 1994–1995 (tequila crisis), Argentina in 1995 (under a currency board), Brazil 1999 (currency crisis), and Ecuador 1999 (currency and financial crises and high inflation). In 2001, Argentina experienced the collapse of its ten-year-old currency board and entered into a severe financial crisis accompanied by a sharp depreciation of the Argentinean peso.

Times changed and a bonanza in terms of trade for Latin American exports took place between 2003 and 2012, accompanied by an expansionary cycle transitorily interrupted by the global financial crisis of 2008–2009. Later on, in 2018, Argentina returned to the IMF to contain strong speculation against the peso, and Venezuela went into hyperinflation in 2017–2018.

Several economies of East Asia in the period 1970–2018 were affected in different ways by the cycles of the international economy, domestic economic policies, and other factors. In general, the frequency of crisis was lower than in Latin America. The worst meltdown was the Asian financial crisis of 1997–1999, examined in this chapter. China and Vietnam had their recessions in the 1970s but avoided output contractions in subsequent decades. The international debt crisis of the early to mid-1980s hit Indonesia hard in 1983–1985, and the Asian crisis of 1997–1999 affected Indonesia, the Philippines, South Korea, Thailand, and Malaysia. Hong Kong and Singapore were hit in a less severe way, with China and Vietnam remaining largely unscathed by the regional shock. Finally, the global financial crisis of 2008–2009 led to small output declines in the Philippines, but effects upon Thailand, Malaysia, Hong Kong, and Singapore were more significant, with China, Korea, Vietnam, and Indonesia avoiding recession.

8.2 A Half-Century of Crises and Output Volatility in Latin America

Table 8.1 presents a summary of episodes of GDP per capita contractions for 11 Latin American countries in the period 1970–2018, showing their intensity, duration, frequency, and recovery rate. The country with the highest frequency of contractions in that period was Venezuela, registering episodes of negative per capita GDP growth in 57 percent of the years in the period (28 years), followed by Argentina, with annual recession in 36 percent of the period (18 years).

Table 8.1. *Episodes of recession in select Latin American countries (percentage of change in GDP per capita, 1970–2018)*

Country	Period	Cumulative decline in GDP per capita (%)	Consecutive years/decline	N° of years for GDP to reach pre-recession levels	Percent (and number) of years of negative growth over sample
Venezuela	1971–1972	−4	2	6	57.14% (28 years)
	1974–1975	−1.44	2	3	
	1978–1985	−24.26	8		
	1989	−10.86	1	4	
	1993–1994	−6.26	2	14	
	1996	−2.23	1	2	
	1998–1999	−9.3	2	9	
	2002–2003	−18.91	2	4	
	2009–2010	−7.56	2		
	2013–2018	−45.84	6		
Argentina	1975–1976	−4.43	2	20	36.73% (18 years)
	1978	−5.99	1	17	
	1980–1982	−11.93	3	15	
	1985	−7.96	1	8	
	1988–1990	−14.04	3	5	
	1995	−4.06	1	2	
	1999–2002	−21.91	2	8	
	2009	−6.88	1	2	
	2012	−2.06	1		
	2014	−3.51	1		
	2016	−2.78	1		
	2018	−3.71	1		

Brazil	1981–1983	−13.41	3	6	30.61% (15 years)
	1988	−2.18	1	8	
	1990–1992	−7.08	3	6	
	1998–1999	−2.23	2	3	
	2001	−0.02	1	2	
	2003	−0.15	1	2	
	2009	−1.11	1	2	
	2014–2016	8.78	3	2	
Peru	1976–1978	−6.40	3	6	26.53% (13 years)
	1982–1983	−17.23	2	25	
	1985	−0.26	1	2	
	1988–1990	−28.17	3	18	
	1992	−2.53	1	2	
	1998	−1.86	1	5	
	2001	−0.71	1	2	
	2009	−0.16	1	2	
Ecuador	1982–1983	−6.84	2	17	26.53% (13 years)
	1987	−8.30	1	8	
	1989	−2.09	1	3	
	1992–1993	−0.53	2	3	
	1996	−0.38	1	2	
	1999–2000	−7.24	2	6	
	2009	−1.10	1	2	
	2015–2016	−4.38	2	—	
	2018	−0.36	1	—	

(Continued)

Table 8.1 (*Continued*)

Country	Period	Cumulative decline in GDP per capita (%)	Consecutive years/decline	N° of years for GDP to reach pre-recession levels	Percent (and number) of years of negative growth over sample
Uruguay	1971–1972	−4.61	2	5	24.49% (12 years)
	1982–1984	−20.17	3	11	
	1988	−0.62	1	2	
	1990	−0.38	1	2	
	1995	−2.16	1	2	
	1999–2002	−15.59	4	9	
Mexico	1982–1983	−9.37	2	17	22.45% (11 years)
	1986–1988	−6.83	3	6	
	1995	−7.98	1	3	
	2001–2002	−2.96	2	4	
	2008–2009	−7.25	2	5	
	2013	−0.06	1	2	
Bolivia	1979–1986	−23.59	8	27	22.45% (11 years)
	1992	−0.34	1	2	
	1999	−1.49	1	5	
	2001	−0.19	1	2	
Chile	1972–1975	−23.65	4	9	16.33% (8 years)
	1982–1983	−18.92	2	8	
	1999	−1.66	1	2	
	2009	−2.54	1	2	

Costa Rica	1975	−0.77	1	2	16.33% (8 years)
	1980–1983	−14.71	4	13	
	1985	−2.07	1	2	
	1996	−1.18	1	2	
	2009	−2.27	1	2	
Colombia	1981–1983	−1.93	3	5	10.20% (5 years)
	1998–1999	−6.50	2	7	

Source: Author's elaboration. Data for 1970–1989 period from Maddison (2013), for 1990–2017 period from World Development Indicators, The World Bank 2018; for GDP per capita growth in 2018 and for Venezuela 2013–2018 from IMF, World Economic Outlook, October, 2018.

Countries with a frequency of recession/depression in the range of 20–30 percent for the whole period were Mexico, Brazil, Peru, Bolivia, Uruguay, and Ecuador with Chile, Cost Rica, and Colombia having frequencies below 20 percent. Colombia had the lowest frequency of recession (10.2 percent) from the group in Table 8.1.

The most severe recessions (except Venezuela in 2014–2018) occurred in the 1980s at the time of the debt crisis.

8.3 Causes and Types of Crisis

Most of the recessions and depressions in Latin American countries over the period under consideration were associated with: (i) adverse terms of trade shocks; (ii) increases in international interest rates; (iii) cutoff of foreign lending from public and/or private sources; (iv) restrictive fiscal, credit, and wage policies; (v) the collapse of exchange-rate regimes (fixed rates, exchange-rate bands, and currency boards); (vi) premature and poorly regulated financial liberalization; (vii) social conflict following periods of democratization and income redistribution; and (viii) natural disasters.

We can identify five types of crisis:

(A) fiscal crisis;
(B) sovereign debt crisis (debt default, forced rescheduling);
(C) high inflation/hyperinflation crisis;
(D) financial crisis (high percent of nonperforming loans in the banking system); and
(E) exchange-rate crisis (collapse of fixed-exchange rates and currency boards).

Table 8.2 provides select country examples of the different types of crisis just outlined. Note that a country may experience multiple crises with elements of the different categories in a given episode. In the following text, we discuss some select examples of crisis episodes.[4]

---

[4] References examining Latin American economic crises are Dornbusch and Edwards (1991), Ocampo (1987), Foxley (1983), Calvo (1998), Végh (1992), and Beckerman and Solimano (2002). The record of inflation-targeting in Latin America is discussed in Céspedes et al. (2014).

Table 8.2. *Economic crisis in Latin America (select episodes, 1970–2018)*

Fiscal crisis	Sovereign debt crisis	High inflation/ hyperinflation crisis	Financial crisis	Exchange-rate crisis
Chile (1972–1973)	Argentina (1981–1985)	Chile (1973)	Chile (1982–1983)	Mexico (1994–1995)
Argentina (1974–1976)	Chile (1983–1984)	Bolivia (1985)	Argentina (1991–1992)	Argentina (2000–2001)
Uruguay (1971–1972)	Mexico (1982–1983)	Argentina (1988–1990)	Ecuador (1999)	Chile (1982)
Venezuela (2013–2018)	Peru (1982–1983)	Peru (1988–1990)	Mexico 1994–1995	Brazil (1999)
	Brazil (1981–1983)	Ecuador (1999)		
	Venezuela (1978–1985)	Venezuela (2014–2018)		
	Uruguay (1982–1984)	Nicaragua (1986–1991)		
	Ecuador (1999)			

8.4 High Frequency of Crisis and Contractions: Argentina and Venezuela

Let us consider in more detail the cases of Argentina and Venezuela, both of which have experienced recurrent crises of the sort identified in the crisis categorization. A main paradox is that chronic instability takes place in two countries that are among the richest economies in South America. Argentina, with fertile lands, a respectable industrial base, and a well-educated population that in the early 1930s was among the top seven advanced economies of the world. Venezuela, in turn, is home of the largest oil reserves in the world, along with reserves of other valuable natural resources (e.g., gold). Of course, instability has prevented these nations from making full use of their economic potential, losing ground in their development levels relative to other nations.

8.4.1 Argentina

In the 1970s, Argentina was affected by escalating political violence, cycles of military rule, and short-lived periods of democratic rule.[5] The Peronist

---

[5] In the period 1973–1976, violence was attributed to the actions of a right-wing civilian death-squad (the AAA, the Argentine Anticommunist Alliance) acting in tandem with the military and the actions of the Montoneros, the radicalized left wing of the Peronist

governments (Héctor José Cámpora, Juan Domingo Perón, and Isabel Martínez de Perón), after the return to democracy in 1973, granted generous wage increases, augmented public spending, and imposed price and exchange-rate controls. Initially, there were output expansions (in 1973 and 1974) followed by negative GDP growth from the third quarter of 1975 through the fourth quarter of 1976 (Sturzenegger, 1991), accompanied by an acceleration of inflation, and fiscal and balance of payments difficulties. In March of 1976, a military coup ousted the government of Martínez de Perón, giving rise to a bloody dictatorship that lasted from 1976 to 1983. The economic policies of the Argentinean junta were oriented to reduce inflation and liberalize markets, restoring financial security to wealthy elites and international capital markets. GDP contracted in 1976 (the year of the coup), in 1978, and again in 1980–1982. These policies were supported, in general, by credit from the IMF, World Bank, and the Inter-American Development Bank (IABD). In March of 1982, the military launched an improvised attempt to recover the Falkland Islands (*Islas Malvinas*) from United Kingdom rule. After two months of war, followed by the United Kingdom's victory, the Argentinian military was forced to call free elections to restore civilian rule.[6]

The return to democracy in 1983, led by President Raúl Alfonsín, had a hard time ensuring economic and political stability. His administration was surrounded by military unrest, currency instability, debt crises, inflation, and two failed stabilization attempts: the Austral Plan and the Primavera Plan. Reducing inflation was a permanent problem for the Alfonsín government and, in 1988, inflation accelerated to 343 percent, further escalating to 3,000 percent in 1989 and 2,300 percent in 1990 (see Figure 8.1a) accompanied by output contraction in 1988–1990 (see Figure 8.1b). Due to the inability to control explosive inflation, President Alfonsín presented his early resignation.

Carlos Saúl Menem, a neoliberal Peronist, was elected president in the elections of May, 1989. He adopted aggressive policies of privatization of state assets and liberalized the economy in line with the prescriptions of the Washington Consensus. In 1991, to stabilize inflation, a currency board was established with a one-to-one parity between the Argentinean peso and the US dollar. For a few years, the currency board and free-market policies seemed to work, with inflation declining and investment and growth

Party, and the guerrilla movement, ERP (*Ejercito Revolucionario del Pueblo*, People's Revolutionary Army). On the economic front, these years also brought episodes of inflation, currency instability, recurrent balance of payments, and fiscal imbalances.

[6] A macro-economic history of Argentina since the nineteenth century is Della Paolera and Taylor (2003).

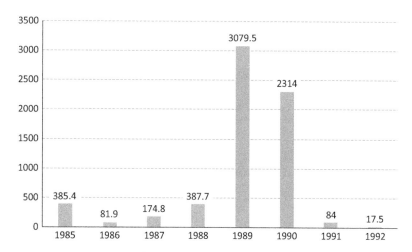

Figure 8.1a. Argentina: inflation, 1985–1992 (annual percentage change, CPI). *Source:* INDEC.

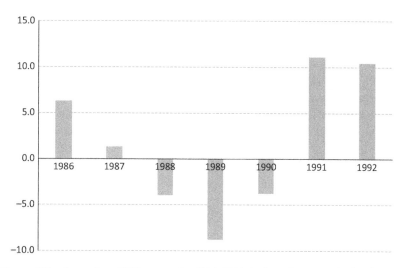

Figure 8.1b. Argentina: GDP per capita 1986–1992, before, during and after hyper-inflation (annual percentage change). *Source:* WDI, The World Bank 2018.

recovering, but this happy phase was interrupted by a recession in 1995. Apparently, markets were uneasy with the high exposure to the short-term debt that Argentina had accumulated in previous years, triggering capital outflow and a recession. In 1999, the economy entered into a new contractionary cycle that strained the currency board, which eventually collapsed

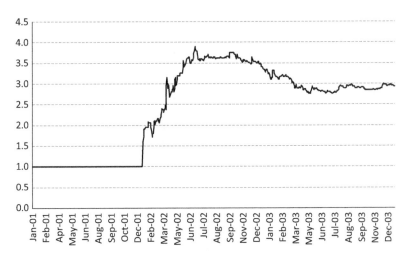

Figure 8.2a. Collapse of the currency board, 2001–2003 (Left-axis: exchange rate, Argentinean pesos per US dollar). *Source:* BCRA.

in 2001. Currency depreciation and a large-scale financial crisis followed as commercial banks could not honor their deposits in terms of the new parity (see Figure 8.2a). Finance minister Domingo Cavallo decreed a freeze on deposits and saving accounts, the so-called "*corralito*." As a consequence of the dual currency and financial crises, GDP per capita contracted by 23.7 percent in 1999–2002 (see Figure 8.2b), the largest economic contraction in Argentina in the period 1970–2018.

Once again, an economic crisis prompted political change. In 2002, Néstor Kirchner of the progressive wing of the Peronist party won the first relative majority over President Menem, who was seeking a second re-election. The arrival of Kirchner implied a strong departure from previous policies: he purged the military, engaged in the repression of the 1970s, and put in place a program of economic recovery to reignite growth and employment creation. Not all the external debt was serviced and relations with the IMF were severed. Economic growth resumed strongly in the period 2003–2008 but stalled in 2009 at the time of the global financial crisis.

In 2010, the government of Christina Fernández de Kirchner (widow of Néstor Kirchner) resorted to price and exchange-rate controls, alienating middle-class support for her government. The fiscal deficit reached 6 percent of GDP in 2015, investment declined, and inflationary pressure

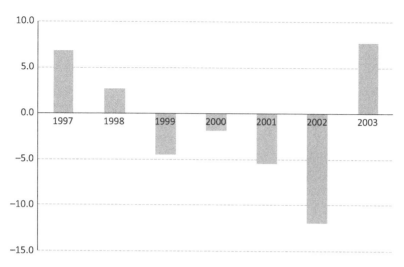

Figure 8.2b. Argentina: GDP per capita, 1997–2003 (annual percentage change). *Source:* WDI, The World Bank 2018.

mounted (the extent of which is difficult to assess, given accusations of government manipulation of the official consumer price index [CPI]).[7]

8.4.1.1 President Macri and the Return of the IMF

The end of the Kirchner's cycle came when liberal entrepreneur Mauricio Macri won the presidential elections and took office in December, 2016. He immediately abolished the exchange-rate controls of the Fernandez era and the peso was left to float. The prices of public utilities were sharply adjusted and inflation accelerated. To counteract inflationary pressures and reduce liquidity, the central bank was selling central bank debt (LABEC) carrying very high interest rates. In an attempt to restore growth and prosperity (not easy with high interest rates) Macri courted foreign investors and the domestic entrepreneurial class to invest again in Argentina, but their response was slow. Currency crisis speculation appeared again and the exchange rate fell from 17 pesos per US dollar in June, 2017, to nearly 40 pesos per US dollar in September, 2018. To avert the possibility of an uncontrolled depreciation of the currency and destabilizing capital outflow, the Macri administration went to the IMF for financial help. In Washington, DC, on October, 2018, a three-year standby program for USD 57 billion was signed with the IMF.

---

[7] The IMF declined to accept the official rate of inflation published by the government and domestic think tanks produced higher estimates of CPI inflation than those delivered by the statistical office (see Table 8.2).

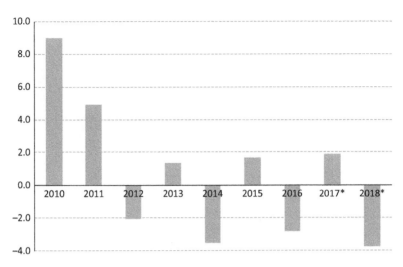

Figure 8.3. Argentina: stop- and go- growth cycles, 2010–2018 (annual percentage change in GDP per capita). *Source:* International Monetary Fund, World Economic Outlook Database, October, 2018.
* IMF estimates.

The conditionality of the loan revolved around a more independent central bank, the strengthening of the level of international reserves, changes in criteria to conduct monetary policy, fiscal adjustment, and labor reforms. Applying to the IMF was certainly a controversial policy of the Macri administration, given the long history of bad relations between the Fund and Argentina. As of late 2018, the IMF loan (to be disbursed in several tranches) managed (for a while) to stop additional devaluation of the peso but the economy contracted in 2018 (Figure 8.3).

8.4.2 Venezuela

In this chapter we have already noted the very high frequency of economic contractions in Venezuela over the last five decades. An important factor behind these cycles is related to fluctuations of public spending following changes in the international price of oil. The revenues from oil represent more than 90 percent of Venezuela's total exports and a high proportion of fiscal revenues in an economy highly dependent on extractive natural resources. In 1998, former army official Hugo Chávez was elected president and launched the "Bolivarian revolution." After his death in 2013, Chávez was succeeded by Nicolás Maduro. The objective of the Bolivarian revolution was to build a "socialism of the twenty-first century" in Venezuela, departing from the neoliberal trends prevailing in other Latin American countries. Income redistribution and access to food, health-care, and housing by low-income groups and working classes were the main economic objectives of the revolution. These aims could be pursued during the expansive cycle in oil prices in the period 2003–2012 but, when oil prices plummeted in 2013, the economic situation deteriorated sharply and has been followed by massive emigration of Venezuelans.[8]

8.4.2.1 Hyperinflation and Output Collapse in 2017–2018

Venezuela provides the most recent cases of hyperinflation in the world. According to IMF statistics, CPI inflation exceeded 1,000 percent in 2017 and escalated to over 1 million percent in 2018 (how to maintain records on prices increasing at very rapid rates on a daily basis remains a mystery).[9] This episode shows the interactions between a high fiscal deficit that is monetized and international sanctions that reduce the supply of foreign exchange, weakening the exchange rate and feeding into higher prices. As shown in Table 8.3, during the phase of rising oil prices in the early 2010s, fiscal revenues went up from 21 percent of GDP in 2010 to 30 percent in 2014 but fiscal spending increased to 46 percent of GDP with the fiscal defi-cit reaching 16.5 percent of GDP. The fiscal situation was further aggravated with a reversal in oil prices, leading to a sharp fall in public revenues to 10 percent of GDP in 2017–2018, while public spending was at 41 percent of GDP. For 2017–2018, the public sector borrowing requirement calculated by the IMF (fiscal deficit) was an astonishing *31 percent of GDP*.

A main consequence of the skyrocketing fiscal deficit was the sharp acceleration in CPI inflation (see Figure 8.4) accompanied by a mas-sive decline in economic activity of 45 percent between 2014 and 2018 that is shown in Figure 8.5.[10] A purely monetary story of hyperinflation, however, has to be qualified. The direct impact of the exchange rate on

---

[8] See Haussman and Rodriguez (2014).
[9] For a critical analysis of IMF estimates of inflation for Venezuela, see Hanke and Bushnell (2017).
[10] It is important to note that as Venezuela has a system of price controls the officially recorded rate of inflation may be under-estimated. Hanke and Bushnell (2017) pro-vide indirect calculations of the rate of inflation in Venezuela using parallel-market exchange rates linked to domestic prices through Purchasing Power Parities, showing that official inflation may have *under-estimated* the actual rate of inflation by a factor of at least 3 to 4 during most of 2015.

Table 8.3. *Venezuela: main macroeconomic indicators, 2010–2018*

	2010	2011	2012	2013	2014	2015	2016	2017	2018
Real GDP (Percent change)	-1.5	4.2	5.6	1.3	-3.9	-6.2	-16.5	-14	-18
GDP per capita (PPP, level in 2011 international dollar)	16,837	17,286	17,996	17,981	17,040	15,764	13,130	11,374	9,743
GDP per capita (PPP, annual change, percent)	-2.9	2.7	4.1	-0.1	-5.2	-7.5	-16.7	-13.4	-14.3
Total investment (Percent of GDP)	22	23.1	26.6	27.3	24.8	49.1	15.4	10	8.5
Gross national savings (Percent of GDP)	31.6	30.6	25.6	19	9.1	31.8	8.6	12.1	14.6
Inflation, average consumer prices (Percent change)	28.2	26.1	21.1	43.5	57.3	111.8	254.4	1,087.50	1,370,000
Volume of imports of goods and services (Percent change)	-2.9	15.4	24.4	-9.7	-18.5	-23.1	-38.4	-19	-15.6
Volume of exports of goods and services (Percent change)	-12.9	4.7	1.6	-6.2	-4.7	-0.9	-8.9	-17.8	-33.1
Current account balance (Percent of GDP)	5.6	16.3	2.6	4.6	4.9	-16.1	-3.9	4.3	5.9
Unemployment rate (Percent of total labor force)	8.5	8.2	7.8	7.5	6.7	7.4	20.6	27.1	34.3
General government revenue (Percent of GDP)	21	27.6	25.1	25.9	30.1	18.9	17.1	9	10.4
General government total expenditure (Percent of GDP)	30.2	38.2	39.7	40	46.6	36.4	34.8	40.9	40.9
General government net lending/borrowing (GDP, negative means borrowing to cover a deficit)	-9.2	-10.6	-14.6	-14.1	-16.5	-17.6	-17.8	-31.8	-30.5

Note: Shaded cells indicate IMF estimates.

Source: International Monetary Fund, World Economic Outlook Database, October, 2018.

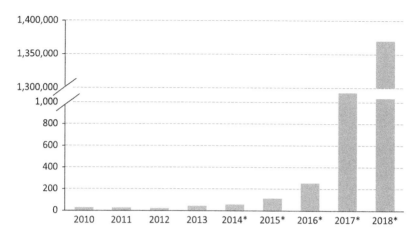

Figure 8.4. Venezuela: inflation, 2010–2018 (annual percentage change in CPI). *Source:* WEO, October, 2018, IMF.
* IMF estimates.

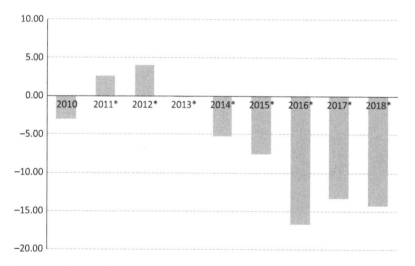

Figure 8.5. Venezuela: GDP per capita, 2010–2018 (annual percentage change). *Source:* International Monetary Fund, World Economic Outlook Database, October, 2018.
* IMF estimates.

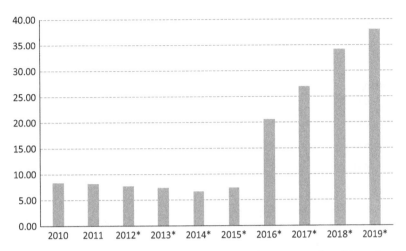

Figure 8.6. Venezuela: unemployment rate, 2010–2018 (percentage of total labor force). *Source:* International Monetary Fund, World Economic Outlook Database, October, 2018.
* IMF estimates.

domestic prices is also important. In turn, the exchange rate is very sensitive to changes in the price of oil, the level of capital flow, and the freeze of Petróleos de Venezuela, S.A. (PDVSA) accounts (Venezuela's main oil exporting company), in the United States (see Figure 8.6).[11]

8.5 Chile: Transition to Fewer and Milder Recessions

The 1970s and 1980s were turbulent decades for the Chilean economy. The swing from the "Chilean Way to Socialism" of Doctor Salvador Allende in 1970–1973 to the radical neoliberalism of General Augusto Pinochet and the "Chicago boys" was daunting. Economic policies shifted from a program of nationalization of copper mines, commercial banks, big industrial companies, and accelerated agrarian reform, coupled with expansive fiscal/credit and wage policies in 1971–1973, to a program of shock treatment to reduce inflation

---

[11] The mechanisms of transmission from very high inflation to economic activity goes through several channels such as the fiscal deficit, the money market, investment, aggregate demand, and aggregate supply. The impact of high inflation on the fiscal deficit is due to a lag in tax collection in which the real value of tax revenues sharply declines at very high rates of inflation (the Keynes–Olivera–Tanzi effect), deteriorating the overall fiscal deficit budget. Moreover, aggregate demand tends to fall as the real stock of money typically declines during hyperinflation (see Cagan, 1956, Bresciani-Turroni, 1937). Investment in physical assets is also severely affected as rational economic calculation of profitability and demand becomes almost impossible at rapidly escalating rates of inflation.

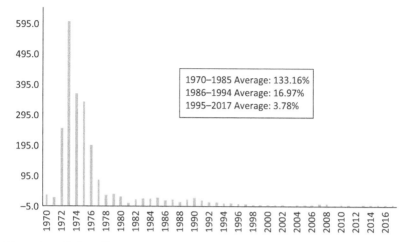

Figure 8.7. Chile: inflation, 1970–2017 (annual percentage change in CPI, percentage). *Source:* Data for 1970–2010 from Díaz, Lüders and Wagner (2016) and for 2011–2017 from Banco Central de Chile.

to squeeze on labor unions, massive privatization of state-owned enterprises, trade, and financial sector liberalization.[12] In the 1990s, democracy was restored but economic policies continued the overall free-market orientation of the Pinochet period, though softened with more social spending and increased public investment.[13] Most of macroeconomic instability affecting Chile centered in the 1970s and early to mid-1980s with a more stable macroeconomic conditions in the 1990s and 2000s,(see Figures 8.7–8.9).[14]

[12] The Allende government macropolicies were followed by an initial expansion of output and higher real wages in 1971. The economic situation deteriorated in 1972 and inflation reached near 600 percent in 1973, accompanied by large fiscal imbalances. Chile started to run out of international reserves. GDP contracted in 1972 and 1973. The external imbalances were difficult to finance due to cuts of external financing from multilateral organizations under the pressure of the United State in retaliation for nationalization of copper mines and the overall socialist orientation of the government. The military coup of September 11, 1973, ousted Allende (who died in the presidential palace), closed parliament, and imposed a harsh dictatorship that lasted for 17 years (see Bitar (1995) for an analysis of the economic policies under Allende). Solimano (2012) provides an analysis of Chilean economic policies and political economy in the last four to five decades, including the Pinochet and post-Pinochet government. Corbo and Solimano (1991) discuss the record of inflation stabilization in the 1970s and 1980s and De Gregorio and Labbé (2011) study the impact of copper price shocks in Chile.

[13] Chile's GDP per capita in 2017 was close to USD 25,000: in purchasing power parity, one of the highest of the Latin American region. Macroeconomic gains, however, have not been matched by equal progress in the fields of income distribution and environmental sustainability. See Solimano and Schaper (2014) and French-Davis (2018).

[14] See Larrain and Parrado (2008).

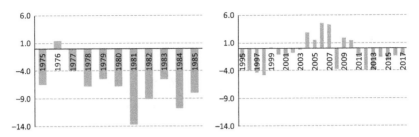

Figure 8.8. Chile: current account balances (percentage of GDP, 1975–1985 and 1995–2017). *Source:* World Development Indicators, The World Bank 2018.

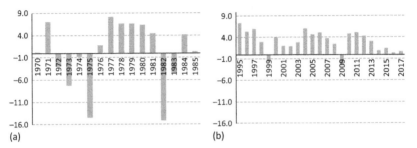

Figure 8.9. Chile: GDP per capita growth (a) annual percentage change in 1970–1985 (b) annual percentage change, 1995–2017. *Source:* Data for 1970–1985 from Maddison (2013) and for 1995–2017 from World Development Indicators, The World Bank 2018.

Following shock treatment to reduce inflation and external deficit, GDP per capita fell by nearly 15 percent in 1975.[15] A main crisis, this time accompanied by a collapse in the banking system, occurred in 1982–1983, when per capita GDP declined by 20 percent and investment by 35 percent. This crisis led to the devaluation of the peso in June, 1982, after three years of a fixed-exchange rate regime to reduce inflation. Currency overvaluation, higher interest rates, and lower terms of trade generated a very large current account deficit (close to 14 percent of GDP in 1981, see Figure 8.8). In addition, unregulated financial liberalization led to an overexpansion of credit and an increase of foreign debt by corporations. In 1984, the economy started to recover, stimulated by

---

[15] This was further complicated by a severe decline in international copper prices.

higher public spending, internal debt rescheduling, a more depreciated real exchange rate, and loans from the IMF, the World Bank, and the IADB.[16]

8.5.1 Milder Recessions in 1999 and 2009

After the crisis of 1982–1983, the Chilean economy suffered milder recessions in 1999 and 2009 (see Figure 8.9).

The transition to more stable macroeconomic conditions in the decades after the crisis of 1982–1983 was associated with an exchange-rate policy oriented to boost exports, an independent central bank, a fiscal rule, more generous loans from multilateral organizations, and the setup of a copper stabilization fund later turned into a sovereign wealth fund.[17] However, growth in Chile has been accompanied also by deindustrialization and chronically high income and wealth inequality (see Solimano, 2012 and 2017; Solimano and Schaper, 2014).

8.6 Mexico: The "Tequila Crisis" and Other Recessions

After rapid economic growth in 1950–1980, Mexico was affected by decades of economic crises, slower and more volatile economic growth, persistent poverty, economic inequality, and massive worker emigration into the United States.[18] The economy became particularly vulnerable to the change of administrations (*sexenios*). Several presidential elections in the 1980s and 1990s were accompanied by currency devaluation and capital outflows. Recessions occurred in 1982–1983 (end of the Jóse López Portillo *sexenio*), in 1986–1988 (end of the Miguel de la Madrid *sexenio*), in 1995 (the "tequila crisis" at the end of Carlos Salinas de Gortari *sexenio*) and in 2008–2009, associated with a recession in the United States, Mexico's main trading partner (see Table 8.1).

---

[16] For an insider's account of the change of policies in 1984 and the firing of the economic team of the Chicago boys by Pinochet, see Escobar-Cerda (1991).

[17] As part of the "fiscal responsibility law" of 2006 a Pension Reserve Fund, PRF, was also created. In addition to the ESSF and PRF there is an opaque fund managed by the Ministry of Defense and the Chilean Armed Forces in which 10 percent of *gross annual revenues* of CODELCO (the copper state-owned company) must be transferred by law to this fund to finance the acquisition of military equipment. This law is not subject to direct congressional oversight in its operation (see Solimano and Calderon, 2017).

[18] In the 1970s the Mexican government engaged in massive improvements in physical infrastructure that were, in part, financed by foreign borrowing. In the early 1980s, it was caught with high levels of external debt at the time of rising international interest rates and declining commodity prices.

8.6.1 The "Tequila Crisis"

A prototypical event was the "tequila crisis" that started in 1994, a very tense year for Mexico. Luis Donaldo Colosio, the appointed presidential candidate of the ruling *Partido Revolucionario Institucional* (PRI) was killed in March. After Colosio's death, the economist Ernesto Zedillo was appointed as the new PRI candidate, being elected in August. In September, the wave of political assassinations continued with the murder of José Francisco Ruiz Massieu, general secretary of the PRI.[19]

In December, 1994, Zedillo devalued the Mexican peso, a move labeled as the "mistake of December" by departing president Salinas de Gortari. Salinas, ruled Mexico from 1994 to 1998, and implemented policies of privatization and economic liberalization. In early 1994, he signed the North American Free Trade Agreement (NAFTA, a free trade agreement with the United States and Canada), followed, almost immediately, by the Zapatista uprising in the southern state of Chiapas. The uprising quickly caught international attention by its simultaneity with the signing of NAFTA presented to the world as proof of the degree of stability, modernization, and integration achieved in Mexico. Certainly, the peasant uprising in the state of Chiapas opaqued the initial euphoria of signing NAFTA. On the economic front, between 1991 and 1994, under Salinas de Gortari, the economy ran a high external current-account deficit (7.5 percent of GDP, see Figure 8.11), accompanied by expansionary fiscal policies and short-term external borrowing. This combination could hardly last for long. In the election year of 1994, there were speculative attacks on central banks reserves and financial capital flew out of Mexico. In 1995, the first year of the Zedillo government, the Clinton administration provided Mexico with a large bilateral loan of USD 20 billion, supplemented by credits from the IMF, the Bank for International Settlements (BIS), the Bank of Canada, and the Brazilian and Argentinean governments. The loan was oriented to stabilize the exchange rate, restore "credibility," and prevent a large-scale crisis that could trigger further emigration into the

---

[19] High profile political assassinations in Mexico in the twentieth century include that of Jose Venustiano Carranza in 1920, (Carranza served as president between 1917 and 1920) and the murder, in 1928, of Alvaro Obregón former leader of the revolution of 1910.

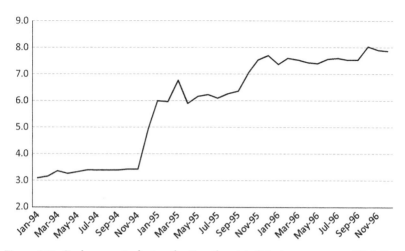

Figure 8.10. Exchange rate during the Tequila crisis (Mexican pesos per US dollars, January 1994 to December 1996). *Source:* IMF Exchange rates report 2018.

Table 8.4. *Mexico: main macroeconomic indicators, 1991–1997*

	GDP per capita growth (Percent)	Inflation, average consumer prices (Percent change)	General government net lending/borrowing (Percent of GDP)	Current account balance (Percent of GDP)
1991	2.17	22.61	−0.84	−6.21
1992	1.58	15.52	0.12	−8.95
1993	2.03	9.76	0.15	−6.82
1994	2.95	6.99	−0.61	−8.13
1995	−7.98	35.06	−3.88	−0.45
1996	4.94	34.35	−4.99	−0.62
1997	5.10	20.60	−5.32	−1.54

Source: International Monetary Fund, World Economic Outlook Database, October, 2018 and for GDP per capita from WDI, The World Bank 2018.

United States. The overall package prevented a relapse of recession following the Asian financial crisis of 1997–1999, but could not avoid a fall of GDP in 2001–2002, at the time of the burst of the dot.com bubble, showing the vulnerability of the Mexican economy to US business cycles/crises (see Figure 8.10; and Table 8.4).[20]

---

[20] In addition, the current account deficit was brought into near balance at the cost of economic contraction with GDP per capita falling by nearly 8 percent and inflation accelerated to 35 percent (from 7 percent in 1994) (see Table 8.4 and Figures 8.10 and 8.11).

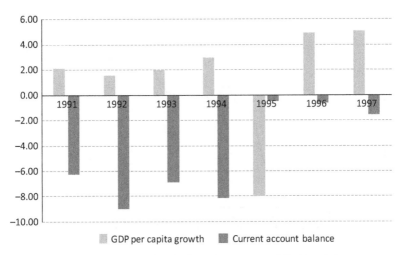

Figure 8.11. Mexico: current account balance (percentage of GDP) and GDP per capita growth (annual percentage change), 1991–1997. *Source:* Data for current account balance from IMF, WEO Database, October, 2018 and for GDP per capita growth from WDI, The World Bank 2018.

8.7 The Asian Crisis of 1997–1998

The East Asian countries most affected by the cycles of capital inflows and then outflows in the period 1993–1998 were Thailand, Indonesia, Korea, Malaysia, and the Philippines (the "Asia-5 countries"). In contrast, China and Vietnam, neither of which had liberalized their financial systems, avoided output contractions in 1997–1999 (see Table 8.5). In turn, Singapore and Hong Kong, two economies with strong international financial integration, experienced output declines in 1998, but avoided financial crises of the type that affected the Asia-5 countries.

The Asian financial crisis came as a big surprise to most external observers – though perhaps not to true insiders – as these economies had undergone a successful transition from being agrarian, low-income countries into industrial powerhouses, at least some of them (see the World Bank report, *The East Asian Miracle*).[21]

In general, the frequency of economic contractions in Asia (last column) is well below that in Latin American countries (see Tables 8.1 and 8.5). The country with the highest recession frequency in the period 1970–2015 was

---

[21] Of course, there also important differences in development levels, with Korea the most developed country and the Philippines the least developed within the Asia-5 countries.

Table 8.5. *Episodes of recession in select Asian Countries (percentage of change in GDP per capita, 1970–2018)*

Country	Period	Cumulative decline in GDP per capita (%)	Consecutive years/decline	N° of years for GDP to reach pre-recession levels	Percent (and number) of years of negative growth over sample
Indonesia	1975	−2.2	1	2	8.16% (4 years)
	1982	−5.56	1	3	
	1998–1999	−14.87	2	8	
Philippines	1983–1985	−18.75	3	21	16.33% (8 years)
	1991–1993	−5.32	3	6	
	1998	−2.74	1	3	
	2009	−0.46	1	2	
Korea	1980	−4.19	1	2	4.08% (2 years)
	1998	−6.15	1	2	
Thailand	1997–1998	−12.29	2	6	6.12% (3 years)
	2009	−1.19	1	2	
Malaysia	1975	−1.48	1	1	12.24% (6 years)
	1985–1986	−4.71	2	4	
	1998	−9.66	1	5	
	2001	−1.66	1	2	
	2009	−3.28	1	2	
China	1974	−0.39	1	2	4.08% (2 years)
	1976	−2.12	1	2	

(Continued)

Table 8.5 (*Continued*)

Country	Period	Cumulative decline in GDP per capita (%)	Consecutive years/decline	N° of years for GDP to reach pre-recession levels	Percent (and number) of years of negative growth over sample
Hong Kong	1974–1975	-1.61	2	3	14.29% (7 years)
	1985	-0.64	1	2	
	1996	-0.27	1	2	
	1998	-6.67	1	3	
	2001	-0.18	1	2	
	2009	-2.67	1	2	
Vietnam	1970	-0.55	1	2	12.24% (6 years)
	1974–1975	-15.09	2	10	
	1978–1980	-7.45	3	6	
Singapore	1985	-2.09	1	3	10.20% (5 years)
	1998	-5.49	1	3	
	2001	-3.59	1	3	
	2008–2009	-6.92	2	3	

Source: Own elaboration. Data for 1970–1989 period from Maddison (2013), for 1990–2017 period from World Development Indicators, The World Bank 2018; and for GDP per capita growth in 2018 from IMF, World Economic Outlook, October, 2018.

Indonesia (16 percent of the years in the sample period[22]), followed by Hong Kong, then Vietnam. In turn, the lowest frequency was in China. In the 1970s, episodes of negative per capita GDP growth were observed in Indonesia, Malaysia, Hong Kong, China (in 1976, at the time of the cultural revolution), and Vietnam, in 1974–1975, at the end of the war with the United States, and again in 1970–1980.

The international debt crisis of the early to mid-1980s, led to recessions in Indonesia (1982), the Philippines (1983–1985), Malaysia (1985–1986), Hong Kong (1985), and Singapore (1985). The most severe output decline was in the Philippines; it took two decades for this economy to recover the level of GDP per capita it had before the crisis. In the other countries, the effects of the debt crises of the 1980s were more moderate. The financial crisis of 2008–2009 led to small output declines in the Philippines, and larger declines in Thailand, Malaysia, Hong Kong, and Singapore.[23]

The East Asian meltdown of 1997–1998 was geared to sudden changes in the size and direction of foreign capital inflow (a capital account crisis) interacting with internal vulnerabilities in the borrowing countries. The crisis led to currency devaluations, cuts in investment and growth, financial fragility, and output contraction (see Table 8.6).[24]

On the causes of the East Asian crisis, it is interesting to note that fundamentals – such as the level of fiscal deficits and current account deficits, inflation and level of the real exchange rate – were not particularly misaligned. The size of external current account deficits – a variable often used to predict "sudden stops" – in Asia-5 countries was not large,[25] fiscal budgets were moderate (with some in surplus), and inflation was below 10 percent in 1994–1996.[26]

The real exchange rates had appreciated in the early to mid-1990s, but much less than in Argentina and Mexico before their crisis of the mid-1990s. External competitiveness was affected by the appreciation of the US dollar (the currency they had pegged to). Also, the devaluation of the Chinese yuan in early 1994 affected the external competitiveness of the Asian-5 economies.

[22] Compared with over 50 percent in Venezuela.
[23] China, Vietnam, Korea, and Indonesia avoided output declines in that crisis.
[24] Useful references for studying the 1997–1998 crisis are Ito (2007), Radelet and Sachs (1998), Berg (1999), and Muchhala (2007).
[25] The average deficit in 1994–1996 was below 4 percent of GDP in Korea, Indonesia and the Philippines and although much higher, in the range of 6–7 percent in Thailand and Malaysia (Table 8.6).
[26] Inflation was near 5.5 percent in Korea and Thailand, 3.5 percent in Malaysia although higher in Indonesia and the Philippines, in the range of 8–9 percent per year in 1994–1996.

Table 8.6. *Asian crisis: main economic indicators (select countries, 1994–2000)*

		1994	1995	1996	1997	1998	1999	2000
GDP per capita (% change)	Thailand	7.0	7.0	4.5	-3.9	-8.7	3.4	3.4
	Indonesia	5.8	6.6	6.2	3.2	-14.3	-0.6	3.5
	Korea	8.1	8.5	6.6	4.9	-6.2	10.5	8.0
	Malaysia	6.5	7.1	7.2	4.6	-9.7	3.6	6.4
	Philippines	2.0	2.3	3.5	2.9	-2.7	0.9	2.2
Current Account Balance (% of GDP)	Thailand	-5.5	-8.0	-8.0	-2.0	12.5	9.8	7.4
	Indonesia	-1.4	-2.8	-2.7	-1.5	3.5	3.4	4.5
	Korea	-1.0	-1.8	-4.0	-1.8	10.7	4.5	1.9
	Malaysia	-5.7	-9.1	-4.1	-5.5	12.3	14.8	8.4
	Philippines	-4.2	-2.4	-4.3	-4.8	2.1	-3.5	-2.8
Inflation (average CPI percent change)	Thailand	5.1	5.8	5.8	5.6	8.0	0.3	1.7
	Indonesia	8.5	9.4	8.4	6.2	58.0	20.8	3.8
	Korea	6.3	4.5	4.9	4.4	7.5	0.8	2.3
	Malaysia	3.7	3.5	3.5	2.7	5.3	2.7	1.6
	Philippines	10.4	6.8	7.5	5.6	9.2	6.0	3.9
General government net lending/ borrowing (Percent of GDP)	Thailand	N.A.	3.1	2.7	-1.7	-6.3	-9.0	-1.8
	Indonesia	0.0	0.6	1.0	-1.0	-1.9	-1.0	-1.9
	Korea	N.A.	2.3	2.4	2.4	1.2	1.2	4.2
	Malaysia	3.6	1.5	1.9	3.7	-0.6	-3.0	-6.1
	Philippines	-0.5	0.0	0.6	0.4	-1.4	-2.4	-3.4

GDP per capita (PPP, 2011 international dollar)	Thailand	8,779	9,384	9,815	9,450	8,643	8,955	9,283
	Indonesia	5,621	5,984	6,378	6,601	5,669	5,649	5,863
	Korea	15,272	16,566	17,656	18,527	17,387	19,216	20,757
	Malaysia	13,585	14,530	15,576	16,298	14,717	15,227	16,135
	Philippines	3,952	4,042	4,071	4,187	4,062	4,098	4,277
Real effective exchange-rate index (2010 = 100)	Thailand	105.68	104.01	109.06	97.15	84.93	89.78	86.58
	Indonesia	105.75	102.22	106.59	95.26	46.31	69.49	67.97
	Korea	121.41	121.56	121.98	110.92	84.67	97.97	105.84
	Malaysia	116.25	117.00	120.52	114.87	92.30	94.53	96.45
	Philippines	99.04	101.23	108.47	106.18	89.21	95.05	89.36

Source: Data for Current Account Balance, Inflation, General government net lending/borrowing and GDP per capita from IMF, WEO Database, October, 2018; for GDP per capita growth and from WDI, The World Bank 2018; and for Real effective exchange rate from Real effective exchange rates Database (Darvas, 2012).

What rendered these economies more vulnerable was the liberalization of their internal financial systems (a rapid increase in the number of financial intermediaries) and the liberalization of short-term capital flows coming from abroad. This set of liberalizations led to an increasing reliance on short-term foreign capital inflows. As a result of these developments, in June, 1997, South Korea, Indonesia, and Thailand had ratios of short-term debt to international reserves between 1.5 and 2, with the Philippines and Malaysia between 0.5 and 1 (see Table 8.3 and Radelet and Sachs, 1998).

8.7.1 Currency Crises and Output Contraction

In 1997, the Indonesian rupiah lost 19 percent of its value against the US dollar, followed by another drop of 70 percent in 1998, accumulating a loss of nearly 90 percent in two years (see Table 8.7).

The currency instability that affected Indonesia, was associated with several factors, such as contagion effects after the devaluation of the Thai baht in June of 1997, the level of international reserves relative to short-term debt and the perceived difficulties of the highly leveraged Indonesian corporate sector to serve its large external debts. In addition, the management of the financial sector during the crisis could have added more uncertainty to an already shaky situation. In November, 1997, the Indonesian government decided to close down 16 commercial banks that were considered financially nonviable. The wave of bank closures led to financial panic and the withdrawal of funds from remaining banks, exacerbating the weakness of the rupiah. In addition, the economic crisis metamorphosed into a political crisis in 1998 that led to the departure, in May, of the autocratic ruler President Suharto after thirty-five years in power.

In Korea, Malaysia, Thailand, and the Philippines, the cumulative loss of value of their currencies in 1997–1998 was in the range of 35 to 45 percent (Table 8.7). Malaysia tried to contain the effects of capital outflow by imposing capital controls, against the wish of the IMF. However, in 1999 and 2000, the national currencies of several of these economies experienced some appreciation in their values after an overshooting in 1998.

The fall in GDP in 1998 in the Asian-5 economies coincided with sharp drops in the value of their currencies. The literature on contractionary devaluation (Krugman and Taylor, 1978, Solimano, 1987) emphasized the *adverse* short-term effects of a depreciation of national currency on output operating through the following mechanisms: (i) cuts in real wages and compression in consumption; (ii) an increase in the local price of imported capital goods that can have adverse effects on capital formation; (iii) an adverse

Table 8.7. *Exchange rates before, during, and after the Asian Crisis (local currency per US dollar, annual averages, 1994–2000)*

	Thailand (Baht)	Indonesia (Rupiah)	Korea (Won)	Malaysia (Ringgit)	Philippines (Peso)
1994	25.1	2,160.8	803.4	2.6	26.4
1995	24.9	2,248.6	771.3	2.5	25.7
1996	25.3	2,342.3	804.5	2.5	26.2
1997	31.4	2,909.4	951.3	2.8	29.5
1998	41.4	10,013.6	1401.4	3.9	40.9
1999	37.8	7,855.2	1188.8	3.8	39.1
2000	40.1	8,421.8	1131.0	3.8	44.2

Source: WDI, The World Bank 2018.

wealth effect upon households indebted in foreign currency that may further depress consumption; and (iv) a positive effect of currency depreciation on competitiveness that stimulates exports. A full empirical evaluation of each of these effects in the Asia-5 countries remains pending but the observed movement of output contraction in 1997–1998, followed by a recovery since 1999 – a sort of V-shape dynamics – suggests that negative consumption and investment effects tend to dominate in the short term, followed by positive export effects (along with some recovery of investment and consumption) in subsequent years (see Figures 8.12 and 8.13 and Table 8.8).

The effects of currency devaluation on inflation is another relevant factor. Again, Indonesia was the country where the fall in the value of the currency led to the highest acceleration in inflation in 1997 and 1998. The change in the CPI jumped from 6.2 percent in 1997 to 58 percent in 1998 and 21 percent in 1999, to converge at levels below 4 percent in 2000. In Korea, Thailand, Malaysia, and the Philippines, inflation also accelerated in 1998, but more modestly, remaining below the 10 percent threshold.

Thailand, Korea, and Malaysia generated external current *surpluses* of several percentage points of GDP in 1998–1999 (see Figure 8.14). Indonesia and the Philippines had smaller current account surpluses (with the Philippines running a deficit in 1999).

8.7.2 The Role of the IMF

The involvement of the IMF in the Asian crisis, through the provision of large loans and technical assistance, was particularly controversial as programs *failed* – initially – on at least three fronts to: (i) stabilize the value of

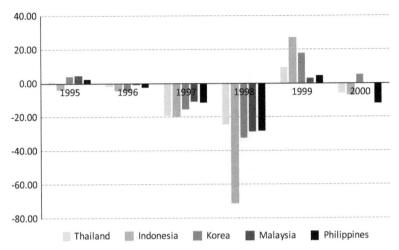

Figure 8.12. Currency depreciations (negative change) and appreciations (positive change) (annual rate of change, 1994–2000). *Source:* WDI, The World Bank 2018.

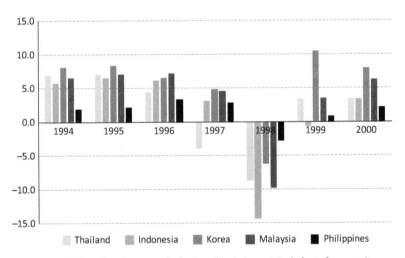

Figure 8.13. GDP per capita growth during the Asian crisis (selected countries, percentage change, 1994–2000). *Source:* World Development Indicators, The World Bank 2018.

Table 8.8. *Annual rate of depreciation of the nominal exchange rate (percentage change, 1994–2000)*

	Thailand	Indonesia	Korea	Malaysia	Philippines
1995	0.9	−3.9	4.2	4.8	2.7
1996	−1.7	−4.0	−4.1	−0.5	−1.9
1997	−19.2	−19.5	−15.4	−10.6	−11.0
1998	−24.2	−70.9	−32.1	−28.3	−27.9
1999	9.4	27.5	17.9	3.3	4.6
2000	−5.7	−6.7	5.1	0.0	−11.5

Source: WDI, The World Bank 2018.

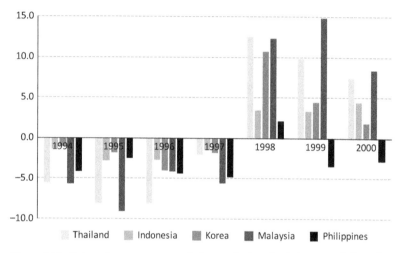

Figure 8.14. External current account balances during the Asian crisis (selected countries, percentage of GDP, 1994–2000). *Source:* IMF, WEO Database, October, 2018.

the domestic currencies; (ii) produce an orderly servicing of external debt; and (iii) avoid massive output and employment losses. Between August and December of 1997, the IMF provided a total of USD 110 billion in loans: USD 57 billion to Korea; USD 35 billion to Indonesia; and USD 18 billion to Thailand.

Criticism of the IMF intervention in the East Asian crisis centered upon four areas: (i) the recommendation of using tight monetary policy and high interest rates in a period of financial panic that needed *additional* liquidity rather than a squeeze on liquidity; (ii) the setting of targets of fiscal surplus at the time of a cutoff in capital inflow, thereby turning fiscal policy into a *procyclical* device that *exacerbated* output and employment contraction; (iii) excessive emphasis in financial restructuring and *liquidation* of banks in a period of financial uncertainty, triggering bank runs, as was the case in Indonesia; and (iv) *secrecy* on the content of program design and overly complex schemes of availability of external resources. It is fair to say, however, the difficulties of the IMF programs implemented during the Asian crisis reflected the complex nature of capital account crisis with a strong element of asymmetric information, uncertainty, and moral hazard. It became apparent that the Fund was probably not in tune with the new character of external crises and its conditionality was corresponding more with previous types of crises.

8.8 Conclusion

The Latin American experience of the last five decades is extremely rich in the variety of cycles, crises, collapses of monetary regimes, and episodes of economic contraction, and in some cases, also the collapse of democracy. The borrowing cycle of the 1970s and the debt crisis of the early 1980s led to significant output contractions in Mexico, Argentina, Brazil, Chile, Uruguay, Peru, Ecuador, and Costa Rica. An exception was Colombia, which experienced a mild decline in GDP per capita at the time the debt crisis hit other Latin American economies. The 1990s and 2000s showed the relevance of a new variety of "capital account crisis" featuring destabilizing capital outflow after waves of financial liberalization and severe strains on existing exchange-rate regimes. The tequila crisis in Mexico (1994–1995), the Argentinean recession of 1995, the Ecuadorean crisis in 1999 (accompanied by a severe banking crisis), currency speculation in Brazil in 1999, and the traumatic end of the convertibility regime in Argentina in 2001 and 2002 are examples of these types of crises. Then, after a bonanza in commodity prices between 2002 and 2012, some countries fell back again into crisis situations in the 2010s. Argentina returned to the IMF in 2018, following a bout of currency speculation and capital outflow, and Venezuela suffered hyperinflation and massive output contraction in 2017–2018.

The economies of East Asia in the period 1970–2018 had fewer episodes of economic contraction and more rapid recoveries than Latin American economies. The worst meltdown was during the financial crisis of 1997–1999 that seriously impacted Indonesia, Korea, Thailand, Malaysia, and the Philippines. Hong Kong and Singapore also experienced output declines unlike China and Vietnam. The global financial crisis of 2008–2009 led to output declines in the Asia-5 countries: a small decline in Philippines with larger declines in Thailand, Malaysia, Hong Kong, and Singapore.

9

Synthesis and Interpretation

9.1 Introduction

The analysis conducted in this book shows that economic contraction can be the consequence of several factors: (i) armed conflicts such as World Wars I and II; (ii) extreme monetary instability and hyperinflation of the sort affecting Central and Eastern European economies and Soviet Russia in the early to mid-1920s; Bolivia, Argentina, Peru, and Nicaragua in the 1980s; Yugoslavia and Bulgaria in the 1990s; Zimbabwe in 2008 and Venezuela in 2017–2018; (iii) collapses in exchange-rate regimes such as those in the 1980s, 1990s, and early 2000s in several Latin American and East Asian economies; (iv) sharp systemic changes such as the end of central planning and the transition to capitalism in the former USSR and Central and Eastern Europe in the 1990s; (v) macroeconomic crises following overexpansionary fiscal/credit and wage policies; (vi) adverse terms of trade shocks; (vii) sudden cuts in capital inflow ; and (viii) premature financial liberalization.

9.2 U, V, and W Cycles of Contraction and Recovery

Cycles of boom/bust and recovery can have a variety of origins and be of varying intensity. Examples of U-cycles include the Great Depression of the 1930s in the United States, European countries, and economies of the periphery of the world economy. Greece in the aftermath of the global financial crisis of 2008-2009 and Japan in the 1990s are also cases of a long depression that fits more in the U-shape.

The deep postsocialist contractions of the early 1990s in Russia, Ukraine, and several Eastern European countries could also be classified as U-cycles, featuring slow recoveries after a big shock. In contrast, the recovery after shock treatment in Poland in the early 1990s and Latvia in the early 2010s resembled more a V-cycle.

The "capital account crises" of the 1990s in Argentina, Mexico, and East Asia are V-shapes: large slumps that last one to two years followed by relatively strong recoveries. W-cycles were observed in the United States in the 1930s, in Argentina in the second half of the 1990s, and in Mexico in the early 2000s.

9.3 Are Wars Economically Contractionary or Expansionary?

As shown in Table A.1 (in the annex to this book), the *largest* declines in real per capita GDP in countries were associated with war.

The evidence from World War I and World War II shows that armed conflicts may lead either to economic stimulus or economic contraction (slump). Both the United States and Great Britain in the initial years of World War I experienced rapid increases in output and employment due to the expansionary effect of defense sector production, especially when labor and capital were not fully utilized. The United States and Great Britain also benefitted from the fact that war was not fought in their territories, saving adverse impacts on human lives, physical infrastructure and economic assets. In contrast, Germany experienced economic contraction during World War I. Moreover, economic contraction was particularly severe in Tsarist Russia and the Austro-Hungarian empire, as their economies were not prepared and flexible enough to stand the rapid war mobilization of labor and capital.

In contrast, the USSR showed great resilience in the early years of World War II. Germany and Japan experienced rapid economic growth in the run-up to World War II when the civilian economy was reoriented to the defense sector but eventually suffered huge destruction of material assets and human capital, bringing large-scale economic debilitation at the end of World War II.

9.4 The Great Depression, Stagflation, and the Global Financial Crisis of 2008–2009

We can distinguish three main *international* slumps in the last eighty years or so: (i) the Great Depression of the 1930s; (ii) the stagflation of the 1970s; and (iii) the global financial crisis of 2008–2009 (the "Great Recession"). The Great Depression affected advanced capitalist economies more severely than the global financial crisis of 2008–2009 and the stagflation of the 1970s. Countries on the periphery of the world economy (primary exporters) were more affected by the Great Depression than by the crisis of 2008–2009. In this latter global crisis, developing and emerging economies were better prepared in terms of exchange-rate flexibility, a higher level of international reserves, and lower fiscal deficits than during previous crises in the 1970s, 1980s, and 1990s. In addition, the continued dynamism of China, a global engine of growth and a main importer of commodities and raw materials from the global periphery, helped to keep economic activity on the periphery, in spite of the contraction in the core capitalist economies. In contrast, in the 1930s, primary exporters depended crucially on the demand coming from the United States and Europe.

A main casualty of the global financial crisis of 2008–2009 was the European periphery: Greece, Spain, Portugal, Ireland, Italy, and the Baltic nations that, in several cases, were forced to adopt "austerity programs" designed by the IMF, the European Commission, and the ECB, with severe and protracted recessive effects.

9.5 Developing Countries and Emerging Economies Crises

A source of economic, and at times political, destabilization are *overexpansionary fiscal/credit and wage policies* of the type experienced by the southern cone of Latin America in the early 1970s, in Peru and Nicaragua in the 1980s, and Venezuela in the 2010s. Another source is *adverse external shocks* to economies dependent on natural resources and commodity exports whose terms of trade fluctuate in unanticipated ways; when these shocks interact with a cutoff in capital inflow, the economies suffer "sudden stops" accompanied by large contractions in economic activity.

Crises also followed episodes of *premature financial liberalization* of internal banking systems and external short-term capital flow: these crises occurred in Chile and Argentina in the late 1970s and early 1980s, and in East Asian countries in the early to mid-1990s. In general, the effects on output, employment, and formation of *capital account reversals* were exacerbated by insolvencies in the domestic banking system. Government bailouts came in the wake of the crisis but they were, in general, fiscally expensive and socially regressive.

9.6 Crashes of Exchange-Rate Regimes

Fixed-exchange rate regimes, exchange-rate bands (managed pegs), and currency boards are often used as devices to control inflation. However, they are vulnerable to reversals in capital inflow, real currency appreciations, widening external current deficits, and the accumulation of short term debt denominated in foreign currency. When countries were forced to devalue and abandon these exchange-rate regimes – often in traumatic fashion – the economy collapsed (inflation, recession, unemployment and, in several cases, banking crises). Examples are Argentina and Chile in the early 1980s; Mexico in 1994–1995; Ecuador in 1999; Argentina in 2001 and 2018; and Thailand, Indonesia, Korea, Malaysia, and the Philippines in 1997–1998.

The timing of the *exit* from the gold standard was relevant during the Great Depression in the early 1930s. Governments staying longer on the gold standard, such as the United States and France, delayed their recoveries more than countries that depreciated their currencies earlier abandoning the gold standard – the United Kingdom, Sweden, and other Nordic countries in 1931.

The stagflation of the 1970s was also preceded by the abandonment of the fixed parity between the US dollar and gold in 1971, and the adoption of flexible exchange-rate regimes in North America and Europe ending, de facto, the Bretton Woods system. In turn, the Great Recession of 2008–2009 originating in the United States did *not* come along with a depreciation of the dollar that was, to an extent, a safe-haven currency in times of turbulence.

In turn, some episodes of output contraction were associated with decisions *not to abandon* the prevailing exchange-rate regime. As shown in Chapter 6, Latvia abstained from devaluing its currency during the depression of 2008–2010 and Greece remained in the euro area during the whole crisis and austerity phase after 2008. Both countries fell into a depression, which was more protracted in Greece.

9.7 Does Economic Contraction Come with Deflation, Inflation, or Hyperinflation?

The relation between episodes of recession/depression and inflation/deflation changed throughout the long twentieth century. In the 1920s, hyperinflation in Central and Eastern Europe and Soviet Russia came along with output declines, although its stabilization has been presented by some authors as virtually costless. In turn, the Great Depression of the 1930s came with *price deflation* (a fall in the price level), a relationship that changed in the 1970s, during which recessions and growth decelerations in the advanced economies were accompanied by an *acceleration in inflation*. A similar situation took place in Latin America and other developing countries in the 1970s, 1980s, and part of the 1990s, when slumps coincided with rising inflation, sometimes reaching very high plateaus.

Countries may accommodate *chronic inflation* through indexation mechanisms (rules for adjusting wages to inflation or the exchange rate to inflation), although this adaptation to inflation often comes at the cost of making inflation irresponsive to cuts in aggregate spending. Stabilization programs in Argentina and Brazil in the 1980s tried to reduce "inertial" inflation through coordinated wage, exchange rate, and price controls, but ultimately failed to succeed. However, Israel was more successful in this regard and managed to permanently reduce inflation with the help of price, wage and exchange rate controls that were accompanied by fiscal reforms. The difficulties in Argentina to stabilize inflation in the late 2010s show that inertial inflation has not disappeared.

The Great Recession of 2008–2009 was not accompanied by serious inflationary pressures in the United States and Europe, although inflation rates on the European periphery during austerity periods was somewhat higher than in core economies over the same period.

9.8 Postsocialist Transitions

Overhauls and restructuring of entire economic systems such as the postsocialist transition to capitalism in the 1990s were accompanied by big contractions in aggregate economic activity in several economies of CEE, Russia, Ukraine, and other former Soviet republics. The explanation of the initial contraction in economic activity in the transition to capitalism identifies both supply-side and demand-side factors. Very rapid integration into the world economy often depressed the industrial sectors of the former socialist countries that had hard times standing foreign competition. The swift dismantling of the state sector implied serious transitional problems in the reallocation of labor, capital, and managerial capacities from the declining public sector to the expanding private sector.

As the transition to a market economy entailed a shift from controlled prices to free prices, and in order to avoid large inflation (an objective not always achieved), monetary and fiscal policies in several transition economies were restrictive and depressed aggregate demand. Also, real wages were squeezed, having an adverse effect on consumption that, in the short term, dominated over competitiveness effects on exports. Privatization of state assets and natural resources implied big wealth accumulation for small oligarchies with a higher propensity to save. Also, the state sector cut public investment with adverse demand and supply-side effects. These effects lasted for a few years and then growth started to accelerate, accompanied in CEE by capital inflow associated with accession to the EU that reduced country and exchange-rate risks. However, these booms preceded internal economic imbalances and subsequent adjustment, often costly, at the time the global financial crisis of 2008–09.

9.9   Countercyclical Policies and Macroeconomic Theory

Main crises spurred changes in dominant economic paradigms. Up until the 1930s, classic macroeconomics – with its faith in wage and price flexibility – was the dominant approach in macroeconomic policies. The events of the early 1930s shattered those beliefs. It took currency depreciation, fiscal expansion, and, above all, monetary easing to start a recovery in the United States in the mid 1930s.

The Keynesian revolution shifted the focus from the supply side to the demand side as the main cause provoking slumps and persistent unemployment. The corollary was active government policies to pull an economy out of recession or depression. The use in the 1950s and 1960s of countercyclical fiscal and monetary policies contributed to maintain economies near full employment although fiscal desequilibria and inflationary pressures were incubated.

The stagflation of the 1970s, however, challenged this view, as inflation could also be an outcome of active government policies. Keynesian macroeconomics retreated and theories of monetarism, real business cycles, efficient markets, and supply-side economics caught the attention of academic economists and policy-makers. Monetary and fiscal policies were considered as ineffective to stabilize the economy around full utilization of capital and labor. In the new paradigm, financial markets are rational, market participants use all available information to make optimal decisions, and savings are transferred to the most profitable investment opportunities. There was no room for financial crisis and big slumps in the rational expectations/new classic macroeconomic schools of the 1970s.

In the 1990s, mainstream macroeconomists argued that we were living in a "great moderation" of steady growth and low inflation. The Great Recession of 2008–2009 was in part a consequence of the adoption of policies of financial deregulation based on these assumptions and beliefs, largely divorced from how the real world operates. Although ideas such as the "great moderation" and the efficient market hypothesis have lost some influence, no new "big idea" after the crisis of 2008–2009 that might reshape the contours of macroeconomic theory has yet emerged.

Still some positive changes have occurred in the ivory tower of academia and the thinking of organizations such as the IMF. There is now a greater appreciation of the importance of financial factors and debt accumulation in generating and propagating financial crises that lead to macroeconomic slumps. There is also growing attention to issues of income and wealth inequality and a concern that deregulated capitalist economies generate a tendency to devote ever-growing proportions of national income to capital to the detriment of labor. Moreover, there is an increasing concentration of financial assets and productive capital in the hands of small economic elites that wield great economic and political power inimical to a genuine democracy. Still, it is likely that the world economy and/or particular economies in the coming years will fall again into cycles of recessions and crises, as debt overhang persists, and the limits to fiscal and monetary policies to counteract adverse shocks and destabilizing forces remain strict. In addition, pervasive economic inequality makes policy consensus more difficult to attain as distributive conflict between capital and labor tend to become more acute.

Appendix

Table A.1. *Episodes of recession and depression in 1900–2017 (declines in per capita GDP above 3 percent; country-episodes are in order according to intensity)*

Country	Period	Intensity (percentage of decline in GDP per capita)	Duration (years)
War Related[a]			
World War I (1913–1919)			
Russia	1916–1919	−58.8	4
	1914	−4.51	1
Greece	1915–1917	−43.55	3
	1919	−10.9	1
Austria-Hungary	1913–1919	−35.55	7
France	1917–1918	−30.83	2
	1913–1914	−7.91	2
Finland	1917–1918	−27.64	2
	1914–1915	−10.85	2
Germany	1914–1915	−20.53	1
	1919	−13.3	1
Norway	1917–1918	−14.65	2
Australia	1914–1918	−10.77	5
	1914–1918	−10.77	5
Italy	1914–1915	−10.2	2
	1918–1919	−6.43	2
Canada	1914	−9.48	1
United States	1914	−9.46	1
Portugal	1917–1918	−6.81	2
Japan	1914	−4.34	1
Average		−17.36	2.35

Country	Period	Intensity (percentage of decline in GDP per capita)	Duration (years)
World War II (1938–1947)			
Greece	1938–1945	−66.14	8
Germany	1945–1946	−63.56	2
Austria	1945	−58.46	1
	1942	−5.56	1
	1940	−3.34	1
Japan	1944–1945	−52.29	2
France	1940–1944	−49.48	5
Italy	1940–1945	−46.03	6
United States	1945–1947	−27.95	3
Turkey	1943–1945	−27.19	3
	1940–1941	−16.88	2
Bulgaria	1944–1945	−27.14	2
	1941–1942	−14.3	2
Costa Rica	1942–1944	−24.91	3
Denmark	1940–1941	−23.68	2
	1945	−8.6	1
Malaysia	1940–1941	−23.05	2
Venezuela	1940–1942	−22.27	3
Singapore	1938	−18	1
United Kingdom	1944–1947	−14.71	4
Australia	1944–1946	−14.38	3
Norway	1942–1944	−12.76	3
	1940	−9.06	1
Finland	1939–1940	−10.28	2
	1944–1945	−6.69	2
Sweden	1940–1941	−10.27	2
Hungary	1940–1941	−7.45	2
Canada	1945–1946	−6.87	2
USSR	1940	−4.16	1
Average		−23.29	2.48
Spanish Civil War			
Spain	1936–1938	−30.69	3
Great Depression of the 1930s			
Chile	1930–1932	−46.62	3
Uruguay	1931–1933	−36.06	3
Singapore	1930–1932	−35.66	3
Canada	1929–1933	−34.83	5
Nicaragua	1930–1932	−32.92	3
United States	1930–1933	−30.76	4
	1938	−4.72	1

(Continued)

Appendix

Table A.1 *(Continued)*

Country	Period	Intensity (percentage of decline in GDP per capita)	Duration (years)
Great Depression of the 1930s *(Continued)*			
Peru	1930–1932	−25.39	3
Poland	1930–1933	−24.92	4
Venezuela	1931–1932	−24.14	2
Austria	1930–1933	−23.4	4
Australia	1927–1931	−21.87	3
Czechoslovakia	1930–1935	−20.79	6
Argentina	1930–1932	−19.35	3
Mexico	1927–1930	−18.75	2
	1932	−16.46	1
Germany	1929–1932	−17.81	4
Yugoslavia	1930–1932	−17.33	3
Malaysia	1930–1932	−16.97	3
France	1930–1932	−15.94	3
	1934–1935	−3.61	2
Indonesia	1931–1934	−13.98	4
Brazil	1929–1931	−13.29	3
Korea	1928–1932	−12.78	5
Costa Rica	1931–1932	−12.6	2
	1929	−6.16	1
Hungary	1930–1932	−11.45	3
Japan	1930–1931	−9.3	2
Switzerland	1930–1932	−8.96	3
Greece	1930–1931	−8.86	2
Norway	1931	−8.37	1
Romania	1927–1929	−8.36	1
Spain	1930–1931	−7.67	2
Turkey	1932	−7.51	1
Italy	1930–1931	−7.17	2
United Kingdom	1930–1931	−6.63	2
Sweden	1931–1932	−6.37	2
Finland	1930–1932	−6.15	3
Bulgaria	1932	−5.17	1
Ecuador	1931–1932	−3.96	2
Colombia	1930–1931	−3.79	2
Philippines	1930–1931	−3.71	2
Denmark	1932	−3.54	1
Average		−15.44	2.60

Country	Period	Intensity (percentage of decline in GDP per capita)	Duration (years)
Stagflation of the 1970s			
Portugal	1974–1975	−7.73	2
Switzerland	1975–1976	−6.76	2
Greece	1974	−3.99	1
Average		−6.16	1.67
Crises in Emerging Economies (Latin America and East Asia)			
Venezuela	2013–2018	−45.84	6
	1978–1985	−24.26	8
	2002–2003	−18.91	2
	1989	−10.86	1
	1998–1999	−9.3	2
	2009–2010	−7.56	2
	1993–1994	−6.26	2
Peru	1988–1990	−28.17	3
	1982–1983	−17.23	2
	1976–1978	−6.4	3
Chile	1972–1975	−23.65	4
	1982–1983	−18.92	2
Bolivia	1979–1986	−23.59	8
Argentina	1999–2002	−21.91	2
	1988–1990	−14.04	3
	1980–1982	−11.93	3
	1980–1982	−11.93	3
	1985	−7.96	1
	2009	−6.88	1
	1978	−5.99	1
Uruguay	1982–1984	−20.17	3
	1999–2002	−15.59	4
Philippines	1983–1985	−18.75	3
	1991–1993	−5.32	3
Vietnam	1974–1975	−15.09	2
	1978–1980	−7.45	3
Indonesia	1998–1999	−14.87	2
	1982	−5.56	1
Costa Rica	1980–1983	−14.71	4
Brazil	1981–1983	−13.41	3
	1990–1992	−7.08	3
Thailand	1997–1998	−12.29	2
Malaysia	1998	−9.66	1

(Continued)

Table A.1 *(Continued)*

Country	Period	Intensity (percentage of decline in GDP per capita)	Duration (years)
Crises in Emerging Economies (Latin America and East Asia) *(Continued)*			
Mexico	1982–1983	−9.37	2
	1995	−7.98	1
	2008–2009	−7.25	2
	1986–1988	−6.83	3
Ecuador	1987	−8.3	1
	1999–2000	−7.24	2
	1982–1983	−6.84	2
Singapore	2008–2009	−6.92	2
	1998	−5.49	1
Hong Kong	1998	−6.67	1
Colombia	1998–1999	−6.5	2
Dominican Republic	1984–1985	−6.45	2
Korea	1998	−6.15	1
Turkey	1979–1980	−5.47	2
Average		−12.32	2.49
Select Hyperinflation Episodes			
Greece	1941–1945	−57.82	5
Yugoslavia	1990–1993	−45.37	4
Peru	1988–1990	−28.17	3
Nicaragua	1986–1991	−26.39	6
Venezuela	2017–2018	−25.78	2
Germany	1923	−17.45	1
Argentina	1988–1990	−14.04	3
Russia	1921	−8.47	1
Bolivia	1985–1986	−7.16	2
Austria	1923	−1.23	1
Bulgaria	1997	−0.48	1
Hungary	1945–1946	N. A.	2
Poland	1923–1924	N. A.	2
Average		−17.46	2.33
Crises in Socialist and Postsocialist Countries			
Ukraine	1990–1998	−60.25	9
	2009	−14.42	1
	2014–2015	−10.48	2
Latvia	1991–1993	−48.75	3
	2008–2010	−17.71	3

Country	Period	Intensity (percentage of decline in GDP per capita)	Duration (years)
Yugoslavia	1990–1993	−45.37	4
	1952	−8.97	1
	1950	−7.59	1
	1956	−5.94	1
	1987–1988	−4.02	2
Lithuania	1991–1994	−43.13	4
	2009	−13.58	1
Russian Federation	1990–1996	−42.09	7
	2009	−7.85	1
	1998	−5.14	1
	2014–2016	−4.44	3
Romania	1987–1992	−29.61	6
	1997–1999	−10.26	3
	2009–2010	−7.02	2
Estonia	1991–1993	−28.09	3
	2008–2009	−18.85	2
Slovenia	1987–1992	−25.35	6
	2009	−8.63	1
	2012–2013	−4.1	2
Bulgaria	1988–1993	−22.43	6
	1999	−5.48	1
	1952	−4.8	1
	1980	−3.22	1
	1985	−3.18	1
Slovak Republic	1991–1992	−20.78	2
	2009	−5.46	1
Hungary	1989–1993	−19.11	5
	2009	−6.47	1
	1956	−5.35	1
Poland	1989–1991	−16.27	3
	1979–1982	−13.46	4
Czech Republic	1991–1993	−11.98	3
	2009	−5.34	1
Soviet Russia	1921	−8.47	1
USSR	1940	−4.16	1
	1963	−3.74	1
Average		−15.4	2.51

(Continued)

Table A.1 *(Continued)*

Country	Period	Intensity (percentage of decline in GDP per capita)	Duration (years)
Great Recession and Aftermath in select OECD Countries			
Greece	2008–2013	−25.96	6
Estonia	2008–2009	−18.85	2
Latvia	2008–2010	−17.71	3
Lithuania	2009	−13.58	1
Ireland	2008–2009	−11.14	2
Spain	2008–2013	−10.63	6
Finland	2009	−8.71	1
	2012–2015	−4.28	4
Slovenia	2009	−8.63	1
	2012–2013	−4.1	2
Italy	2008–2009	−7.51	2
	2012–2014	−6.61	3
Mexico	2008–2009	−7.25	2
Sweden	2008–2009	−7.24	2
Japan	2008–2009	−6.48	2
Hungary	2009	−6.47	1
Denmark	2008–2009	−6.45	2
Turkey	2008–2009	−6.25	2
United Kingdom	2008–2009	−6.1	2
Portugal	2011–2013	−5.81	3
	2009	−3.07	1
Slovak Republic	2009	−5.46	1
Germany	2009	−5.38	1
Czech Republic	2009	−5.34	1
United States	2008–2009	−4.81	2
Norway	2008–2011	−4.51	4
Canada	2008–2009	−4.14	2
Austria	2009	−4.02	1
France	2008–2009	−3.79	2
Switzerland	2009	−3.44	1
Average		−7.79	2.17

[a] Before, during and after.
Source: Author's elaboration based on data from Maddison (2013); World Development Indicators, The World Bank 2017; OECD (2017); National Accounts Main Aggregates Database (United Nations); and World Economic Outlook, FMI October, 2017.

References

Abelshauser, W. (2005). *The Dynamics of German Industry: Germany's Path Toward the New Economy and the American Challenge* (Vol. 6). Oxford: Berghahn Books.

Amsden, A. H., J. Kochanowicz and L. Taylor (2004). *The Market Meets Its Match: Restructuring the Economies of Eastern Europe*. Cambridge, MA: Harvard University Press.

Angell, N. (1911). *The Great Illusion*. New York and London: G.P. Putnam & Sons.

Atkinson, A. B. (2015). *Inequality*. Cambridge, MA: Harvard University Press.

Avramov, R. and D. Gnjatovic (2008). "Stabilization Policies in Bulgaria and Yugoslavia during Communism's-Terminal Years: The 1980s economic visions in retrospect." *South-Eastern European Monetary History Network SEEMHN*, 81, Bank of Greece.

Ban, C. (2012). "Sovereign Debt, Austerity and Regime Change: The Case of Nicolas Ceausescu's Romania." *East European Politics and Societies and Cultures*, 26: 743–76, Sage Publications.

Becker, J. (2016). "Europe's other Periphery." *New Left Review*, 99, May/June.

Beckerman, P. and Solimano, A. (eds.). (2002). *Crisis and Dollarization in Ecuador: Stability, Growth, and Social Equity*. Washington, DC: The World Bank.

Berg, M. A. (1999). *The Asia Crisis: Causes, Policy Responses and Outcomes* (No. 99–138). Washington, DC.

Bernanke, B. (2000). *Essays on the Great Depression*. Princeton: (IMF Working Paper 138/99), International Monetary Fund, Washington, DC.

(2004). "Money, Gold and the Great Depression." Federal Reserve Board, Remarks by Governor Ben S. Bernanke at the H. Parker Willis Lecture in Economic Policy, Washington and Lee University, Lexington, Virginia, March, 2004, vol. 2, pp. 1867–960.

Bértola, L. and J. A. Ocampo (2013). *El desarrollo económico de América Latina desde la independencia*. Mexico: Fondo de Cultura Económica.

Bitar, S. (1995). *Chile 1970-1973, Asumir la Historia para Construir el Futuro*. Santiago: Pehuen ed. Santiago.

Blanchard, O., M. Griffiths and B. Gruss (2012). "Boom, Bust and Recovery: Forensics of the Latvian Crisis". *Brookings Papers on Economic Activity*, Fall 2013.

Bordo, M. (2006). "Sudden Stops, financial Crises and Original Sin in Emerging Countries: Déjà vu?" Paper prepared for the conference: Global Imbalances and Risk Management. Has the Center become the Periphery? Madrid, Spain.

Bresciani-Turroni, C. (1937). *The Economics of Inflation: A Study of Currency Depreciation in Post-War Germany, 1914–1923.* Oxfordshire: Routledge.

Broadberry, S. and M. Harrison (eds.). (2005). *The Economics of World War I,* Cambridge: Cambridge University Press.

Brown, C. E. (1940). "Fiscal Policies in the 1930s: A Reappraisal." *American Economic Review,* 46: 857–79.

Bruner, R. F. and S. D. Carr (2009). *The Panic of 1907: Lessons Learned from the Market's Perfect Storm.* Hoboken: John Wiley & Sons.

Bruno, M. and J. D Sachs (1985). *Economics of Worldwide Stagflation.* Cambridge, MA: Harvard University Press.

Bruno, M., S. Fischer, E. Helpman, N. Liviatan and L. Meridor (eds.). (1991). *Lessons of Economic Stabilization and Its Aftermath.* Cambridge, MA: MIT Press.

Burk, K. and A. Caincross (1992). *"Goodbye Great Britain": The 1976 IMF Crisis.* New Haven and London: Yale University Press.

Cagan, P. (1956). "The Monetary Dynamics of Hyperinflation," in M. Friedman (ed.). *Studies in the Quantity Theory of Money.* Chicago: University of Chicago Press.

Calvo, G. A. (1998). "Capital Flows and Capital-Market Crises: The Simple Economics of Sudden Stops." *Journal of Applied Economics,* 1(1): 35–54.

(2007). "Crises in Emerging Market Economies: A Global Perspective." NBER Working Paper 11305.

(2016). *Macroeconomics in Times of Liquidity Crises: Searching for Economic Essentials.* Cambridge, MA: MIT Press.

Calvo, G. and F. Coricelli (1990). *Stagflationary Effects of Stabilization Programs in Reforming Socialist Countries: Supply Side vs. Demand Side Factors.* Washington, DC: International Monetary Fund and World Bank.

Campos, N. and F. Coricelli (2002). "Growth in Transition: What We Know, What We Don't and What We Should." *Journal of Economic Literature,* 40: 793–836.

Cassidy, J. (2009). *How Markets Fail.* New York: Farrar, Straus and Giroux.

Cerra, V. and S. W. Saxena (2008). "Growth Dynamics: The Myth of Economic Recovery." *American Economic Review,* 98(1): 439–57.

(2016). "Booms, Crises and Recoveries." International Monetary Fund, draft paper.

Céspedes, L., R. Chang and A. Velasco (2014). "Is Inflation Targeting Still on Target? The Recent Experience of Latin America." *International Finance,* 17: 185–207.

Corbo, V. and A. Solimano (1991). "Stabilization Policies in Chile Revisited." in M. Bruno, S. Fischer, H. Helpman and N. Liviatan (eds.). *Lessons from Economic Stabilization and Its Aftermath.* Cambridge, MA: MIT Press.

De Gregorio, J. and F. Labbé (2011). "Copper, the Real Exchange Rate and Macroeconomic Fluctuations in Chile." in R. Arezki, T. Gylfason and A. Sy (eds.). *Beyond the Curse: Policies to Harness the Power of Natural Resources.* Washington, DC: International Monetary Fund.

De Long, J. B. (1990). "Liquidation" Cycles: Old-Fashioned Real Business Cycle Theory and the Great Depression (NBER Working Paper 3546). National Bureau of Economic Research.

Della Paolera, G. and A. M. Taylor (eds.). (2003). *A New Economic History of Argentina* (Vol. 1). Cambridge: Cambridge University Press.

Díaz, J., R. Lüders and G. Wagner (2016). *"Chile 1810–2010. La República en cifras. Historical Statistics."* Santiago: Ediciones Universidad Católica de Chile.

Dornbusch, R. and S. Edwards (1991). *The Macroeconomics of Populism: In the Macroeconomics of Populism in Latin America* (pp. 7–13). Chicago: University of Chicago Press.

Dornbusch, R. and S. Fischer (1986). "Stopping Hyperinflations Past and Present." *Weltwirtschaftliches Archiv*, 122(1): 1–47.

Easterly, W. and S. Fischer (1995). "The Soviet Economic Decline." *World Bank Economic Review*, 9(3): 341–71.

Edwards, S. (2018). *American Default: The Untold Story of FDR, the Supreme Court, and the Battle over Gold*. Princeton: Princeton University Press.

Eichengreen, B. (1992). *Golden Fetters: The Gold Standard and the Great Depression 1919–1939*. Oxford: Oxford University Press.

Eichengreen, B. and J. D. Sachs (1985). "Exchange Rates and Economic Recovery in the 1930s." *The Journal of Economic History*, 45: 925–46.

    (2002). "Still Fettered after All These Years." NBER Working Paper 9276.

Eichengreen, B., D. Park and K. Shin (2013). "Growth Slowdowns Redux: New Evidence on the Middle-Income Trap." NBER Working Paper 18673.

Eloranta, J. (2007). "From the Great Illusion to the Great War: Military Spending Behaviour of the Great Powers, 1870–1913." *European Review of Economic History*, 11(2): 255–83.

    (2013). "World War I" in Parker, R. and R. Whales (eds.). 2013, *Handbook of Major Events in Economic History*. Abingdon: Routledge.

Escobar Cerda, L. (1991). *Mi Testimonio*. Santiago: Editorial Ver.

Feinstein, C., P. Temin and G. Toniolo (2008), *The World Economy Between the Wars*. New York and Oxford: Oxford University Press.

Feldman, G. (1928). "On the Theory of Growth Rates of National Incomes." Reprinted and translated in N. Spulber (ed.). *Foundations of Soviet Strategies of Economic Growth, Selected Essays, 1924–1930*. Bloomington IN: Indiana University Press, 1964.

Ferguson, N. (1998). *The Pity of War*. London: Penguin Books.

French-Davis, R. (2018). *Reformas económicas en Chile, 1973–2017*. 6ª ed. Santiago: Taurus.

Frieden, J. A. (2007). *Global Capitalism: Its Fall and Rise in the Twentieth Century*. New York: W. W. Norton & Company.

Foxley, A. (1983). *Experimentos neoliberales en América latina*. México: Fondo de Cultura Económica.

Galbraith, J. K. (2016). *Welcome to the Poisoned Chalice: The Destruction of Greece and the Future of Europe*. New Haven: Yale University Press.

Gale, D. (ed.). (2011). *First Transition, Then the Crash: Eastern Europe in the 2000s*. London: Pluto Press.

Gatrell, P. (2005). "Poor Russia, Poor Show: Mobilizing a Backward Economy" Chapter 8, table 8.2. in S. Broadberry and M. Harrison (eds.). *The Economics of World War I*. Cambridge: Cambridge University Press.

Gatrell, P. and M. Harrison (1993). "The Russian and Soviet Economies in Two World Wars: A Comparative View 1." *The Economic History Review*, 46(3): 425–52.

Gourinchas, P.-O., T. Philippn and D. Vayanos (2016). "The Analytics of the Greek Crisis." NBER Working Paper 22370, Cambridge, MA.

Graham, F. D. (1930). *Exchange, Prices, and Production in Hyper-Inflation: Germany, 1920–1923* (Vol. 1). Auburn: Ludwig von Mises Institute.

Grant, J. (2014). *The Forgotten Depression: 1921 – The Crash that Cured Itself.* New York: Simon & Schuster.

Gregory, P. and M. Harris (2005). "Allocation Under Dictatorship: Research in Stalin's Archives." *Journal of Economic Literature*, 43: 721–61.

Hanke, S. H. and C. Bushnell (2017). "On Measuring Hyperinflation." *World Economics*, 18(3): 1–18.

Hanke, S. H. and N. Krus (2013). "World Hyperinflations."in R. Parker and R. Whaples (eds.). *The Handbook of Major Events in Economic History*. Oxfordshire: Routledge.

Hansen, A. (1938). *Full Recovery or Stagnation?* New York: W. W. Norton & Company.

Hara, A. (2005). "Japan: Guns before Rice." in M. Harrison (ed.). *The Economics of World War II: Six Great Powers in International Comparison*, 1st ed. New York: Mark Harrison, pp. 177–218.

Harrison, M. (1998a). "The Economics of World War II: An Overview. in M. Harrison (ed.). *The Economics of World War II: Six Great Powers in International Comparison*, 1st ed. New York: Mark Harrison, pp. 1–40.

Harrison, M. (1998b). "The Soviet Union: The Defeated Victor." in M. Harrison (ed.). *The Economics of World War II: Six Great Powers in International Comparison*, 1st ed. New York: Mark Harrison, pp. 268–96.

Hatton, T. J. and J. G. Williamson (2005). *Global Migration and the World Economy: Two Centuries of Policy and Performance* (p. 290). Cambridge, MA: MIT Press.

Hausmann, R. and F. R. Rodríguez (eds.). (2014). *Venezuela Before Chávez: Anatomy of an Economic Collapse*. University Park: Penn State Press.

Hausmann, R., L. Pritchet and D. Rodrik (2005). "Growth Accelerations." *Journal of Economic Growth*, 10(4): 973–87.

Hausmann, R., F. Rodriguez and R. Wagner (2006). "Growth Collapses." CID Working Paper # 136, Harvard University.

Hicks, J. K. (1974). *The Crisis of Keynesian Economics*. New York: Basic Books.

Hobson, J. A. (1902[1988]). *Imperialism: A Study*. 3rd ed. London, Boston, MA, Sydney, Wellington: Unwin Hyman,

International Monetary Fund (2009). Greece: Staff Report for the 2009 Article IV Consultation. IMF Country Report No. 09/244.

Ito, T. (2007). "Asian Currency Crisis and the International Monetary Fund, 10 years Later: Overview." *Asian Economic Policy Review*, 2(1): 16–49.

James, H. (2002). *The End of Globalization: Lessons from the Great Depression*. Cambridge, MA: Harvard University Press.

Kalecki, M. (1944). "Professor Pigou on the 'Classical Stationary State' a Comment." *The Economic Journal*, 54(213): 131–2.

Katzenellennbaum, S. (1925). *Russian Currency and Banking*. London: Orchard house.

Kennedy, P. (1989). *The Rise and of Economic Powers: Economic Change and Military Conflict from 1500 to 2000*. London: Fontana Press.

Keynes, J. M. (1920). "The Economic Consequences of the Peace (1919)." *The Collected Writings of John Maynard Keynes*, 2: 8.

(1925). *The Economic Consequences of Mr. Churchill*, Reprinted in Donald Moggridge (ed.), *The Collected Writings of John Maynard Keynes*, Vol. IX, 1972. New York: St Martin's Press, pp. 207–30.

(1927). *The End of Laissez-Faire* (p. 17). Wm. C. Brown Reprint Library. Hogarth Press.

(1931). "An Economic Analysis of Unemployment." (University of Chicago: 1931 Harris Foundation lectures). reprinted in J. M. Keynes, *The General Theory and After: Part 1*, Preparation, voL Xffl, pt. I of The Collected Writings of John Maynard Keynes, Donald Moggridge (eds.), Cambridge, UK: Cambridge University Press, 1972.

Kindleberger, C. P. (1967). *Europe's Postwar Growth: The Role of Labor Supply*. Cambridge, MA: Harvard University Press.

(1973[2013]). *The World in Depression 1929–1939*. Oakland: University of California Press.

Kodolko, G. (2000). "Globalization and Catching-up: From Recession to Growth in Transition Economies." WP/00/100, IMF.

Kornai, J. (1992). *The Socialist System: The Political Economy of Communism*. Princeton: Princeton University Press.

(2006). "The Great Transformation of Central and Eastern Europe. Success and Disappointment." *Economics of Transition*, 14(2): 207–44.

Krugman, P. and L. Taylor (1978). "Contractionary Effects of Devaluation." *Journal of International Economics*, 8(3): 445–56.

Larraín, F. and E. Parrado (2008). "'Chile menos volátil' [A 'Less Volatile Chile']." *El Trimestre Económico*, 75(299): 563–96.

Lazaretou, S. (2003). "Greek Monetary Economics in Retrospect: The Adventures of the Drachma." Working Paper #2, Bank of Greece, Athens.

Lenin, V. I. (1939[1972]). *Imperialism: The Highest Stage of capitalism*, A Popular Outline. New York: International Publishers.

Macmillan, M. (2014). *The War that Ended Peace, How Europe Abandoned Peace for the First World War*. Great Britain: Profile Books.

Maddison, A. (2013). The Maddison-Project, http://www.ggdc.net/maddison/maddison-project/home.htm, 2013 version.

Muchhala, B. (ed.). (2007). Ten years after: Revisiting the Asian financial crisis: Essays. Woodrow Wilson International Center for Scholars, Asia Program.

Nenovsky, N. (2015). "The Soviets monetary experience (1917–1924) through the perspective of the discussion on unity and diversity of money." CRIISEA, University of Picardie Jules Verne, France, RUDN, Russia.

Nove, A. (1990). *An Economic History of the USSR*. London: Penguin Books.

Nuti, M. (1981). "The Polish Crisis: Economic Factors and Constraints." *Socialist Register*, 18(18).

Ocampo, J. A. (1987). *Planes antinflacionarios recientes en la América Latina: un debate teórico en la práctica*. Fondo de Cultura Económica.

OECD (2017a). General government deficit (indicator). doi:10.1787/77079edb-en (Accessed on 7 May 2017).

OECD (2017b). Household debt (indicator). doi:10.1787/f03b6469-en (Accessed on 7 May 2017).

Offer, G. (1987). "Soviet Economic Growth: 1928–1985." *Journal of Economic Literature*, 25: 1767–833.

Palairet, M. (2000). *The Four Ends of the Greek Hyperinflation of 1941–1946*. Copenhagen: Museum Tusculanum Press, University of Copenhagen.

Patinkin, D. (1948). "Price Flexibility and Full Employment." *The American Economic Review*, 38(4): 543–64.

Picketty, T. (2012). *Capital in the Twenty First Century*, Cambridge, MA: Harvard University Press.

Pigou, A. C. (1943). "The Classic Stationary State." *Economic Journal*, 53(212): 343–51.

Pilisuk, M. and J. A. Rountree (2008). *Who Benefits from Global Violence and War: Uncovering a Destructive System*. Westport: Greenwood Publishing Group, p. 136.

Pindyck, R. and A. Solimano (1993). "Economic Instability and Aggregate Investment." in O. Blanchard and S. Fischer (eds.). *NBER Macroeconomic Annual, 1993*. MIT Press.

Podkaminer, I. (2013). "Development Patterns of Central and Eastern European Countries (in Transition and Following EU accession)." *Research Reports* 388, July, WIID. The Vienna Institute for International Economic Studies, Oxford.

Popov, V. (2014). *Mixed Fortunes: An Economic History of China, Russia and the West*. Oxford: Oxford University Press.

Preobrazhensky, E. (1926). "On Primary Socialist Accumulation" Reprinted and translated in N. Spulber (ed.). *Foundations of Soviet Strategies of Economic Growth, Selected Essays, 1924–1930*. Bloomington, IN: Indiana University Press, 1964.

Purfield, C. and C. B. Rosenberg (2013). "Adjustment under a Currency peg: Estonia, Latvia and Lithuania during the Global Financial Crisis 2008–2009." IMF Working Paper, WP/10/213, Washington, DC.

Radelet, S., & Sachs, J. (1998). The onset of the East Asian financial crisis (NBER Working Paper 6680). National Bureau of Economic Research.

Reinhart, C. M., & Rogoff, K. S. (2009). *This Time Is Different: Eight Centuries of Financial Folly*. Princeton: Princeton University Press.

(2010). "From Financial Crash to Debt Crisis." NBER Working Paper 15795.

Ritschl, A. (2005). "The Pity of Peace: Germany's Economy at War, 1914–1918 and Beyond." Chapter 2 in S. Broadberry and M. Harrison (eds.). *The Economics of World War I*. Cambridge: Cambridge University Press.

Roberts, M. (2016). *The Long Depression*. Chicago, IL: Haymarket Books.

Rockoff, H. (1998). "The United States: From Ploughshares to Swords." in M. Harrison (ed.). *The Economics of World War II: Six Great Powers in International Comparison*, 1st ed. New York: Mark Harrison, pp. 81–121.

Rockoff, H. (2005). "Until It Is Over, Over There: The US economy in WWI." Chapter 10 in S. Broadberry and M. Harrison (eds.). *The Economics of World War I*. Cambridge: Cambridge University Press.

Roemer. C. (1988). "World War I and the Postwar Depression, A Reinterpretation based on Alternative Estimates of GDP." *Journal of Monetary Economics*, 22(9): 91–115.

Romer, C. D. (1990). "The Great Crash and the Onset of the Great Depression." *The Quarterly Journal of Economics*, 105(3): 597–624.

(1992). "What Ended the Great Depression?" *The Journal of Economic History*, 52: 4.

Sargent, T. J. (1982). "The Ends of Four Big Inflations." In *Inflation: Causes and Effects* (pp. 41–98). Chicago: University of Chicago Press.

Schulze, M.-S. (2005). "Austria-Hungary's Economy in World War I." Chapter 3 in S. Broadberry and M. Harrison (eds.). (2005). *The Economics of World War I*. Cambridge: Cambridge University Press.

Solimano, A. (1987). "Desempleo estructural en Chile: un análisis macroeconómico." *Estudios de Economía*, 14(2): 273–310.

(1989). "Inflation and the Costs of Stabilization: Country Experience, Conceptual Issues and Policy Lessons." *The World Bank Research Observer*, 5. Washington, DC.

(1990). "Inflation and Growth in the Transition from Socialism: The Case of Bulgaria." World Bank Policy Research Working Paper Series # 659. World Bank.

(1991). "The Economies of Central and Eastern Europe: An Historical and International Perspective." in V. Corbo, F. Coricelli and J. Bossak (eds.). *Reforming Central and Eastern European Economies: Initial Results and Challenges.* New York: A World Bank Symposium.

(2010). *International Migration in the Age of Crisis and Globalization: Historical and Recent Experiences.* New York: Cambridge University Press.

(2012). *Chile and the Neoliberal Trap: The Post-Pinochet Era.* Cambridge, UK and New York: Cambridge University Press.

(2017). *Global Capitalism in Disarray, Inequality, Debt and Austerity.* New York: Oxford University Press.

Solimano, A. and D. Calderón Guajardo (2017). "The Copper Sector, Fiscal Rules, and Stabilization Funds in Chile: Scope and Limits." Working Paper 2017/53. Helsinki: UNU-WIDER.

Solimano, A. and M. Schaper (2014). "The Paradoxes of Chilean Economic Development: Growth, Inequality, Deindustrialization and Sustainability Risks." in A. Hansen and U. Wethal (eds.). *Emerging Economies and Challenges to Sustainability.* London: Routledge.

Stevenson, D. (1996). *Armaments and the Coming of War: Europe, 1904–1914.* Oxford: Oxford University Press.

Sturzenegger, F. A. (1991). "Descriptions of a Populist Experience: Argentina, 1973–1976." in R. Donbursch and S. Edwards (eds.). *The Macroeconomics of Populism in Latin America.* Chicago: NBER, University of Chicago Press.

Summers, L. (2014). "U.S. Economic Prospects: Secular Stagnation, Hysteresis and the Zero Lower Bound." *Business Economics*, 49(2): 65–73.

Taylor, L. (2010). *Maynard's Revenge.* Cambridge, MA: Harvard University Press.

Temin, P. and B. Wigmore (1990). "The End of a Big Deflation." *Explorations in Economic History*, 27: 483–502.

Twoney, M. J. (1983). "The Great Depression in Latin America; A Macro Analysis." *Explorations in Economic History*, 20: 221–47.

US Central Intelligence Agency (1986). "Poland: Economic Stagnation Ahead." A Research Paper, Directorate of Intelligence.

Végh, C. A. (1992). "Stopping High Inflation: An Analytical Overview." *Staff Papers (International Monetary Fund)*, 39(3): 626–95.

Vonyo, T. and A. Klein (2016). "Why did Socialist Economies Fail? The Role of Inputs Reconsidered." Working Paper Series No. 276. Centre for Competitive Advantage in the Global Economy. University of Warwick.

Weisbrot, M. and R. Reiss (2011). "Latvia's Internal Devaluation: A Success Story?" Center for Economic and Policy Research, CEPR, Washington, DC.

Wicker, E. (1986). "Terminating Hyperinflation in the Dismembered Habsburg Monarchy." *American Economic Review*, 76: 350–63.

World Bank (2017). *World Development Indicators*. Washington, DC.
  (2018). *World Development Indicators*. Washington, DC.
Wyplosz, Ch. and Sgherri, S (2016). "The IMF Role in Greece in the Context of the 2010 Stand-By Arrangement." IEO Background paper 16. Washington, DC.
Zamagni, V. (1998). "Italy: How to Lose the War and Win the Peace." in M. Harrison (ed.). *The Economics of World War II: Six great Powers in International Comparison*, 1st ed. New York: Mark Harrison, pp. 177–218.

Index